Here are three eighteenth-century English comedies that remain vividly alive and vastly entertaining to today's readers and theatregoers. In satirizing the follies of their own age, these dramatists speak to those people of every generation who can laugh at human frailty and foibles.

JOHN BETTENBENDER

is Associate Professor of Speech at St. Joseph's College, Calumet Campus. He has taught at Catholic University of America, University of Maryland, Loyola University, New York University and Jersey City State College. A producer, director, writer and actor, he has been involved in several hundred plays on radio, television and in the theatre.

THE LAUREL-LEAF LIBRARY brings together under a single imprint outstanding works of fiction and nonfiction particularly suitable for young adult readers, both in and out of the classroom. This series is under the editorship of M. Jerry Weiss, Distinguished Professor of Communications, Jersey City State College and Dr. Charles F. Reasoner, Professor, Elementary Education, New York University.

THREE ENGLISH COMEDIES

Oliver Goldsmith's
SHE STOOPS TO CONQUER

Richard Brinsley Sheridan's
THE RIVALS
and
THE SCHOOL FOR SCANDAL

Edited, with an introduction and notes, by John Bettenbender

Published by Dell Publishing Co., Inc.
750 Third Avenue, New York, N.Y. 10017
Copyright © 1966 by Dell Publishing Co., Inc.
Laurel-Leaf Library ® TM 766734, Dell Publishing Co., Inc.
First Printing: April, 1966
Second Printing: January, 1968
Third Printing: August, 1970
Fourth Printing: August, 1971
Fifth Printing: October, 1972

Printed in U.S.A.

CONTENTS

Introduction

A good work of art, and a play is certainly a work of art, is deeply rooted in its own times. But to survive beyond its own age, it must have something to say to men of other ages. Goldsmith and Sheridan were very much men of the eighteenth century and the plays they wrote are eighteenth-century pieces. Their language is clearly English, but quite different from our way of speaking English. At first glance, their characters seem to be artificial and strange—not like the type of people we know—yet these plays have held the boards for nearly two hundred years. They are still today among the most widely read and frequently revived plays in our language.

Each generation discovers anew the bumptious Tony Lumpkin, the scatterbrained Mrs. Malaprop, and the acid-tongued Lady Sneerwell. Year after year these plays are enjoyed because Goldsmith and Sheridan had insight into aspects of human nature that are universal for all men.

Young people, when first approaching these plays, frequently do so with a sense that they are relics of a dead culture. This is a natural enough reaction since most young people feel they have burst upon the world full blown and what they have discovered about life was never known before. They have little sense of each generation standing on the shoulders of the previous generation. But if these young readers persist in their study of these plays, they find that the works are vividly alive, filled with action, wit and humor, and have something to say to them.

The eighteenth century is called the Age of Reason. Great changes were taking place in religion, science, philosophy, government, economics and social life. England was becoming a great international power. Wars in America

and Europe and Clive's conquest of India all contributed
to the Englishman's sense of greatness. Philosophers and
social thinkers were beginning to hold man responsible
for his own destiny, and as a result they blamed social
evil on the conditions created by man. They also believed
that man had the power within him to remedy these evils.
Large attempts to remedy political and social injustice
resulted in the American Revolution (1776) and in the
French Revolution (1789). Though in England social reform was often slow in coming, the conscience of the
nation was being aroused.

The English theatre was also going through a period of
change. The drama had reached its greatest heights at the
end of the sixteenth and the beginning of the seventeenth
centuries with the works of Shakespeare, Jonson, Webster
and others. Theirs was a great theatre that appealed to all
classes of society. It began to decline, however, and was
finally outlawed by the Puritans after they overthrew the
monarchy in 1642.

When Charles II was restored to power in 1660, the
theatres reopened, but they were quite different from what
they had been. The plays were mostly cold, classical
tragedies, or brilliant but amoral comedies of manners.
The audience was almost entirely aristocratic and the
theatre catered to its tastes. Though many consider these
tastes to be effete and decadent, we must keep in mind that
at its best the Restoration was unsurpassed for clever and
glittering comedy. After the pleasure-loving Stuarts were
deposed by the Glorious Revolution and the austere
William III was put on the throne, the middle class began
to flourish and the power of the aristocracy was curtailed.

The rise of the middle class saw a reawakening of
Puritan values. The old drama of the Restoration was attacked as "immoral and profane." The monarchy and the
nobility began to drift away from the theatre. Where the
gay Stuart kings had loved playgoing, doughty Queen
Anne and her Hanoverian successors had little or no use
for it. In fact the first two Georges, who ruled England
from 1714 to 1760, could not even speak the English
language. When the aristocracy left the theatre, the
merchant princes moved in.

The dramatists began to woo the new audiences by writing sentimental plays with neat little morals. Several men, notably John Gay and Henry Fielding, wrote plays satirizing the new comedy and its middle-class audience, but in 1737 a Theatre Licensing Act was passed and censorship was established. Fielding, in disgust, gave up writing plays and took to the novel, achieving literary immortality with his comic masterpiece *Tom Jones*. The theatre was left to the sentimentalists.

To a society that believed in man's innate goodness and saw itself getting better and better in this harmonious and perfect universe, this sentimental drama was very appealing. The characters depicted were people of high and noble virtues. If they suffered, it was because society was cruel to them, but society could be made better. If they did bad things, one had only to appeal to their essential goodness and they reformed. The characters suffered bittersweet sorrows but the plays ended happily, often with a sinner reforming and making things right for everyone. The members of the audience cried freely and felt much better, because to be able to recognize suffering and respond to it emotionally proved their own essential goodness.

True, Shakespeare's plays were still performed, but even they suffered at the hands of sentiment. Many of Shakespeare's lines were considered coarse and so were changed into more genteel speeches. His tragedies often had new endings in which everything came out right. King Lear and his daughter Cordelia no longer died; Lear got well and Cordelia found a new husband. Macbeth still died but not until after he had a long speech of repentance.

The comedies of the eighteenth century were not very funny. People attempting to be high-minded are unwilling intentionally to make fools of themselves in the theatre. Servants and other members of the lower classes provided whatever humor the plays had.

Not only were the plays censored but the number of theatres was also limited. Only two houses, Drury Lane and Covent Garden, were allowed legally to put on legitimate plays. Several other theatres presented musicals and pantomimes, and they occasionally "bootlegged" plays under the guise of recitals. But with all these limitations the theatre flourished for it was an age of actors, the greatest of them being David Garrick, who also managed the Drury Lane Theatre. The plays, bad as they were, provided vehicles for Garrick and others, and they pleased their audiences. Many people, however, were growing tired of these plays and were ready for a change. Goldsmith and Sheridan, at least for a few brief years, gave them that change.

Oliver Goldsmith was born in Ireland in 1730, one of seven children. His father was a minister, and Oliver studied for the church but finally turned to medicine. He graduated from Trinity College in Dublin in 1750 and two years later entered medical school at Edinburgh. Whether he ever received his doctor's degree is doubtful, but he used the title in later years and he did practice medicine. (Many did in those days without doctor's degrees.)

After spending two years traveling about Europe, Goldsmith settled in London. Besides practicing medicine, he taught school and wrote book reviews for the *Monthly Review*. In 1759 he published his first book, *An Inquiry into the Present State of Polite Learning in Europe*. With this book, he began a literary career, though he did not completely abandon medicine.

Before the eighteenth century, writers were supported for the most part by patrons, but Goldsmith was one of a new breed who made their living from public sales of their works. He became well known in literary circles and became a charter member of Dr. Samuel Johnson's famous Literary Club. He seems to have been well liked generally, but he had the unfortunate ability to spend money faster than he made it. He frequently found himself in embarrassing straits. In order to survive, he had to do much hack writing, but he also wrote more ambitious works. Among these were the long poems *The Traveller* and *The Deserted Village* and the novel *The Vicar of Wakefield*. His first play, *The Good-Natured Man*, was presented in 1768, and was fairly well received. His second play, *She Stoops to Conquer* was done in 1773. Goldsmith died the next year.

She Stoops to Conquer was attacked by some in its

own time as crude and vulgar. Both Colman and Garrick, who managed Covent Garden and Drury Lane respectively, were reluctant to produce the play, and it was only after Johnson interceded that Colman agreed to a production. Even the actors had little confidence in the script. One outstanding comedian, Woodward, refused to play Tony Lumpkin. The opening-night audience roared with laughter, however, and though voices were raised against the play, it was generally acclaimed an outstanding success. It has been attacked since because many feel that it is an impure mixture of high comedy and low farce. But the play has two assets that make it stand up. First of all it is funny. It is funny when read and even funnier when seen in the theatre. Secondly, the characters are warm and likable, which is not always the case with comedy. In achieving this Goldsmith was harking back to Shakespeare.

Many people when reading comedies miss much of the humor because they respond only to the gag lines and the epigrams. The greatest laughter comes not from lines but from comic situations, and *She Stoops to Conquer* has several hilarious ones.

When we see two elements placed together in such a way that they look absurd—the fat wife and the skinny husband, for instance—we have incongruity and the basis of comedy. The writer of comedy shows us the ludicrous, the unexpected, the absurd, the folly in human character. When Tony convinces Marlow and Hastings that Hardcastle's home is an inn, he sets up the basic incongruity of the plot. Maybe the situation would not work in real life —though Goldsmith is said to have had a similar experience in his youth—but if we go along with it, Goldsmith will show us a merry time. Hardcastle, a brusque, friendly man, expects to find Marlow shy and withdrawn, as indeed he is in polite company, but is outraged to find him high-handed and aggressive. Marlow, thinking he is in an inn treats Hardcastle as though he were a pushy innkeeper. The fun is compounded when Marlow, who is terribly shy with nice young ladies, mistakes Hardcastle's daughter, Kate, for a barmaid. Kate, taking full advantage of the situation, is able to see Marlow behave with a boldness he would never have used had he known who she was.

Comedy also has its victims. Someone has to be made a fool. This is particularly well done in *She Stoops to Conquer* in the scene where Mrs. Hardcastle is taken on a merry-go-round night ride by Tony. As things get more difficult for her, and as she becomes more frightened the harder we laugh. If we are to laugh, it is also important that we not worry about consequences. Marlow makes a fool of himself by taking Kate for a barmaid, but we do not worry that he will lose the girl. Mrs. Hardcastle suffers a ducking in the horsepond, but we do not worry that she will catch pneumonia.

Serious plays are always concerned with consequences. In the more sentimental ones, human nature is conveniently altered to produce desired ends. Comedy is concerned with what absurd fools people make of themselves. In warmer comedies, such as *She Stoops to Conquer*, the people, though often foolish, are basically sympathetic. We can see our own foibles mirrored in them. In this way Goldsmith reflected the best attitudes of the eighteenth-century middle class, and, incidentally, reflected attitudes we in the twentieth century can still appreciate.

For those who insist on categories, *She Stoops to Conquer* might be called high comedy with extensive farce elements. It also has its share of sentiment. Like all great comedies, this play has strong situation humor. It may lack the brilliant dialogue of *The School for Scandal* or some of the great Restoration plays, but the language is good enough, the characters are amusing and likable, and the plot serves them well.

A word must be said about the characters. All comic characters tend to fall more or less into types. In Tony we see elements of Shakespeare's Falstaff, and our own Groucho Marx and Jackie Gleason. But Goldsmith manages to make Tony unique. His real stroke of comic genius is in giving Mrs. Hardcastle, an imperious woman with social airs, such a nonconforming and earthy son. Here again is brilliant incongruity. Each of the other characters is clearly drawn. Each has distinct characteristics that type him, but each is warm and individual— saucy, pert Kate, bashful Marlow, garrulous Mr. Hardcastle, and sensible, lovely Constance.

Richard Brinsley Sheridan was also an Irishman. He was born in Dublin in 1751. His grandfather, a teacher, was a friend of the famous Jonathan Swift. His father, an outstanding actor and teacher of elocution, was a friend of Dr. Samuel Johnson. His mother was a novelist and playwright of considerable ability. When Richard was nineteen, he and his family settled in Bath, England, the scene of *The Rivals*. Bath was known for its hot springs and baths, and was a fashionable resort of the upper middle class.

While in Bath Sheridan began to dabble with literature, but he became involved with romantic concerns, which occupied more of his time. He was attracted to Miss Elizabeth Linley, a beautiful, young concert singer. She had many suitors, but one of them, a married man, Major Matthews, made life difficult for her with his unwelcome advances. Sheridan ran away with her to France, where they were secretly married. Her father brought her home and refused to recognize her marriage to Sheridan. Sheridan's troubles were compounded when Major Matthews challenged him to a duel. Sheridan, an excellent fencer, disarmed Matthews. In a subsequent duel, however, Matthews wounded Sheridan, but Sheridan recovered. He retired to a life of study, but a year later he openly married Elizabeth with her father's consent.

Sheridan had little money, and he was too proud to allow his wife to work. He wrote *The Rivals* in order to make money. It was produced at Covent Garden in 1775 when Sheridan was not yet twenty-four. The play was too long and was not well received. He immediately revised it and it became a great hit. The same year he wrote a short farce, *St. Patrick's Day,* and a comic opera, *The Duenna.* The next year he and his father-in-law bought out David Garrick, and Sheridan became the manager of the Drury Lane Theatre. He wrote three more plays in 1777; the last of them, *The School for Scandal,* was his most successful play. A satire, *The Critic,* followed in 1779, and, except for an attempt at writing a tragedy twenty years later, Sheridan, at twenty-eight years of age, stopped writing for the theatre. He became a member of parliament and achieved renown as a great orator. He continued to live

off the profits of Drury Lane until it was destroyed by fire
in 1805. He fell into debt and drank heavily. He even spent
a short time in debtor's prison, but his friends came to his
rescue. He died in London in 1816 and was buried with
great pomp in the poet's corner of Westminster Abbey.
Lord Byron, the great romantic poet, said of Sheridan,
"Whatever he tried he did better than anyone else. He
wrote the best comedy, *The School for Scandal*, the best
opera, *The Duenna*, the best farce, *The Critic*, and the
best address, 'The Monologue' on Garrick. And to crown
it all, he delivered the very best oration ever conceived or
heard in this country, the famous Begum speech."

The Rivals and *The School for Scandal* are both
comedies of manners. They depict the language, customs
and fashions of a limited social group, the leisure class.
The Rivals tends more to broad comedy and its language
is seldom as brilliant as is that in *The School for Scandal*.
It has an extremely complex plot, and is filled with dis-
guises and surprises. Some critics have attacked it as a
"hodgepodge" of high and low comedy. But it works in the
theatre. Audiences love it and so do actors. It has so many
fine roles that actors, for years, have used it for all-star
revivals.

The intricate plot may give readers a little difficulty at
first, but after a while it becomes clear enough. Sheridan
uses all the various plots and counterplots to set up one
hilarious scene after another. The play satirizes eighteenth-
century sentimental comedy as well as the artificial social
set at Bath. Neither of these institutions means much to
us today, but Sheridan goes beyond his topical material.
Even in our own day we still know these comic types and
we recognize their follies: Lydia, who is more interested in
the intrigues of romance than she is in true love; Acres, the
country boob who tries to put on airs; Mrs. Malaprop,
whose romantic pretensions make her almost as absurd as
do her linguistic pretensions; Faulkland, who must drama-
tize every scrap of his romance; and Sir Lucius O'Trigger,
who tries to make a fortune out of marriage but still
wants a pretty girl. All of these types we recognize as
universal phonies. We laugh at them, we understand them,
and we even like them.

The School for Scandal treats more serious and more dangerous aspects of human behavior. Among the play's characters are an arch hypocrite, a group of scandalmongers, a wife who seeks an adulterous attachment, and a young man who is wasting his life in wild living. But Sheridan is not preaching a sermon. True unlike Restoration playwrights, he is on the side of virtue. The good people triumph and the bad people are undone. But he does not belabor the serious consequences of his characters' follies and vices. He uses them to provoke laughter.

Here is a true manners comedy. We are presented with a very special group of society. The language they use is as artificial as they are, but it is witty and masterful. Here we have juxtaposed the hypocritical sentiment of Joseph with the natural, though wild, behavior of Charles; the vicious values of the scandalmongers, Lady Sneerwell, Mrs. Candour and Sir Benjamin, with the humane values of the honest people, Sir Oliver, Rowley and Maria. But the play never gets nasty. It is all very good fun.

We still have elements of the sentimental comedy here. Lady Teazle's reform in the end is pure sentiment. But the sentiment in the play only provides geniality and good humor, never mawkishness.

The plot is masterfully handled. All the way through, the various story elements cross and crisscross each other until Sheridan weaves a tight structural pattern from them. In the famous screen scene he manages to pull together his major and minor plots into an hilarious climax.

The characters are beautifully drawn. Here again we have universal types. The very names of the characters indicate their natures—Sneerwell, Candour, Surface, Backbite, Snake—but they are deftly delineated. Notice, for example, how he distinguishes between the types of scandalmongers in Lady Sneerwell and Mrs. Candour. And Sir Benjamin Backbite is quite unlike either of them.

All the elements of comedy come together in a happy blend in *The School for Scandal*. It is not only generally recognized as Sheridan's best play but it is also considered by many to be one of the finest comedies in the English language.

A last word should be said about the staging of the plays. The theatres had stages not unlike our own conventional stages. The scenery consisted of elaborately painted back drops and side pieces, called "wings." Little furniture was used and most of the action took place on the apron of the stage, an extended area down near the audience. Costumes were lavish, makeup heavy and lighting poor by our standards. Candles supplied the illumination. Plays began at 6 P.M. A play was usually introduced by a prologue which set the tone and theme of the play. An epilogue frequently concluded the evening. A device, now rarely used in the modern theatre, the aside, was quite popular. At certain times the actor simply stepped to the end of the apron and addressed the audience. By convention the characters on the stage could not hear him at that time. This device enabled characters to get information to the audience that could not be revealed in dialogue. The aside was also used for comic effects.

The best way to enjoy any play is to see it on stage. The costumes, lights, scenery, makeup; the sounds of the actors' voices; their movement and gestures; and the audience itself are all part of the theatre experience. In lieu of seeing plays, however, reading them can give us great pleasure. These three plays, which so lighted up the eighteenth-century stage, still are part of our own theatre, and they still delight thousands of readers every year. Because they are great examples of dramatic art, they not only reflect their own times but continue to speak to men of all ages.

JOHN BETTENBENDER

SHE STOOPS TO CONQUER

or, The Mistakes of a Night

by OLIVER GOLDSMITH

Dramatis Personae

—MEN	—WOMEN
SIR CHARLES MARLOW	MRS HARDCASTLE
YOUNG MARLOW, *his son*	MISS HARDCASTLE
HARDCASTLE	MISS NEVILLE
HASTINGS	MAID
TONY LUMPKIN	LANDLORD, SERVANTS, *etc.*
DIGGORY	

Prologue

BY DAVID GARRICK, ESQ.[1]

[*Enter* MR WOODWARD,[2] *dressed in black, and holding a handkerchief to his eyes.*]

Excuse me, sirs, I pray—I can't yet speak—
  I'm crying now—and have been all the week.
"Tis not alone this mourning suit,' good masters;
  'I've that within'—for which there are no plasters![3]
Pray would you know the reason why I'm crying?
  The comic muse, long sick, is now a-dying!
And if she goes, my tears will never stop;
  For as a player, I can't squeeze out one drop:
I am undone, that's all—shall lose my bread—
  I'd rather, but that's nothing—lose my head.
When the sweet maid is laid upon the bier,
  Shuter[4] and I shall be chief mourners here.
To her a mawkish drab of spurious breed,
  Who deal in Sentimentals will succeed!
Poor Ned and I are dead to all intents;
  We can as soon speak Greek as Sentiments.
Both nervous grown, to keep our spirits up,
  We now and then take down a hearty cup.
What shall we do?—If Comedy forsake us!
  They'll turn us out, and no one else will take us,
But, why can't I be moral?—Let me try—
  My heart thus pressing—fix'd my face and eye—
With a sententious look, that nothing means
  (Faces are blocks, in sentimental scenes),
Thus I begin—'All is not gold that glitters,
  'Pleasure seems sweet, but proves a glass of bitters.
'When ignorance enters, folly is at hand:
  'Learning is better far than house and land.

'Let not your virtue trip, who trips may stumble,
  'And virtue is not virtue, if she tumble.'
I give it up—morals won't do for me;
  To make you laugh, I must play tragedy.
One hope remains—hearing the maid was ill,
  A Doctor⁵ comes this night to show his skill.
To cheer her heart, and give your muscles motion,
  He in Five Draughts⁶ prepar'd, presents a potion:
A kind of magic charm—for be assur'd,
  If you will swallow it, the maid is cur'd.
But desperate the Doctor, and her case is,
  If you reject the dose, and make wry faces!
This truth he boasts, will boast it while he lives,
  No poisonous drugs are mix'd in what he gives.
Should he succeed, you'll give him his degree;
  If not, within⁷ he will receive no fee!
The college You, must his pretensions back,
  Pronounce him Regular, or dub him Quack.

Act one.

SCENE I

[*A chamber in an old-fashioned house.*]
[*Enter* MRS HARDCASTLE *and* MR HARDCASTLE.]

MRS HARDCASTLE

I vow, Mr Hardcastle, you're very particular. Is there a
creature in the whole country, but ourselves, that does not
take a trip to town now and then, to rub off the rust a
little? There's the two Miss Hoggs, and our neighbour,
Mrs Grigsby, go to take a month's polishing every winter.

HARDCASTLE

Ay, and bring back vanity and affectation to last them the
whole year. I wonder why London cannot keep its own
fools at home. In my time, the follies of the town crept
slowly among us, but now they travel faster than a stage-
coach. Its fopperies come down, not only as inside passengers, but in the very basket.[8]

MRS HARDCASTLE

Ay, your times were fine times, indeed; you have been
telling us of them for many a long year. Here we live in an
old rambling mansion, that looks for all the world like an
inn, but that we never see company. Our best visitors are
old Mrs Oddfish, the curate's wife, and little Cripplegate,
the lame dancing-master: and all our entertainment your
old stories of Prince Eugene and the Duke of Marlborough.[9] I hate such old-fashioned trumpery.

HARDCASTLE

And I love it. I love everything that's old: old friends,
old times, old manners, old books, old wine; and, I believe,

Dorothy [*Taking her hand.*], you'll own I have been pretty
fond of an old wife.

MRS HARDCASTLE

Lord, Mr Hardcastle, you're for ever at your Dorothys
and your old wives. You may be a Darby, but I'll be no
Joan,[10] I promise you. I'm not so old as you'd make me,
by more than one good year. Add twenty to twenty, and
make money of that.

HARDCASTLE

Let me see; twenty added to twenty makes just fifty and
seven.

MRS HARDCASTLE

It's false, Mr Hardcastle: I was but twenty when Tony was
born, the son of Mr Lumpkin, my first husband; and he's
not come to years of discretion yet.

HARDCASTLE

Nor ever will, I dare answer for him. Ay, you have taught
him finely!

MRS HARDCASTLE

No matter, Tony Lumpkin has a good fortune. My son is
not to live by his learning. I don't think a boy wants much
learning to spend fifteen hundred a-year.

HARDCASTLE

Learning, quotha![11] a mere composition of tricks and
mischief!

MRS HARDCASTLE

Humour, my dear: nothing but humour. Come, Mr Hardcastle, you must allow the boy a little humour.

HARDCASTLE

I'd sooner allow him a horse-pond![12] If burning the footmen's shoes, frightening the maids, and worrying the kittens
be humour, he has it. It was but yesterday he fastened my
wig to the back of my chair, and when I went to make a
bow, I popt my bald head in Mrs Frizzle's face!

MRS HARDCASTLE

And am I to blame? The poor boy was always too sickly
to do any good. A school would be his death. When he
comes to be a little stronger, who knows what a year or
two's Latin may do for him?

HARDCASTLE

Latin for him! A cat and fiddle! No, no, the alehouse and

the stable are the only schools he'll ever go to.

MRS HARDCASTLE

Well, we must not snub[13] the poor boy now, for I believe
we shan't have him long among us. Anybody that looks
in his face may see he's consumptive.

HARDCASTLE

Ay, if growing too fat be one of the symptoms.

MRS HARDCASTLE

He coughs sometimes.

HARDCASTLE

Yes, when his liquor goes the wrong way.

MRS HARDCASTLE

I'm actually afraid of his lungs.

HARDCASTLE

And truly, so am I; for he sometimes whoops like a speak-
ing-trumpet—[TONY *halloing behind the scenes.*]—O, there
he goes—a very consumptive figure, truly!

   [*Enter* TONY, *crossing the stage.*]

MRS HARDCASTLE

Tony, where are going, my charmer? Won't you give papa
and I a little of your company, lovee?

TONY

I'm in haste, mother; I cannot stay.

MRS HARDCASTLE

You shan't venture out this raw evening, my dear; you
look most shockingly.

TONY

I can't stay, I tell you. The Three Pigeons[14] expects me
down every moment. There's some fun going forward.

HARDCASTLE

Ay; the alehouse, the old place: I thought so.

MRS HARDCASTLE

A low, paltry set of fellows.

TONY

Not so low, neither. There's Dick Muggins the exciseman,[15]
Jack Slang the horse doctor, Little Aminadab that grinds
the music-box, and Tom Twist that spins the pewter
platter.

MRS HARDCASTLE

Pray, my dear, disappoint them for one night, at least.

TONY

As for disappointing them I should not so much mind; but
I can't abide to disappoint myself!

MRS HARDCASTLE

[*Detaining him.*] You shan't go.

TONY

I will, I tell you.

MRS HARDCASTLE

I say you shan't.

TONY

We'll see which is strongest, you or I.

[*Exit, hauling her out.* HARDCASTLE *solus.*]

HARDCASTLE

Ay, there goes a pair that only spoil each other. But is not
the whole age in a combination to drive sense and discretion out of doors? There's my pretty darling Kate! the
fashions of the times have almost infected her too. By
living a year or two in town, she's as fond of gauze and
French frippery as the best of them. [*Enter* MISS HARD-
CASTLE.] Blessing on my pretty innocence! drest out as
usual, my Kate. Goodness! What a quantity of superfluous
silk hast thou got about thee, girl! I could never teach the
fools of this age, that the indigent world could be clothed
out of the trimmings of the vain.

MISS HARDCASTLE

You know our agreement, sir. You allow me the morning
to receive and pay visits, and to dress in my own manner;
and in the evening I put on my housewife's dress to please
you.

HARDCASTLE

Well, remember, I insist on the terms of our agreement;
and, by the by, I believe I shall have occasion to try your
obedience this very evening.

MISS HARDCASTLE

I protest, sir, I don't comprehend your meaning.

HARDCASTLE

Then, to be plain with you, Kate, I expect the young
gentleman I have chosen to be your husband from town
this very day. I have his father's letter, in which he informs
me his son is set out, and that he intends to follow himself
shortly after.

MISS HARDCASTLE

Indeed! I wish I had known something of this before. Bless me, how shall I behave? It's a thousand to one I shan't like him; our meeting will be so formal, and so like a thing of business, that I shall find no room for friendship or esteem.

HARDCASTLE

Depend upon it, child, I never will control your choice; but Mr Marlow, whom I have pitched upon, is the son of my old friend, Sir Charles Marlow, of whom you have heard me talk so often. The young gentleman has been bred a scholar, and is designed for an employment in the service of his country. I am told he's a man of an excellent understanding.

MISS HARDCASTLE

Is he?

HARDCASTLE

Very generous.

MISS HARDCASTLE

I believe I shall like him.

HARDCASTLE

Young and brave.

MISS HARDCASTLE

I am sure I shall like him.

HARDCASTLE

And very handsome.

MISS HARDCASTLE

My dear papa, say no more. [*Kissing his hand.*] He's mine, I'll have him.

HARDCASTLE

And, to crown all, Kate, he's one of the most bashful and reserved young fellows in all the world.

MISS HARDCASTLE

Eh! you have frozen me to death again. That word *reserved* has undone all the rest of his accomplishments. A reserved lover, it is said, always makes a suspicious husband.

HARDCASTLE

On the contrary, modesty seldom resides in a breast that is not enriched with nobler virtues. It was the very feature in his character that first struck me.

MISS HARDCASTLE

He must have more striking features to catch me, I
promise you. However, if he be so young, so handsome,
and so everything as you mention, I believe he'll do still. I
think I'll have him.

HARDCASTLE

Ay, Kate, but there is still an obstacle. It is more than an
even wager, he may not have you.

MISS HARDCASTLE

My dear papa, why will you mortify one so? Well, if he
refuses, instead of breaking my heart at his indifference,
I'll only break my glass for its flattery, set my cap to some
newer fashion, and look out for some less difficult admirer.

HARDCASTLE

Bravely resolved! In the meantime I'll go prepare the
servants for his reception; as we seldom see company, they
want as much training as a company of recruits the first
day's muster. [*Exit.*]

MISS HARDCASTLE

[*Alone.*] Lud, this news of papa's puts me all in a flutter.
Young, handsome; these he put last; but I put them fore-
most. Sensible, good-natured; I like all that. But then
reserved, and sheepish, that's much against him. Yet can't
he be cured of his timidity, by being taught to be proud
of his wife? Yes, and can't I—but I vow I'm disposing of
the husband before I have secured the lover. [*Enter* MISS
NEVILLE.] I'm glad you're come, Neville, my dear. Tell
me, Constance, how do I look this evening? Is there anything whimsical [16] about me? Is it one of my well-looking
days, child? Am I in face to-day?

MISS NEVILLE

Perfectly, my dear. Yet, now I look again—bless me!—
sure no accident has happened among the canary birds or
the goldfishes? Has your brother or the cat been meddling?
Or has the last novel been too moving?

MISS HARDCASTLE

No nothing of all this. I have been threatened—I can
scarce get it out—I have been threatened with a lover.

MISS NEVILLE

And his name—

MISS HARDCASTLE
Is Marlow.
MISS NEVILLE
Indeed!
MISS HARDCASTLE
The son of Sir Charles Marlow.
MISS NEVILLE
As I live, the most intimate friend of Mr Hastings, my admirer. They are never asunder. I believe you must have seen him when we lived in town.
MISS HARDCASTLE
Never.
MISS NEVILLE
He's a very singular character, I assure you. Among women of reputation he is the modestest man alive but his acquaintance give him a very different character among creatures of another stamp: you understand me.
MISS HARDCASTLE
An odd character, indeed. I shall never be able to manage him. What shall I do? Pshaw, think no more of him, but trust to occurrences for success. But how goes on your own affair, my dear? Has my mother been courting you for my brother Tony as usual?
MISS NEVILLE
I have just come from one of our agreeable *tête-à-têtes*. She has been saying a hundred tender things, and setting off her pretty monster as the very pink of perfection.
MISS HARDCASTLE
And her partiality is such, that she actually thinks him so. A fortune like yours is no small temptation. Besides, as she has the sole management of it, I'm not surprised to see her unwilling to let it go out of the family.
MISS NEVILLE
A fortune like mine, which chiefly consists in jewels, is not such mighty temptation. But at any rate, if my dear Hastings be but constant, I make no doubt to be too hard for her at last. However, I let her suppose that I am in love with her son, and she never once dreams that my affections are fixed upon another.
MISS HARDCASTLE
My good brother holds out stoutly. I could almost love

him for hating you so.

MISS NEVILLE

It is a good-natured creature at bottom, and I'm sure would
wish to see me married to anybody but himself. But my
aunt's bell rings, for our afternoon's walk around the improvements.[17] *Allons.*[18] Courage is necessary, as our affairs
are critical.

MISS HARDCASTLE

'Would it were bed-time and all were well.' [*Exeunt.*]

SCENE II

[*An alehouse room.*]

[*Several shabby fellows, with punch and tobacco.*
TONY *at the head of the table, a little higher than the
rest, a mallet in his hand.*]

OMNES

Hurrea! hurrea! hurrea! bravo!

FIRST FELLOW

Now, gentlemen, silence for a song. The 'squire is going
to knock himself down[19] for a song.

OMNES

Ay, a song, a song.

TONY

Then I'll sing you, gentlemen, a song I made upon this
alehouse, the Three Pigeons.

Song

Let school-masters puzzle their brain
    With grammar, and nonsense, and learning;
Good liquor, I stoutly maintain,
    Gives genius a better discerning,
Let them brag of their heathenish gods,
    Their Lethes, their Styxes, and Stygians; [20]
Their Quis, and their Quaes, and their Quods,[21]

They're all but a parcel of pigeons.
      Toroddle, toroddle, toroll!

When Methodist [22] preachers come down,
   A-preaching that drinking is sinful,
I'll wager the rascals a crown,
   They always preach best with a skinful.
But when you come down with your pence,
   For a slice of their scurvy religion,
I'll leave it to all men of sense,
   But you, my good friend, are the pigeon. [23]
      Toroddle, toroddle, toroll!

Then come, put the jorum [24] about,
   And let us be merry and clever,
Our hearts and our liquors are stout,
   Here's the Three Jolly Pigeons for ever.
Let some cry up woodcock or hare,
   Your bustards, your ducks, and your widgeons;
But of all the birds in the air,
   Here's a health to the Three Jolly Pigeons.
      Toroddle, toroddle, toroll!

OMNES
Bravo, bravo!
FIRST FELLOW
The 'squire has got spunk in him.
SECOND FELLOW
I loves to hear him sing, bekeays he never gives us nothing
that's low.
FIRST FELLOW
O damn anything that's low, I cannot bear it.
FOURTH FELLOW
The genteel thing is the genteel thing at any time: if so
be that a gentleman bees in a concatenation accordingly.
THIRD FELLOW
I like the maxum of it, Master Muggins. What, though I
am obligated to dance a bear, a man may be a gentleman
for all that. May this be my poison if my bear ever dances
but to the very genteelest of tunes; Water Parted, [25] or the
minuet in *Ariadne.* [26]

SECOND FELLOW

What a pity it is the 'squire is not come to his own. It would
be well for all the publicans within ten miles round of him.

TONY

Ecod, and so it would, Master Slang. I'd then show what it
was to keep choice of company.

SECOND FELLOW

Oh, he takes after his own father for that. To be sure,
old 'squire Lumpkin was the finest gentleman I ever set
my eyes on. For winding the straight horn, or beating a
thicket for a hare, or a wench, he never had his fellow. It
was a saying in the place, that he kept the best horses, dogs,
and girls, in the whole county.

TONY

Ecod, and when I'm of age I'll be no bastard, I promise
you. I have been thinking of Bet Bouncer and the miller's
grey mare to begin with. But come, my boys, drink about
and be merry, for you pay no reckoning. Well, Stingo,
what's the matter?

[*Enter* LANDLORD.]

LANDLORD

There be two gentlemen in a postchaise[27] at the door. They
have lost their way upo' the forest; and they are talking
something about Mr Hardcastle.

TONY

As sure as can be, one of them must be the gentleman
that's coming down to court my sister. Do they seem to be
Londoners?

LANDLORD

I believe they may. They look woundily[28] like Frenchmen.

TONY

Then desire them to step this way, and I'll set them right
in a twinkling. [*Exit* LANDLORD.] Gentlemen, as they
mayn't be good enough company for you, step down for
a moment, and I'll be with you in the squeezing of a
lemon. [*Exeunt* MOB.] Father-in-law[29] has been calling me
whelp and hound this half-year. Now, if I pleased, I could
be so revenged upon the old grumbletonian. But then I'm
afraid—afraid of what? I shall soon be worth fifteen hundred a year, and let him frighten me out of that if he can!

[*Enter the* LANDLORD, *conducting* MARLOW *and*
HASTINGS.]

MARLOW

What a tedious uncomfortable day have we had of it! We
were told it was but forty miles across the country, and we
have come above threescore!

HASTINGS

And all, Marlow, from that unaccountable reserve of
yours that would not let us inquire more frequently on the
way.

MARLOW

I own, Hastings, I am unwilling to lay myself under an
obligation to everyone I meet, and often stand the chance
of an unmannerly answer.

HASTINGS

At present, however, we are not likely to receive any
answer.

TONY

No offence, gentlemen. But I'm told you have been inquiring for one Mr Hardcastle in these parts. Do you know
what part of the country you are in?

HASTINGS

Not in the least, sir, but should thank you for information.

TONY

Nor the way you came?

HASTINGS

No, sir; but if you can inform us—

TONY

Why, gentlemen, if you know neither the road you are
going, nor where you are, nor the road you came, the
first thing I have to inform you is, that—you have lost your
way.

MARLOW

We wanted no ghost[30] to tell us that.

TONY

Pray, gentlemen, may I be so bold as to ask the place from
whence you came?

MARLOW

That's not necessary towards directing us where we are
to go.

TONY

No offence; but question for question is all fair, you
know.—Pray, gentlemen, is not this same Hardcastle a
cross-grained, old-fashioned, whimsical fellow with an
ugly face, a daughter, and a pretty son?

HASTINGS

We have not seen the gentleman; but he has the family
you mention.

TONY

The daughter, a tall, trapesing, trolloping, talkative may-
pole—the son, a pretty, well-bred, agreeable youth, that
everybody is fond of?

MARLOW

Our information differs in this. The daughter is said to be
well-bred, and beautiful; the son, an awkward booby,
reared up and spoiled at his mother's apron-string.

TONY

He-he-hem!—Then gentlemen, all I have to tell you is,
that you won't reach Mr Hardcastle's house this night, I
believe.

HASTINGS

Unfortunate!

TONY

It's a damned long, dark, boggy, dirty, dangerous way.
Stingo, tell the gentlemen the way to Mr Hardcastle's.
[*Winking upon the* LANDLORD.] Mr Hardcastle's of Quag-
mire Marsh, you understand me.

LANDLORD

Master Hardcastle's! Lock-a-daisy, my masters, you're
come a deadly deal wrong! When you came to the bottom
of the hill, you should have crossed down Squash Lane.

MARLOW

Cross down Squash Lane!

LANDLORD

Then you were to keep straight forward, until you came
to four roads.

MARLOW

Come to where four roads meet!

TONY

Ay, but you must be sure to take only one of them.

MARLOW

O, sir, you're facetious!

TONY

Then, keeping to the right, you are to go sideways till you come upon Crack-skull common: there you must look sharp for the track of the wheel, and go forward, till you come to Farmer Murrain's barn. Coming to the farmer's barn, you are to turn to the right, and then to the left, and then to the right about again, till you find out the old mill.

MARLOW

Zounds, man! we could as soon find out the longitude!

HASTINGS

What's to be done, Marlow?

MARLOW

This house promises but a poor reception; though perhaps the landlord can accommodate us.

LANDLORD

Alack, master, we have but one spare bed in the whole house.

TONY

And to my knowledge, that's taken up by three lodgers already. [*After a pause, in which the rest seem disconcerted.*] I have hit it. Don't you think, Stingo, our landlady could accommodate the gentlemen by the fireside, with— three chairs and a bolster?

HASTINGS

I hate sleeping by the fireside.

MARLOW

And I detest your three chairs and a bolster.

TONY

You do, do you?—then let me see—what if you go on a mile farther, to the Buck's Head; the old Buck's Head on the hill, one of the best inns in the whole county?

HASTINGS

Oho! so we have escaped an adventure for this night, however.

LANDLORD

[*Apart to* TONY.] Sure, you ben't sending them to your father's as an inn, be you?

TONY

Mum, you fool, you. Let them find that out. [*To them.*]
You have only to keep on straight forward, till you come
to a large old house by the roadside. You'll see a pair of
large horns over the door. That's the sign. Drive up the
yard, and call stoutly about you.

HASTINGS

Sir, we are obliged to you. The servants can't miss the way?

TONY

No, no: but I tell you, though, the landlord is rich, and
going to leave off business; so he wants to be thought a
gentleman, saving your presence, he! he! he! He'll be for
giving you his company, and, ecod, if you mind him, he'll
persuade you that his mother was an alderman, and his
aunt a justice of peace!

LANDLORD

A troublesome old blade, to be sure; but 'a keeps as good
wines and beds as any in the whole country.

MARLOW

Well, if he supplies us with these, we shall want no further
connexion. We are to turn to the right, did you say?

TONY

No, no; straight forward. I'll just step myself, and show
you a piece of the way. [*To the* LANDLORD.] Mum.

LANDLORD

Ah, bless your heart for a sweet, pleasant—damned, mis-
chievous son of a whore.

Act two.

[*An old-fashioned house.*]

[HARDCASTLE, *followed by three or four awkward* SERVANTS.]

HARDCASTLE
Well, I hope you're perfect in the table exercise I have been teaching you these three days. You all know your posts and your places, and can shew that you have been used to good company, without ever stirring from home.
OMNES
Ay, ay.
HARDCASTLE
When company comes, you are not to pop out and stare, and then run in again, like frightened rabbits in a warren.
OMNES
No, no.
HARDCASTLE
You, Diggory, whom I have taken from the barn, are to make a shew at the side-table; and you, Roger, whom I have advanced from the plough, are to place yourself behind my chair. But you're not to stand so, with your hands in your pockets. Take your hands from your pockets, Roger; and from your head, you blockhead, you. See how Diggory carries his hands. They're a little too stiff indeed, but that's no great matter.
DIGGORY
Ay, mind how I hold them. I learned to hold my hands this way, when I was upon drill for the militia. And so being upon drill—
HARDCASTLE
You must not be so talkative, Diggory. You must be all

attention to the guests. You must hear us talk, and not think of talking; you must see us drink, and not think of drinking; you must see us eat, and not think of eating.

DIGGORY

By the laws, your worship, that's parfectly unpossible. Whenever Diggory sees yeating going forward, ecod, he's always wishing for a mouthful himself.

HARDCASTLE

Blockhead! Is not a bellyful in the kitchen as good as a bellyful in the parlour? Stay your stomach with that reflection.

DIGGORY

Ecod. I thank your worship, I'll make a shift to stay my stomach with a slice of cold beef in the pantry.

HARDCASTLE

Diggory, you are too talkative.—Then, if I happen to say a good thing, or tell a good story at table, you must not all burst out a-laughing, as if you made part of the company.

DIGGORY

Then, ecod, your worship must not tell the story of old Grouse in the gun-room: I can't help laughing at that—he! he! he!—for the soul of me! We have laughed at that these twenty years—ha! ha! ha!

HARDCASTLE

Ha! ha! ha! The story is a good one. Well, honest Diggory, you may laugh at that—but still remember to be attentive. Suppose one of the company should call for a glass of wine, how will you behave? A glass of wine, sir, if you please [*To* DIGGORY.]—Eh, why don't you move?

DIGGORY

Ecod, your worship, I never have courage till I see the eatables and drinkables brought upo' the table, and then I'm as bauld as a lion.

HARDCASTLE

What, will nobody move?

FIRST SERVANT

I'm not to leave this pleace.

SECOND SERVANT

I'm sure it's no pleace of mine.

THIRD SERVANT

Nor mine, for sartain.

DIGGORY

Wauns, and I'm sure it canna be mine.

HARDCASTLE

You numskulls! and so while, like your betters, you are quarrelling for places, the guests must be starved. Oh, you dunces! I find I must begin all over again.——But don't I hear a coach drive into the yard? To your posts, you block-heads. I'll go in the meantime and give my old friend's son a hearty reception at the gate. [*Exit* HARDCASTLE.]

DIGGORY

By the elevens, my pleace is gone quite out of my head.

ROGER

I know that my pleace is to be everywhere!

FIRST SERVANT

Where the devil is mine?

SECOND SERVANT

My pleace is to be nowhere at all; and so I'ze go about my business!

[*Exeunt* SERVANTS, *running about as if frighted, different ways. Enter* SERVANT *with lighted candles, showing in* MARLOW *and* HASTINGS.]

SERVANT

Welcome, gentlemen, very welcome! This way.

HASTINGS

After the disappointments of the day, welcome once more, Charles, to the comforts of a clean room and a good fire. Upon my word, a very well-looking house; antique but creditable.

MARLOW

The usual fate of a large mansion. Having first ruined the master by good house-keeping, it at last comes to levy contributions as an inn.

HASTINGS

As you say, we passengers are to be taxed to pay for all these fineries. I have often seen a good sideboard, or a marble chimney-piece, though not actually put in the bill, inflame a reckoning confoundedly.

MARLOW

Travellers, George, must pay in all places. The only difference is, that in good inns you pay dearly for luxuries, in bad inns, you are fleeced and starved.

HASTINGS

You have lived pretty much among them. In truth, I have been often surprised, that you who have seen so much of the world, with your natural good sense, and your many opportunities, could never yet acquire a requisite share of assurance.

MARLOW

The Englishman's malady. But tell me, George, where could I have learned that assurance you talk of? My life has been chiefly spent in a college or an inn, in seclusion from that lovely part of the creation that chiefly teach men confidence. I don't know that I was ever familiarly acquainted with a single modest woman—except my mother—but among females of another class, you know—

HASTINGS

Ay, among them you are impudent enough of all conscience!

MARLOW

They are of *us,* you know.

HASTINGS

But in the company of women of reputation I never saw such an idiot, such a trembler; you look for all the world as if you wanted an opportunity of stealing out of the room.

MARLOW

Why, man, that's because I do want to steal out of the room. Faith, I have often formed a resolution to break the ice, and rattle away at any rate. But I don't know how, a single glance from a pair of fine eyes has totally overset my resolution. An impudent fellow may counterfeit modesty, but I'll be hanged if a modest man can ever counterfeit impudence.

HASTINGS

If you could but say half the fine things to them, that I have heard you lavish upon the barmaid of an inn, or even a college bed-maker—

MARLOW

Why, George, I can't say fine things to them. They freeze, they petrify me. They may talk of a comet, or a burning mountain, or some such bagatelle; but to me, a modest woman, drest out in all her finery, is the most tremendous object of the whole creation.

HASTINGS

Ha! ha! ha! At this rate, man, how can you ever expect to marry!

MARLOW

Never; unless, as among kings and princes, my bride were to be courted by proxy. If, indeed, like an eastern bridegroom, one were to be introduced to a wife he never saw before, it might be endured. But to go through all the terrors of a formal courtship, together with the episode of aunts, grandmothers, and cousins, and at last to blurt out the broad staring question of, Madam, will you marry me? No, no, that's a strain much above me, I assure you!

HASTINGS

I pity you. But how do you intend behaving to the lady you are come down to visit at the request of your father?

MARLOW

As I behave to all other ladies. Bow very low; answer yes, or no, to all her demands.—But for the rest, I don't think I shall venture to look in her face, till I see my father's again.

HASTINGS

I'm surprised that one who is so warm a friend can be so cool a lover.

MARLOW

To be explicit, my dear Hastings, my chief inducement down was to be instrumental in forwarding your happiness, not my own. Miss Neville loves you, the family don't know you; as my friend you are sure of a reception, and let honour do the rest.

HASTINGS

My dear Marlow! But I'll suppress the emotion. Were I a wretch, meanly seeking to carry off a fortune, you should be the last man in the world I would apply to for assistance. But Miss Neville's person is all I ask, and that is mine, both from her deceased father's consent, and her own inclination.

MARLOW

Happy man! You have talents and art to captivate any woman. I'm doomed to adore the sex, and yet to converse with the only part of it I despise. This stammer in my address, and this awkward unprepossessing visage of mine, can never permit me to soar above the reach of a milliner's apprentice, or one of the duchesses of Drury-Lane.[31] Pshaw! this fellow here to interrupt us.

[*Enter* HARDCASTLE.]

HARDCASTLE

Gentlemen, once more you are heartily welcome. Which is Mr Marlow? Sir, you're heartily welcome. It's not my way, you see, to receive my friends with my back to the fire. I like to give them a hearty reception in the old style at my gate. I like to see their horses and trunks taken care of.

MARLOW

[*Aside.*] He has got our names from the servants already. [*To him.*] We approve your caution and hospitality, sir. [*To Hastings.*] I have been thinking, George, of changing our travelling dresses in the morning. I am grown confoundedly ashamed of mine.

HARDCASTLE

I beg, Mr Marlow, you'll use no ceremony in this house. [*Both ignore him.*]

HASTINGS

I fancy, George, you're right: the first blow is half the battle. I intend opening the campaign with the white and gold.

HARDCASTLE

Mr Marlow—Mr Hastings—gentlemen—pray be under no constraint in this house. This is Liberty Hall, gentlemen. You may do just as you please here.

MARLOW

Yet, George, if we open the campaign too fiercely at first, we may want ammunition before it is over. I think to reserve the embroidery to secure a retreat.

HARDCASTLE

Your talking of a retreat, Mr Marlow, puts me in mind of the Duke of Marlborough, when we went to besiege Denain.[32] He first summoned the garrison—

MARLOW

Don't you think the *ventre d'or*[33] waistcoat will do with the plain brown?

HARDCASTLE

He first summoned the garrison, which might consist of

about five thousand men—

HASTINGS

I think not: brown and yellow mix but very poorly.

HARDCASTLE

I say, gentlemen, as I was telling you, he summoned the garrison, which might consist of about five thousand men—

MARLOW

The girls like finery.

HARDCASTLE

Which might consist of about five thousand men, well appointed with stores, ammunition, and other implements of war. 'Now,' says the Duke of Marlborough to George Brooks, that stood next to him—you must have heard of George Brooks; 'I'll pawn my Dukedom,' says he, 'but I take that garrison without spilling a drop of blood.' So—

MARLOW

What, my good friend, if you gave us a glass of punch in the meantime, it would help us to carry on the siege with vigour.

HARDCASTLE

Punch, sir! [*Aside.*] This is the most unaccountable kind of modesty I ever met with.

MARLOW

Yes, sir, punch! A glass of warm punch, after our journey, will be comfortable. This is Liberty Hall, you know.

HARDCASTLE

Here's a cup, sir.

MARLOW

[*Aside.*] So this fellow, in his Liberty Hall, will only let us have just what he pleases.

HARDCASTLE

[*Taking the cup.*] I hope you'll find it to your mind. I have prepared it with my own hands, and I believe you'll own the ingredients are tolerable. Will you be so good as to pledge me, sir? Here, Mr Marlow, here is our better acquaintance! [*Drinks.*]

MARLOW

[*Aside.*] A very impudent fellow this! but he's a character, and I'll humour him a little. Sir, my service to you. [*Drinks.*]

HASTINGS

[*Aside.*] I see this fellow wants to give us his company, and

forgets that he's an innkeeper, before he has learned to be
a gentleman.

MARLOW

From the excellence of your cup, my old friend, I suppose
you have a good deal of business in this part of the country.
Warm work, now and then, at elections, I suppose?

HARDCASTLE

No, sir, I have long given that work over. Since our betters
have hit upon the expedient of electing each other, there's
no business 'for us that sell ale'.[34]

HASTINGS

So, then you have no turn for politics, I find.

HARDCASTLE

Not in the least. There was a time, indeed, I fretted
myself about the mistakes of government, like other people
but, finding myself every day grow more angry, and the
government growing no better, I left it to mend itself.
Since that, I no more trouble my head about Heyder Ally
or Ally Cawn, than about Ally Croaker.[35] Sir, my service
to you.

HASTINGS

So that, with eating above stairs, and drinking below, with
receiving your friends within, and amusing them without,
you lead a good pleasant bustling life of it.

HARDCASTLE

I do stir about a great deal, that's certain. Half the differ-
ences of the parish are adjusted in this very parlour.

MARLOW

[*After drinking.*] And you have an argument in your cup,
old gentleman, better than any in Westminster Hall.[36]

HARDCASTLE

Ay, young gentleman, that, and a little philosophy.

MARLOW

[*Aside.*] Well, this is the first time I ever heard of an innkeeper's philosophy.

HASTINGS

So then, like an experienced general, you attack them on
every quarter. If you find their reason manageable, you
attack it with your philosophy; if you find they have no
reason, you attack them with this. Here's your health, my
philosopher. [*Drinks.*]

HARDCASTLE

Good, very good, thank you; ha! ha! Your generalship puts me in mind of Prince Eugene, when he fought the Turks at the battle of Belgrade. You shall hear.

MARLOW

Instead of the battle of Belgrade,[37] I believe it's almost time to talk about supper. What has your philosophy got in the house for supper?

HARDCASTLE

For supper, sir! [*Aside.*] Was ever such a request to a man in his own house!

MARLOW

Yes, sir, supper, sir; I begin to feel an appetite. I shall make devilish work tonight in the larder, I promise you.

HARDCASTLE

[*Aside.*] Such a brazen dog sure never my eyes beheld. [*To him.*] Why, really, sir, as for supper I can't well tell. My Dorothy, and the cook-maid, settle these things between them. I leave these kind of things entirely to them.

MARLOW

You do, do you?

HARDCASTLE

Entirely. By the by, I believe they are in actual consultation upon what's for supper this moment in the kitchen.

MARLOW

Then I beg they'll admit me as one of their privy council. It's a way I have got. When I travel I always choose to regulate my own supper. Let the cook be called. No offence, I hope, sir.

HARDCASTLE

Oh no, sir, none in the least; yet, I don't know how: our Bridget, the cook-maid, is not very communicative upon these occasions. Should we send for her, she might scold us all out of the house.

HASTINGS

Let's see your list of the larder, then. I ask it as a favour. I always match my appetite to my bill of fare.

MARLOW

[*To* HARDCASTLE, *who looks at them with surprise.*] Sir, he's very right, and it's my way, too.

HARDCASTLE

Sir, you have a right to command here. Here, Roger, bring us the bill of fare for tonight's supper. I believe it's drawn out.—Your manner, Mr Hastings, puts me in mind of my uncle, Colonel Wallop. It was a saying of his, that no man was sure of his supper till he had eaten it.

HASTINGS

[*Aside.*] All upon the high rope! [38] His uncle a colonel! We shall soon hear of his mother being a justice of peace. [HARDCASTLE *gives the paper to* MARLOW.] But let's hear the bill of fare.

MARLOW

[*Perusing.*] What's here? For the first course; for the second course; for the desert. The devil, sir, do you think we have brought down the whole Joiners' Company, or the Corporation [39] of Bedford, to eat up such a supper? Two or three little things, clean and comfortable, will do.

HASTINGS

But let's hear it.

MARLOW

[*Reading.*] For the first course at the top, a pig, and pruin sauce.

HASTINGS

Damn your pig, I say!

MARLOW

And damn your pruin sauce, say I!

HARDCASTLE

And yet, gentlemen, to men that are hungry, pig with pruin sauce is very good eating.

MARLOW

At the bottom a calf's tongue and brains.

HASTINGS

Let your brains be knocked out, my good sir, I don't like them.

MARLOW

Or you may clap them on a plate by themselves. I do.

HARDCASTLE

[*Aside.*] Their impudence confounds me. [*To them.*] Gentlemen, you are my guests, make what alterations you please. Is there anything else you wish to retrench or alter, gentlemen?

MARLOW

A pork pie, a boiled rabbit and sausages, a Florentine, a shaking pudding, and a dish of tiff—taff—taffety cream! [40]

HASTINGS

Confound your made dishes; [41] I shall be as much at a loss in this house as at a green and yellow dinner at the French ambassador's table, I'm for plain eating.

HARDCASTLE

I'm sorry, gentlemen, that I have nothing you like, but if there be anything you have a particular fancy to—

MARLOW

Why really, sir, your bill of fare is so exquisite, that any one part of it is full as good as another. Send us what you please. So much for supper. And now to see that our beds are aired, and properly taken care of.

HARDCASTLE

I entreat you'll leave all that to me. You shall not stir a step.

MARLOW

Leave that to you! I protest, sir, you must excuse me, I always look to these things myself.

HARDCASTLE

I must insist, sir, you'll make yourself easy on that head.

MARLOW

You see I'm resolved on it. [*Aside.*] A very troublesome fellow this, as ever I met with.

HARDCASTLE

Well, sir, I'm resolved at least to attend you. [*Aside.*] This may be modern modesty, but I never saw anything look so like old-fashioned impudence.

[*Exeunt* MARLOW *and* HARDCASTLE.]

HASTINGS

[*Alone.*] So I find this fellow's civilities begin to grow troublesome. But who can be angry at those assiduities which are meant to please him? Ha! what do I see! Miss Neville, by all that's happy!

[*Enter* MISS NEVILLE.]

MISS NEVILLE

My dear Hastings! To what unexpected good fortune, to what accident, am I to ascribe this happy meeting?

HASTINGS

Rather let me ask the same question, as I could never have hoped to meet my dearest Constance at an inn.

MISS NEVILLE

An inn! sure you mistake: my aunt, my guardian, lives here. What could induce you to think this house an inn?

HASTINGS

My friend, Mr Marlow, with whom I came down, and I, have been sent here as to an inn, I assure you. A young fellow, whom we accidentally met at a house hard by, directed us thither.

MISS NEVILLE

Certainly it must be one of my hopeful cousin's tricks, of whom you have heard me talk so often: ha! ha! ha!

HASTINGS

He whom your aunt intends for you? He of whom I have such just apprehensions?

MISS NEVILLE

You have nothing to fear from him, I assure you. You'd adore him if you knew how heartily he despises me. My aunt knows it, too, and has undertaken to court me for him, and actually begins to think she has made a conquest.

HASTINGS

Thou dear dissembler! You must know, my Constance, I have just seized this happy opportunity of my friend's visit here to get admittance into the family. The horses that carried us down are now fatigued with their journey, but they'll soon be refreshed; and then, if my dearest girl will trust in her faithful Hastings, we shall soon be landed in France, where even among slaves the laws of marriage are respected.

MISS NEVILLE

I have often told you, that though ready to obey you, I yet should leave my little fortune behind with reluctance. The greatest part of it was left me by my uncle, the India Director,[42] and chiefly consists in jewels. I have been for some time persuading my aunt to let me wear them. I fancy I'm very near succeeding. The instant they are put into my possession you shall find me ready to make them and my-self yours.

HASTINGS

Perish the baubles! Your person is all I desire. In the meantime, my friend Marlow must not be let into his mistake. I know the strange reserve of his temper is such that, if abruptly informed of it, he would instantly quit the house before our plan was ripe for execution.

MISS NEVILLE

But how shall we keep him in the deception? Miss Hardcastle is just returned from walking; what if we still continue to deceive him?—This, this way—[*They confer. Enter* MARLOW.]

MARLOW

The assiduities of these good people tease me beyond bearing. My host seems to think it ill manners to leave me alone, and so he claps not only himself, but his old-fashioned wife on my back. They talk of coming to sup with us, too; and then, I suppose, we are to run the gauntlet through all the rest of the family.—What have we got here?—

HASTINGS

My dear Charles! Let me congratulate you!—The most fortunate accident!—Who do you think is just alighted?

MARLOW

Cannot guess.

HASTINGS

Our mistresses, boy, Miss Hardcastle and Miss Neville. Give me leave to introduce Miss Constance Neville to your acquaintance. Happening to dine in the neighbourhood, they called, on their return, to take fresh horses here. Miss Hardcastle has just stepped into the next room, and will be back in an instant. Wasn't it lucky? eh!

MARLOW

[*Aside.*] I have just been mortified enough of all conscience, and here comes something to complete my embarrassment.

HASTINGS

Well! but wasn't it the most fortunate thing in the world?

MARLOW

Oh! yes. Very fortunate—a most joyful encounter.—But our dresses, George, you know, are in disorder.—What if we should postpone the happiness till tomorrow?—Tomorrow at her own house.—It will be every bit as con-

venient—and rather more respectful.—Tomorrow let it
be. [*Offering to go.*]

MISS NEVILLE

By no means, sir. Your ceremony will displease her. The
disorder of your dress will shew the ardour of your impatience. Besides, she knows you are in the house, and will
permit you to see her.

MARLOW

Oh! the devil! how shall I support it? Hem! hem! Hastings,
you must not go. You are to assist me, you know. I shall
be confoundedly ridiculous. Yet, hang it! I'll take courage.
Hem!

HASTINGS

Pshaw, man! it's but the first plunge, and all's over. She's
but a woman, you know.

MARLOW

And of all women, she that I dread most to encounter!

   [*Enter* MISS HARDCASTLE, *as returned from walking.*]

HASTINGS

[*Introducing them.*] Miss Hardcastle. Mr Marlow. I'm
proud of bringing two persons of such merit together, that
only want to know, to esteem each other.

MISS HARDCASTLE

[*Aside.*] Now, for meeting my modest gentleman with a
demure face, and quite in his own manner. [*After a pause,
in which he appears very uneasy and disconcerted.*] I'm
glad of your safe arrival, sir—I'm told you had some accidents by the way.

MARLOW

Only a few, madam. Yes, we had some. Yes, madam, a
good many accidents, but should be sorry—madam—or
rather glad of any accidents—that are so agreeably concluded. Hem!

HASTINGS

[*To him.*] You never spoke better in your whole life.
Keep it up, and I'll insure you the victory.

MISS HARDCASTLE

I'm afraid you flatter, sir. You that have seen so much of
the finest company can find little entertainment in an
obscure corner of the country.

MARLOW

[*Gathering courage.*] I have lived, indeed, in the world, madam; but I have kept very little company. I have been but an observer upon life, madam, while others were enjoying it.

MISS NEVILLE

But that, I am told, is the way to enjoy it at last.

HASTINGS

[*To him.*] Cicero never spoke better. Once more, and you are confirmed in assurance for ever.

MARLOW

[*To him.*] Hem! Stand by me, then, and when I'm down, throw in a word or two to set me up again.

MISS HARDCASTLE

An observer, like you, upon life, were, I fear, disagreeably employed, since you must have had much more to censure than to approve.

MARLOW

Pardon me, madam. I was always willing to be amused. The folly of most people is rather an object of mirth than uneasiness.

HASTINGS

[*To him.*] Bravo, bravo. Never spoke so well in your whole life. Well, Miss Hardcastle, I see that you and Mr Marlow are going to be very good company. I believe our being here will but embarrass the interview.

MARLOW

Not in the least, Mr Hastings. We like your company of all things. [*To him.*] Zounds! George, sure you won't go? How can you leave us?

HASTINGS

Our presence will but spoil conversation, so we'll retire to the next room. [*To him.*] You don't consider, man, that we are to manage a little *tête-à-tete* of our own. [*Exeunt.*]

MISS HARDCASTLE

[*After a pause.*] But you have not been wholly an observer, I presume, sir: the ladies, I should hope, have employed some part of your addresses.

MARLOW

[*Relapsing into timidity.*] Pardon me, madam, I—I—I— as yet have studied—only—to—deserve them.

MISS HARDCASTLE

And that some say is the very worst way to obtain them.

MARLOW

Perhaps so, madam. But I love to converse only with the
more grave and sensible part of the sex.—But I'm afraid
I grow tiresome.

MISS HARDCASTLE

Not at all, sir; there is nothing I like so much as grave conversation myself: I could hear it for ever. Indeed, I have
often been surprised how a man of sentiment could ever
admire those light airy pleasures, where nothing reaches
the heart.

MARLOW

It's—a disease—of the mind, madam. In the variety of
tastes there must be some who, wanting a relish for—um-
a-um.

MISS HARDCASTLE

I understand you, sir. There must be some, who, wanting a
relish for refined pleasures, pretend to despise what they
are incapable of tasting.

MARLOW

My meaning, madam, but infinitely better expressed. And
I can't help observing—a—

MISS HARDCASTLE

[*Aside.*] Who could ever suppose this fellow impudent
upon some occasions. [*To him.*] You were going to observe, sir—

MARLOW

I was observing, madam—I protest, madam, I forget what
I was going to observe.

MISS HARDCASTLE

[*Aside.*] I vow and so do I. [*To him.*] You were observing,
sir, that in this age of hypocrisy—something about hypocrisy, sir.

MARLOW

Yes, madam. In this age of hypocrisy, there are few who
upon strict inquiry do not—a—a—a—

MISS HARDCASTLE

I understand you perfectly, sir.

MARLOW

[*Aside.*] Egad! and that's more than I do myself!

MISS HARDCASTLE

You mean that in this hypocritical age there are few that do not condemn in public what they practise in private, and think they pay every debt to virtue when they praise it.

MARLOW

True, madam; those who have most virtue in their mouths, have least of it in their bosoms. But I'm sure I tire you, madam.

MISS HARDCASTLE

Not in the least, sir; there's something so agreeable and spirited in your manner, such life and force—pray, sir, go on.

MARLOW

Yes, madam. I was saying—that there are some occasions —when a total want of courage, madam, destroys all the —and puts us—upon a—a—a—

MISS HARDCASTLE

I agree with you entirely, a want of courage upon some occasions assumes the appearance of ignorance, and betrays us when we most want to excel. I beg you'll proceed.

MARLOW

Yes, madam. Morally speaking, madam—but I see Miss Neville expecting us in the next room. I would not intrude for the world.

MISS HARDCASTLE

I protest, sir, I never was more agreeably entertained in all my life. Pray go on.

MARLOW

Yes, madam. I was—but she beckons us to join her. Madam, shall I do myself the honour to attend you?

MISS HARDCASTLE

Well then, I'll follow.

MARLOW

[*Aside.*] This pretty smooth dialogue has done for me. [*Exit.*]

MISS HARDCASTLE

[*Alone.*] Ha! ha! ha! Was there ever such a sober sentimental interview? I'm certain he scarce looked in my face the whole time. Yet the fellow, but for his unaccountable bashfulness, pretty well, too. He has good sense, but then so buried in his fears, that it fatigues one more than

ignorance. If I could teach him a little confidence, it
would be doing somebody that I know of a piece of
service. But who is that somebody?—that, faith, is a
question I can scarce answer. [*Exit. Enter* TONY *and*
MISS NEVILLE, *followed by* MRS HARDCASTLE *and* HASTINGS.]

TONY

What do you follow me for, cousin Con? I wonder you're
not ashamed to be so very engaging.

MISS NEVILLE

I hope, cousin, one may speak to one's own relations, and
not be to blame.

TONY

Ay, but I know what sort of a relation you want to make
me though; but it won't do. I tell you, cousin Con, it won't
do; so I beg you'll keep your distance, I want no nearer
relationship.

[*She follows, coquetting him to the back scene.*]

MRS HARDCASTLE

Well! I vow, Mr Hastings, you are very entertaining.
There's nothing in the world I love to talk of so much as
London, and the fashions, though I was never there myself.

HASTINGS

Never there! You amaze me! From your air and manner, I
concluded you had been bred all your life either at
Ranelagh, St James's, or Tower Wharf.[43]

MRS HARDCASTLE

Oh! sir, you're only pleased to say so. We country persons
can have no manner at all. I'm in love with the town, and
that serves to raise me above some of our neighbouring
rustics; but who can have a manner, that has never seen
the Pantheon, the Grotto Gardens, the Borough, and such
places where the nobility chiefly resort? All I can do is to
enjoy London at second-hand. I take care to know every
tête-à-tête[44] from the Scandalous Magazine, and have all the
fashions as they come out, in a letter from the two Miss
Rickets of Crooked Lane. Pray how do you like this head,[45]
Mr Hastings?

HASTINGS

Extremely elegant and *dégagée*,[46] upon my word, madam.
Your friseur[47] is a Frenchman, I suppose?

MRS HARDCASTLE

I protest. I dressed it myself from a print in the Ladies'
Memorandum-book for the last year.

HASTINGS

Indeed. Such a head in a side-box, at the play-house, would
draw as many gazers as my Lady Mayoress at a city ball.

MRS HARDCASTLE

I vow, since inoculation[48] began, there is no such thing to
be seen as a plain woman; so one must dress a little particular, or one may escape in the crowd.

HASTINGS

But that can never be your case, madam, in any dress!
[*Bowing.*]

MRS HARDCASTLE

Yet, what signifies my dressing when I have such a piece
of antiquity by my side as Mr Hardcastle: all I can say
will never argue down a single button from his clothes. I
have often wanted him to throw off his great flaxen wig,
and where he was bald, to plaster it over like my Lord
Pately, with powder.

HASTINGS

You are right, madam; for, as among the ladies there are
none ugly, so among the men there are none old.

MRS HARDCASTLE

But what do you think his answer was? Why, with his
usual Gothic vivacity, he said I only wanted him to throw
off his wig to convert it into a *tête*[49] for my own wearing!

HASTINGS

Intolerable! At your age you may wear what you please,
and it must become you.

MRS HARDCASTLE

Pray, Mr. Hastings, what do you take to be the most
fashionable age about town?

HASTINGS

Some time ago forty was all the mode; but I'm told the
ladies intend to bring up fifty for the ensuing winter.

MRS HARDCASTLE

Seriously? Then I shall be too young for the fashion!

HASTINGS

No lady begins now to put on jewels till she's past forty.
For instance, Miss there, in a polite circle, would be con-

sidered as a child, as a mere maker of samplers.

MRS HARDCASTLE

And yet Mrs Niece[50] thinks herself as much a woman, and is as fond of jewels as the oldest of us all.

HASTINGS

Your niece, is she? And that young gentleman, a brother of yours, I should presume?

MRS HARDCASTLE

My son, sir. They are contracted to each other. Observe their little sports. They fall in and out ten times a day, as if they were man and wife already. [*To them.*] Well, Tony child, what soft things are you saying to your cousin Constance this evening?

TONY

I have been saying no soft things; but that it's very hard to be followed about so! Ecod! I've not a place in the house now that's left to myself but the stable.

MRS HARDCASTLE

Never mind him, Con, my dear. He's in another story behind your back.

MISS NEVILLE

There's something generous in my cousin's manner. He falls out before faces to be forgiven in private.

TONY

That's a damned confounded—crack.

MRS HARDCASTLE

Ah! he's a sly one. Don't you think they're like each other about the mouth, Mr Hastings? The Blenkinsop mouth to a T. They're of a size, too. Back to back, my pretties, that Mr Hastings may see you. Come, Tony.

TONY

You had as good not make me, I tell you. [*Measuring.*]

MISS NEVILLE

Oh lud! he has almost cracked my head.

MRS HARDCASTLE

Oh, the monster! For shame, Tony. You a man, and behave so!

TONY

If I'm a man, let me have my fortin. Ecod! I'll not be made a fool of no longer.

MRS HARDCASTLE

Is this, ungrateful boy, all that I'm to get for the pains I have taken in your education? I that have rocked you in your cradle, and fed that pretty mouth with a spoon! Did not I work that waistcoat to make you genteel? Did not I prescribe for you every day, and weep while the receipt was operating?

TONY

Ecod! you had reason to weep, for you have been dosing me ever since I was born. I have gone through every receipt in the complete housewife[61] ten times over; and you have thoughts of coursing me through Quincy[62] next spring. But, ecod! I tell you, I'll not be made a fool of no longer.

MRS HARDCASTLE

Wasn't it all for your good, viper? Wasn't it all for your good?

TONY

I wish you'd let me and my good alone, then. Snubbing this way when I'm in spirits. If I'm to have any good, let it come of itself; not to keep dinging it, dinging it into one so.

MRS HARDCASTLE

That's false; I never see you when you're in spirits. No, Tony, you then go to the alehouse or kennel. I'm never to be delighted with your agreeable wild notes, unfeeling monster!

TONY

Ecod! Mamma, your own notes are the wildest of the two.

MRS HARDCASTLE

Was ever the like? But I see he wants to break my heart, I see he does.

HASTINGS

Dear Madam, permit me to lecture the young gentleman a little. I'm certain I can persuade him to his duty.

MRS HARDCASTLE

Well, I must retire. Come, Constance, my love. You see, Mr Hastings, the wretchedness of my situation. Was ever poor woman so plagued with a dear, sweet, pretty, provoking, undutiful boy. [*Exeunt* MRS HARDCASTLE *and* MISS NEVILLE.]

TONY

[*Singing.*] 'There was a young man riding by, and fain
would have his will. Rang do didlo dee.'
Don't mind her. Let her cry. It's the comfort of her heart.
I have seen her and sister cry over a book for an hour
together, and they said they liked the book the better the
more it made them cry.

HASTINGS

Then you're no friend to the ladies, I find, my pretty
young gentleman?

TONY

That's as I find 'um.

HASTINGS

Not to her of your mother's choosing, I dare answer! And
yet she appears to me a pretty, well-tempered girl.

TONY

That's because you don't know her as well as I. Ecod! I
know every inch about her; and there's not a more bitter
cantankerous toad in all Christendom!

HASTINGS

[*Aside.*] Pretty encouragement this for a lover!

TONY

I have seen her since the height of that. She has as many
tricks as a hare in a thicket, or a colt the first day's breaking.

HASTINGS

To me she appears sensible and silent.

TONY

Ay, before company. But when she's with her playmates,
she's as loud as a hog in a gate.

HASTINGS

But there is a meek modesty about her that charms me.

TONY

Yes, but curb her never so little, she kicks up, and you're
flung in a ditch.

HASTINGS

Well, but you must allow her a little beauty.—Yes, you
must allow her some beauty.

TONY

Bandbox! She's all a made-up thing, mun. Ah! could you
but see Bet Bouncer of these parts, you might then talk of

beauty. Ecod, she has two eyes as black as sloes, and cheeks as broad and red as a pulpit cushion. She'd make two of she.

HASTINGS

Well, what say you of a friend that would take this bitter bargain off your hands?

TONY

Anon? [58]

HASTINGS

Would you thank him that would take Miss Neville, and leave you to happiness and your dear Betsy?

TONY

Ay; but where is there such a friend, for who would take her?

HASTINGS

I am he. If you but assist me, I'll engage to whip her off to France, and you shall never hear more of her.

TONY

Assist you! Ecod, I will, to the last drop of my blood. I'll clap a pair of horses to your chaise that shall trundle you off in a twinkling, and may be get you a part of her fortin beside in jewels that you little dream of.

HASTINGS

My dear 'squire, this looks like a lad of spirit.

TONY

Come along then, and you shall see more of my spirit before you have done with me.

[*Singing.*]

> We are the boys
> That fears no noise
> Where the thundering cannons roar.

[*Exeunt.*]

Act three.

[*Enter* HARDCASTLE *alone.*]

HARDCASTLE

What could my old friend Sir Charles mean by recommending his son as the modestest young man in town? To me he appears the most impudent piece of brass that ever spoke with a tongue. He has taken possession of the easy chair by the fireside already. He took off his boots in the parlour, and desired me to see them taken care of. I'm desirous to know how his impudence affects my daughter. —She will certainly be shocked at it.

[*Enter* MISS HARDCASTLE *plainly dressed.*]

HARDCASTLE

Well, my Kate, I see you have changed your dress, as I bid you; and yet, I believe, there was no great occasion.

MISS HARDCASTLE

I find such a pleasure, sir, in obeying your commands, that I take care to observe them without ever debating their propriety.

HARDCASTLE

And yet, Kate, I sometimes give you some cause, particularly when I recommended my modest gentleman to you as a lover today.

MISS HARDCASTLE

You taught me to expect something extraordinary, and I find the original exceeds the description!

HARDCASTLE

I was never so surprised in my life! He has quite confounded all my faculties!

MISS HARDCASTLE

I never saw anything like it: and a man of the world, too!

HARDCASTLE

Ay, he learned it all abroad,—what a fool was I, to think a young man could learn modesty by travelling. He might as soon learn wit at a masquerade.

MISS HARDCASTLE

It seems all natural to him.

HARDCASTLE

A good deal assisted by bad company and a French dancing-master.

MISS HARDCASTLE

Sure, you mistake, papa! A French dancing-master could never have taught him that timid look—that awkward address—that bashful manner—

HARDCASTLE

Whose look? whose manner, child?

MISS HARDCASTLE

Mr Marlow's: his *mauvaise honte*,[54] his timidity, struck me at the first sight.

HARDCASTLE

Then your first sight deceived you; for I think him one of the most brazen first sights that ever astonished my senses!

MISS HARDCASTLE

Sure, sir, you rally! I never saw anyone so modest.

HARDCASTLE

And can you be serious! I never saw such a bouncing swaggering puppy since I was born. Bully Dawson[55] was but a fool to him.

MISS HARDCASTLE

Surprising! He met me with a respectful bow, a stammering voice, and a look fixed on the ground.

HARDCASTLE

He met me with a loud voice, a lordly air, and a familiarity that made my blood freeze again.

MISS HARDCASTLE

He treated me with diffidence and respect; censured the manners of the age; admired the prudence of girls that never laughed; tired me with apologies for being tiresome; then left the room with a bow, and 'Madam, I would not for the world detain you.'

HARDCASTLE

He spoke to me as if he knew me all his life before; asked

twenty questions, and never waited for an answer; interrupted my best remarks with some silly pun, and when I was in my best story of the Duke of Marlborough and Prince Eugene, he asked if I had not a good hand at making punch. Yes, Kate, he asked your father if he was a maker of punch!

MISS HARDCASTLE

One of us must certainly be mistaken.

HARDCASTLE

If he be what he has shown himself, I'm determined he shall never have my consent.

MISS HARDCASTLE

And if he be the sullen thing I take him, he shall never have mine.

HARDCASTLE

In one thing then we are agreed—to reject him.

MISS HARDCASTLE

Yes: but upon conditions. For if you should find him less impudent, and I more presuming; if you find him more respectful, and I more importunate—I don't know—the fellow is well enough for a man.—Certainly we don't meet many such at a horse-race in the country.

HARDCASTLE

If we should find him so—but that's impossible. The first appearance has done my business. I'm seldom deceived in that.

MISS HARDCASTLE

And yet there may be many good qualities under that first appearance.

HARDCASTLE

Ay, when a girl finds a fellow's outside to her taste, she then sets about guessing the rest of his furniture. With her, a smooth face stands for good sense, and a genteel figure for every virtue.

MISS HARDCASTLE

I hope, sir, a conversation begun with a compliment to my good sense won't end with a sneer at my understanding?

HARDCASTLE

Pardon me, Kate. But if young Mr Brazen can find the art of reconciling contradictions, he may please us both, perhaps.

MISS HARDCASTLE

And as one of us must be mistaken, what if we go to make further discoveries?

HARDCASTLE

Agreed. But depend on't I'm in the right.

MISS HARDCASTLE

And depend on't I'm not much in the wrong. [*Exeunt. Enter* TONY, *running in with a casket.*]

TONY

Ecod! I have got them. Here they are. My cousin Con's necklaces, bobs[56] and all. My mother shan't cheat the poor souls out of their fortin neither. Oh! my genius, is that you?

[*Enter* HASTINGS.]

HASTINGS

My dear friend, how have you managed with your mother? I hope you have amused her with pretending love for your cousin, and that you are willing to be reconciled at last? Our horses will be refreshed in a short time, and we shall soon be ready to set off.

TONY

And here's something to bear your charges by the way. [*Giving the casket.*] Your sweetheart's jewels. Keep them, and hang those, I say, that would rob you of one of them.

HASTINGS

But how have you procured them from your mother?

TONY

Ask me no questions, and I'll tell you no fibs. I procured them by the rule of thumb. If I had not a key to every drawer in mother's bureau, how could I go to the alehouse so often as I do? An honest man may rob himself of his own at any time.

HASTINGS

Thousands do it every day. But to be plain with you, Miss Neville is endeavouring to procure them from her aunt this very instant. If she succeeds, it will be the most delicate way at least of obtaining them.

TONY

Well, keep them, till you know how it will be. But I know how it will be well enough; she'd as soon part with the only sound tooth in her head!

HASTINGS

But I dread the effects of her resentment, when she finds she has lost them.

TONY

Never you mind her resentment, leave *me* to manage that. I don't value her resentment the bounce of a cracker.[57] Zounds! here they are! Morrice![58] prance!

[*Exit* HASTINGS. TONY, MRS HARDCASTLE, *and* MISS NEVILLE.]

MRS HARDCASTLE

Indeed, Constance, you amaze me. Such a girl as you want jewels? It will be time enough for jewels, my dear, twenty years hence, when your beauty begins to want repairs.

MISS NEVILLE

But what will repair beauty at forty, will certainly improve it at twenty, madam.

MRS HARDCASTLE

Yours, my dear, can admit of none. That natural blush is beyond a thousand ornaments. Besides, child, jewels are quite out at present. Don't you see half the ladies of our acquaintance, my Lady Kill-daylight, and Mrs Crump, and the rest of them, carry their jewels to town, and bring nothing but paste and marcasites[59] back?

MISS NEVILLE

But who knows, madam, but somebody that shall be nameless would like me best with all my little finery about me?

MRS HARDCASTLE

Consult your glass, my dear, and then see, if with such a pair of eyes, you want any better sparklers. What do you think, Tony, my dear, does your cousin Con want any jewels, in your eyes, to set off her beauty?

TONY

That's as thereafter may be.

MISS NEVILLE

My dear aunt, if you knew how it would oblige me.

MRS HARDCASTLE

A parcel of old-fashioned rose and table-cut things.[60] They would make you look like the court of King Solomon at a puppet-show. Besides, I believe I can't readily come at them. They may be missing, for aught I know to the contrary.

TONY

[*Apart to* MRS HARDCASTLE.] Then why don't you tell her so at once, as she's so longing for them. Tell her they're lost. It's the only way to quiet her. Say they're lost, and call me to bear witness.

MRS HARDCASTLE

[*Apart to* TONY.] You know, my dear, I'm only keeping them for you. So if I say they're gone, you'll bear me witness, will you? He! he! he!

TONY

Never fear me. Ecod! I'll say I saw them taken out with my own eyes.

MISS NEVILLE

I desire them but for a day, madam. Just to be permitted to shew them as relics, and then they may be locked up again.

MRS HARDCASTLE

To be plain with you, my dear Constance, if I could find them, you should have them. They're missing, I assure you. Lost, for aught I know; but we must have patience wherever they are.

MISS NEVILLE

I'll not believe it; this is but a shallow pretence to deny me. I know they're too valuable to be so slightly kept, and as you are to answer for the loss—

MRS HARDCASTLE

Don't be alarmed, Constance. If they be lost, I must restore an equivalent. But my son knows they are missing, and not to be found.

TONY

That I can bear witness to. They are missing, and not to be found, I'll take my oath on't.

MRS HARDCASTLE

You must learn resignation, my dear; for though we lose our fortune, yet we should not lose our patience. See me, how calm I am.

MISS NEVILLE

Ay, people are generally calm at the misfortunes of others.

MRS HARDCASTLE

Now, I wonder a girl of your good sense should waste a thought upon such trumpery. We shall soon find them;

and, in the meantime, you shall make use of my garnets till your jewels be found.

MISS NEVILLE

I detest garnets.

MRS HARDCASTLE

The most becoming things in the world to set off a clear complexion. You have often seen how well they look upon me. You shall have them. [*Exit.*]

MISS NEVILLE

[*Trying to detain her.*] I dislike them of all things. You shan't stir. Was ever anything so provoking to mislay my own jewels, and force me to wear her trumpery.

TONY

Don't be a fool. If she gives you the garnets, take what you can get. The jewels are your own already. I have stolen them out of her bureau, and she does not know it. Fly to your spark, he'll tell you more of the matter. Leave me to manage her.

MISS NEVILLE

My dear cousin!

TONY

Vanish. She's here, and has missed them already. Zounds! how she fidgets and spits about like a catherine wheel![61]

[*Enter* MRS HARDCASTLE.]

MRS HARDCASTLE

Confusion! thieves! robbers! We are cheated, plundered, broke open, undone!

TONY

What's the matter, what's the matter, mamma? I hope nothing has happened to any of the good family!

MRS HARDCASTLE

We are robbed. My bureau has been broke open, the jewels taken out, and I'm undone!

TONY

Oh! is that all? Ha! ha! ha! By the laws, I never saw it better acted in my life. Ecod, I thought you was ruined in earnest, ha, ha, ha!

MRS HARDCASTLE

Why, boy, I am ruined in earnest. My bureau has been broke open, and all taken away.

TONY

Stick to that; ha, ha, ha! stick to that. I'll bear witness, you know, call me to bear witness.

MRS HARDCASTLE

I tell you, Tony, by all that's precious, the jewels are gone, and I shall be ruined for ever.

TONY

Sure I know they're gone, and I am to say so.

MRS HARDCASTLE

My dearest Tony, but hear me. They're gone, I say.

TONY

By the laws, mamma, you make me for to laugh, ha! ha! I know who took them well enough, ha! ha! ha!

MRS HARDCASTLE

Was there ever such a blockhead, that can't tell the difference between jest and earnest. I tell you I'm not in jest, booby!

TONY

That's right, that's right: you must be in a bitter passion, and then nobody will suspect either of us. I'll bear witness that they are gone.

MRS HARDCASTLE

Was there ever such a cross-grained brute, that won't hear me! Can you bear witness that you're no better than a fool? Was ever poor woman so beset with fools on one hand, and thieves on the other?

TONY

I can bear witness to that.

MRS HARDCASTLE

Bear witness again, you blockhead you, and I'll turn you out of the room directly. My poor niece, what will become of her? Do you laugh, you unfeeling brute, as if you enjoyed my distress?

TONY

I can bear witness to that.

MRS HARDCASTLE

Do you insult me, monster? I'll teach you to vex your mother, I will.

TONY

I can bear witness to that.

[*He runs off, she follows him. Enter* MISS HARDCASTLE

and MAID.]

MISS HARDCASTLE

What an unaccountable creature is that brother of mine, to
send them to the house as an inn, ha! ha! I don't wonder
at his impudence.

MAID

But what is more, madam, the young gentleman as you
passed by in your present dress, asked me if you were the
barmaid. He mistook you for the barmaid, madam!

MISS HARDCASTLE

Did he? Then as I live I'm resolved to keep up the delusion.
Tell me, Pimple, how do you like my present dress? Don't
you think I look something like Cherry in the *Beaux'
Stratagem*[62]?

MAID

It's the dress, madam, that every lady wears in the country,
but when she visits or receives company.

MISS HARDCASTLE

And are you sure he does not remember my face or
person?

MAID

Certain of it.

MISS HARDCASTLE

I vow, I thought so; for though we spoke for some time
together, yet his fears were such, that he never once looked
up during the interview. Indeed, if he had, my bonnet
would have kept him from seeing me.

MAID

But what do you hope from keeping him in his mistake?

MISS HARDCASTLE

In the first place, I shall be seen, and that is no small advantage to a girl who brings her face to market. Then I
shall perhaps make an acquaintance, and that's no small
victory gained over one who never addresses any but the
wildest of her sex. But my chief aim is to take my gentleman off his guard, and like an invisible champion of
romance, examine the giant's force before I offer to combat.

MAID

But you are sure you can act your part, and disguise your
voice, so that he may mistake that, as he has already mistaken your person?

MISS HARDCASTLE

Never fear me. I think I have got the true bar cant. Did your honour call?—Attend the Lion there.—Pipes and tobacco for the Angel.—The Lamb⁶⁸ has been outrageous this half-hour.

MAID

It will do, madam. But he's here. [*Exit* MAID. *Enter* MARLOW.]

MARLOW

What a bawling in every part of the house; I have scarce a moment's repose. If I go to the best room, there I find my host and his story. If I fly to the gallery, there we have my hostess with her curtsy down to the ground. I have at last got a moment to myself, and now for recollection. [*Walks and muses.*]

MISS HARDCASTLE

Did you call, sir? Did your honour call?

MARLOW

[*Musing.*] As for Miss Hardcastle, she's too grave and sentimental for me. [*Paces to left.*]

MISS HARDCASTLE

Did your honour call? [*She still places herself before him, he turning away.*]

MARLOW

No, child. [*Musing.*] Besides from the glimpse I had of her, I think she squints.

MISS HARDCASTLE

I'm sure, sir, I heard the bell ring.

MARLOW

No, no. [*Musing.*] I have pleased my father, however, by coming down, and I'll tomorrow please myself by returning. [*Taking out his tablets, and perusing.*]

MISS HARDCASTLE

Perhaps the other gentleman called, sir?

MARLOW

I tell you, no.

MISS HARDCASTLE

I should be glad to know, sir. We have such a parcel of servants.

MARLOW

No, no, I tell you. [*Looks full in her face.*] Yes, child, I

think I did call. I wanted—I wanted—I vow, child, you are
vastly handsome.

MISS HARDCASTLE

O la, sir, you'll make one ashamed.

MARLOW

Never saw a more sprightly malicious eye. Yes, yes, my
dear, I did call. Have you got any of your—a—what d'ye
call it in the house?

MISS HARDCASTLE

No, sir, we have been out of that these ten days.

MARLOW

One may call in this house, I find, to very little purpose.
Suppose I should call for a taste, just by way of trial, of
the nectar of your lips; perhaps I might be disappointed in
that, too.

MISS HARDCASTLE

Nectar! nectar! that's a liquor there's no call for in these
parts. French, I suppose. We keep no French wines here,
sir.

MARLOW

Of true English growth, I assure you.

MISS HARDCASTLE

Then it's odd I should not know it. We brew all sorts of
wines in this house, and I have lived here these eighteen
years.

MARLOW

Eighteen years! Why one would think, child, you kept the
bar before you were born. How old are you?

MISS HARDCASTLE

O! sir, I must not tell my age. They say women and music
should never be dated.

MARLOW

To guess at this distance, you can't be much above forty.
[*Approaching.*] Yet nearer I don't think so much. [*Approaching.*] By coming close to some women they look
younger still; but when we come very close indeed—[*Attempting to kiss her.*]

MISS HARDCASTLE

Pray, sir, keep your distance. One would think you wanted
to know one's age as they do horses, by mark of mouth.

MARLOW

I protest, child, you use me extremely ill. If you keep me at this distance, how is it possible you and I can ever be acquainted?

MISS HARDCASTLE

And who wants to be acquainted with you? I want no such acquaintance, not I. I'm sure you did not treat Miss Hardcastle that was here awhile ago in this obstropalous manner. I'll warrant me, before her you looked dashed, and kept bowing to the ground, and talked, for all the world, as if you was before a justice of peace.

MARLOW

[*Aside.*] Egad! she has hit it, sure enough. [*To her.*] In awe of her, child? Ha! ha! ha! A mere awkward, squinting thing, no, no. I find you don't know me. I laughed, and rallied her a little; but I was unwilling to be too severe. No, I could not be too severe, curse me!

MISS HARDCASTLE

Oh! then, sir, you are a favourite, I find, among the ladies?

MARLOW

Yes, my dear, a great favourite. And yet, hang me, I don't see what they find in me to follow. At the ladies' club in town I'm called their agreeable Rattle. Rattle, child, is not my real name, but one I'm known by. My name is Solomons. Mr Solomons, my dear, at your service. [*Offering to salute*[64] *her.*]

MISS HARDCASTLE

Hold, sir; you are introducing me to your club, not to yourself. And you're so great a favourite there, you say?

MARLOW

Yes, my dear. There's Mrs Mantrap, Lady Betty Blackleg, the Countess of Sligo, Mrs Langhorns, old Miss Biddy Buckskin and your humble servant, keep up the spirit of the place.

MISS HARDCASTLE

Then it's a very merry place, I suppose?

MARLOW

Yes, as merry as cards, suppers, wine, and old women can make us.

MISS HARDCASTLE

And their agreeable Rattle, ha! ha! ha!

MARLOW

[*Aside.*] Egad! I don't quite like this chit. She looks knowing, methinks. You laugh, child!

MISS HARDCASTLE

I can't but laugh to think what time they all have for minding their work or their family.

MARLOW

[*Aside.*] All's well, she don't laugh at me. [*To her.*] Do you ever work, child?

MISS HARDCASTLE

Ay, sure. There's not a screen or a quilt in the whole house but what can bear witness to that.

MARLOW

Odso! Then you must show me your embroidery. I embroider and draw patterns myself a little. If you want a judge of your work you must apply to me. [*Seizing her hand.*]

MISS HARDCASTLE

Ay, but the colours don't look well by candlelight. You shall see all in the morning. [*Struggling.*]

MARLOW

And why not now, my angel? Such beauty fires beyond the power of resistance.—Pshaw! the father here! My old luck: I never nicked seven that I did not throw ames-ace[65] three times following. [*Exit* MARLOW. *Enter* HARDCASTLE, *who stands in surprise.*]

HARDCASTLE

So, madam. So I find this is your modest lover. This is your humble admirer that kept his eyes fixed on the ground, and only adored at humble distance. Kate, Kate, art thou not ashamed to deceive your father so?

MISS HARDCASTLE

Never trust me, dear papa, but he's still the modest man I first took him for, you'll be convinced of it as well as I.

HARDCASTLE

By the hand of my body. I believe his impudence is infectious! Didn't I see him seize your hand? Didn't I see him haul you about like a milkmaid? and now you talk of his respect and his modesty, forsooth!

MISS HARDCASTLE

But if I shortly convince you of his modesty, that he has

only the faults that will pass off with time, and the virtues
that will improve with age, I hope you'll forgive him.

HARDCASTLE

The girl would actually make one run mad! I tell you I'll
not be convinced. I am convinced. He has scarcely been
three hours in the house, and he has already encroached
on all my prerogatives. You may like his impudence, and
call it modesty. But my son-in-law, madam, must have
very different qualifications.

MISS HARDCASTLE

Sir, I ask but this night to convince you.

HARDCASTLE

You shall not have half the time, for I have thoughts of
turning him out this very hour.

MISS HARDCASTLE

Give me that hour then, and I hope to satisfy you.

HARDCASTLE

Well, an hour let it be then. But I'll have no trifling with
your father. All fair and open, do you mind me?

MISS HARDCASTLE

I hope, sir, you have ever found that I consider your
commands as my pride; for your kindness is such, that
my duty as yet has been inclination.

Act four.

[*Enter* HASTINGS *and* MISS NEVILLE.]

HASTINGS

You surprise me! Sir Charles Marlow expected here this
night? Where have you had your information?

MISS NEVILLE

You may depend upon it. I just saw his letter to Mr Hardcastle, in which he tells him he intends setting out a few
hours after his son.

HASTINGS

Then, my Constance, all must be completed before he
arrives. He knows me; and should he find me here, would
discover my name, and perhaps my designs, to the rest
of the family.

MISS NEVILLE

The jewels, I hope, are safe.

HASTINGS

Yes, yes. I have sent them to Marlow, who keeps the keys
of our baggage. In the meantime, I'll go to prepare matters
for our elopement. I have had the 'squire's promise of a
fresh pair of horses; and, if I should not see him again, will
write him further directions. [*Exit.*]

MISS NEVILLE

Well! success attend you. In the meantime, I'll go amuse
my aunt with the old pretence of a violent passion for my
cousin. [*Exit. Enter* MARLOW *followed by* SERVANT.]

MARLOW

I wonder what Hastings could mean by sending me so
valuable a thing as a casket to keep for him, when he
knows the only place I have is the seat of a post-coach at

an inn-door. Have you deposited the casket with the landlady, as I ordered you? Have you put it into her own hands?

SERVANT

Yes, your honour.

MARLOW

She said she'd keep it safe, did she?

SERVANT

Yes, she said she'd keep it safe enough; she asked me how I came by it, and she said she had a great mind to make me give an account of myself. [*Exit* SERVANT.]

MARLOW

Ha! ha! ha! They're safe, however. What an unaccountable set of beings have we got amongst! This little barmaid, though, runs in my head most strangely, and drives out the absurdities of all the rest of the family. She's mine, she must be mine, or I'm greatly mistaken.

[*Enter* HASTINGS.]

HASTINGS

Bless me! I quite forgot to tell her that I intended to prepare at the bottom of the garden. Marlow here, and in spirits too!

MARLOW

Give me joy, George! Crown me, shadow me with laurels! Well, George, after all, we modest fellows don't want for success among the women.

HASTINGS

Some women, you mean. But what success has your honour's modesty been crowned with now, that it grows so insolent upon us?

MARLOW

Didn't you see the tempting, brisk, lovely little thing that runs about the house with a bunch of keys to its girdle?

HASTINGS

Well! and what then?

MARLOW

She's mine, you rogue you. Such fire, such motions, such eyes, such lips—but, egad! she would not let me kiss them though.

HASTINGS

But are you so sure, so very sure of her?

MARLOW

Why man, she talked of showing me her work above stairs
and I am to improve the pattern.

HASTINGS

But how can you, Charles, go about to rob a woman of
her honour?

MARLOW

Pshaw! pshaw! We all know the honour of a barmaid of
an inn. I don't intend to rob her, take my word for it,
there's nothing in this house I shan't honestly pay for.

HASTINGS

I believe the girl has virtue.

MARLOW

And if she has, I should be the last man in the world that
would attempt to corrupt it.

HASTINGS

You have taken care, I hope, of the casket I sent you to
lock up? It's in safety?

MARLOW

Yes, yes. It's safe enough. I have taken care of it. But how
could you think the seat of a post-coach at an inn-door a
place of safety? Ah! numbskull! I have taken better pre-
cautions for you than you did for yourself.—I have—

HASTINGS

What?

MARLOW

I have sent it to the landlady to keep for you.

HASTINGS

To the landlady!

MARLOW

The landlady.

HASTINGS

You did?

MARLOW

I did. She's to be answerable for its forthcoming, you know.

HASTINGS

Yes, she'll bring it forth with a witness.

MARLOW

Wasn't I right? I believe you'll allow that I acted prudently
upon this occasion?

HASTINGS

[*Aside.*] He must not see my uneasiness.

MARLOW

You seem a little disconcerted, though, methinks. Sure nothing has happened?

HASTINGS

No, nothing. Never was in better spirits in all my life. And so you left it with the landlady, who, no doubt, very readily undertook the charge?

MARLOW

Rather too readily. For she not only kept the casket, but, through her great precaution, was going to keep the messenger too. Ha! ha! ha!

HASTINGS

He! he! he! They're safe, however.

MARLOW

As a guinea in a miser's purse.

HASTINGS

[*Aside.*] So now all hopes of fortune are at an end, and we must set off without it. [*To him.*] Well, Charles, I'll leave you to your meditations on the pretty barmaid, and, he! he! he! may you be as successful for yourself as you have been for me. [*Exit.*]

MARLOW

Thank ye, George! I ask no more. Ha! ha! ha!

[*Enter* HARDCASTLE.]

HARDCASTLE

I no longer know my own house. It's turned all topsy-turvy. His servants have got drunk already. I'll bear it no longer, and yet, from my respect for his father, I'll be calm. [*To him.*] Mr Marlow, your servant. I'm your very humble servant. [*Bowing low.*]

MARLOW

Sir, your humble servant. [*Aside.*] What's to be the wonder now?

HARDCASTLE

I believe, sir, you must be sensible, sir, that no man alive ought to be more welcome than your father's son, sir. I hope you think so?

MARLOW

I do, from my soul, sir. I don't want much entreaty. I

generally make my father's son welcome wherever he goes.

HARDCASTLE

I believe you do, from my soul, sir. But though I say nothing to your own conduct, that of your servants is insufferable. Their manner of drinking is setting a very bad example in this house, I assure you.

MARLOW

I protest, my very good sir, that's no fault of mine. If they don't drink as they ought they are to blame. I ordered them not to spare the cellar. I did, I assure you. [*To the side scene.*[66]] Here, let one of my servants come up. [*To him.*] My positive directions were, that as I did not drink myself, they should make up for my deficiencies below.

HARDCASTLE

Then they had your orders for what they do! I'm satisfied!

MARLOW

They had, I assure you. You shall hear from one of themselves. [*Enter* SERVANT, *drunk.*] You, Jeremy! Come forward, sirrah! What were my orders? Were you not told to drink freely, and call for what you thought fit, for the good of the house?

HARDCASTLE

[*Aside.*] I begin to lose my patience.

JEREMY

[*Staggering forward.*] Please your honour, liberty and Fleet Street for ever![67] Though I'm but a servant, I'm as good as another man. I'll drink for no man before supper, sir, dammy! Good liquor will sit upon a good supper, but a good supper will not sit upon—hiccup—upon my conscience, sir.

MARLOW

You see, my old friend, the fellow is as drunk as he can possibly be. I don't know what you'd have more, unless you'd have the poor devil soused in a beer-barrel.

HARDCASTLE

Zounds! He'll drive me distracted if I contain myself any longer. Mr Marlow, Sir; I have submitted to your insolence for more than four hours, and I see no likelihood of its coming to an end. I'm now resolved to be master here, sir, and I desire that you and your drunken pack may leave my house directly.

MARLOW

Leave your house!—Sure, you jest, my good friend! What, when I'm doing what I can to please you!

HARDCASTLE

I tell you, sir, you don't please me; so I desire you'll leave my house.

MARLOW

Sure, you cannot be serious! At this time o' night, and such a night! You only mean to banter me!

HARDCASTLE

I tell you, sir, I'm serious; and, now that my passions are roused, I say this house is mine, sir; this house is mine, and I command you to leave it directly.

MARLOW

Ha! ha! ha! A puddle in a storm. I shan't stir a step, I assure you. [*In a serious tone.*] This your house, fellow! It's my house. This is my house. Mine, while I choose to stay. What right have you to bid me leave this house, sir? I never met with such impudence, curse me, never in my whole life before.

HARDCASTLE

Nor I, confound me if ever I did! To come to my house, to call for what he likes, to turn me out of my own chair, to insult the family, to order his servants to get drunk, and then to tell me *This house is mine, sir.* By all that's impudent, it makes me laugh. Ha! ha! ha! Pray sir, [*bantering*] as you take the house, what think you of taking the rest of the furniture? There's a pair of silver candlesticks, and there's a firescreen, and here's a pair of brazen-nosed bellows, perhaps you may take a fancy to them?

MARLOW

Bring me your bill, sir, bring me your bill, and let's make no more words about it.

HARDCASTLE

There are a set of prints, too. What think you of the Rake's Progress[66] for your own apartment?

MARLOW

Bring me your bill, I say; and I'll leave you and your infernal house directly.

HARDCASTLE

Then there's a mahogany table, that you may see your own face in.

MARLOW

My bill, I say.

HARDCASTLE

I had forgot the great chair, for your own particular slumbers, after a hearty meal.

MARLOW

Zounds! bring me my bill, I say, and let's hear no more on't.

HARDCASTLE

Young man, young man, from your father's letter to me, I was taught to expect a well-bred modest man, as a visitor here, but now I find him no better than a coxcomb and a bully; but he will be down here presently, and shall hear more of it. [*Exit.*]

MARLOW

How's this! Sure I have not mistaken the house! Everything looks like an inn. The servants cry 'coming'. The attendance is awkward; the barmaid, too, to attend us. But she's here, and will further inform me. Whither so fast, child? A word with you.

  [*Enter* MISS HARDCASTLE.]

MISS HARDCASTLE

Let it be short, then. I'm in a hurry. [*Aside.*] I believe he begins to find out his mistake, but it's too soon quite to undeceive him.

MARLOW

Pray, child, answer me one question. What are you, and what may your business in this house be?

MISS HARDCASTLE

A relation of the family, sir.

MARLOW

What, a poor relation?

MISS HARDCASTLE

Yes, sir. A poor relation appointed to keep the keys, and to see that the guests want nothing in my power to give them.

MARLOW

That is, you act as the barmaid of this inn.

MISS HARDCASTLE

Inn. O law!—What brought that in your head? One of the best families in the country keep an inn! Ha, ha, ha, old Mr Hardcastle's house an inn!

MARLOW

Mr Hardcastle's house! Is this house Mr Hardcastle's house, child?

MISS HARDCASTLE

Ay, sure. Whose else should it be?

MARLOW

So then all's out, and I have been damnably imposed on. O, confound my stupid head, I shall be laughed at over the whole town. I shall be stuck up in caricatura in all the print-shops. The Dullissimo Maccaroni.⁶⁹ To mistake this house of all others for an inn, and my father's old friend for an innkeeper. What a swaggering puppy must he take me for. What a silly puppy do I find myself. There again, may I be hanged, my dear, but I mistook you for the barmaid.

MISS HARDCASTLE

Dear me! dear me! I'm sure there's nothing in my behaviour to put me upon a level with one of that stamp.

MARLOW

Nothing, my dear, nothing. But I was in for a list of blunders, and could not help making you a subscriber. My stupidity saw everything the wrong way. I mistook your assiduity for assurance, and your simplicity for allurement. But it's over.—This house I no more show my face in!

MISS HARDCASTLE

I hope, sir, I have done nothing to disoblige you. I'm sure I should be sorry to affront any gentleman who has been so polite, and said so many civil things to me. I'm sure I should be sorry [*pretending to cry*] if he left the family upon my account. I'm sure I should be sorry people said anything amiss, since I have no fortune but my character.

MARLOW

[*Aside.*] By heaven, she weeps. This is the first mark of tenderness I ever had from a modest woman, and it touches me. [*To her.*] Excuse me, my lovely girl, you are the only part of the family I leave with reluctance. But to be plain with you, the difference of our birth, fortune and education, make an honourable connexion impossible.

MISS HARDCASTLE

[*Aside.*] Generous man! I now begin to admire him. [*To him.*] But I'm sure my family is as good as Miss Hardcastle's, and though I'm poor, that's no great misfortune to a contented mind, and, until this moment, I never thought that it was bad to want fortune.

MARLOW

And why now, my pretty simplicity?

MISS HARDCASTLE

Because it puts me at a distance from one, that if I had a thousand pound I would give it all to.

MARLOW

[*Aside.*] This simplicity bewitches me, so that if I stay I'm undone. I must make one bold effort, and leave her. [*To her.*] Your partiality in my favour, my dear, touches me most sensibly, and were I to live for myself alone, I could easily fix my choice. But I owe too much to the opinion of the world, too much to the authority of a father, so that —I can scarcely speak it—it affects me. Farewell. [*Exit.*]

MISS HARDCASTLE

I never knew half his merit till now. He shall not go, if I have power or art to detain him. I'll still preserve the character in which I stooped to conquer, but will undeceive my papa, who, perhaps, may laugh him out of his resolution. [*Exit. Enter* TONY, MISS NEVILLE.]

TONY

Ay, you may steal for yourselves the next time. I have done my duty. She has got the jewels again, that's a sure thing; but she believes it was all a mistake of the servants.

MISS NEVILLE

But, my dear cousin, sure, you won't forsake us in this distress. If she in the least suspects that I am going off, I shall certainly be locked up, or sent to my Aunt Pedigree's which is ten times worse.

TONY

To be sure, aunts of all kinds are damned bad things. But what can I do? I have got you a pair of horses that will fly like Whistlejacket,[70] and I'm sure you can't say but I have courted you nicely before her face. Here she comes, we

must court a bit or two more, for fear she should suspect
us. [*They retire, and seem to fondle. Enter* MRS HARD-
CASTLE.]

MRS HARDCASTLE

Well, I was greatly fluttered, to be sure. But my son tells
me it was all a mistake of the servants. I shan't be easy,
however, till they are fairly married, and then let her keep
her own fortune. But what do I see? Fondling together, as
I'm alive! I never saw Tony so sprightly before. Ah! have
I caught you, my pretty doves! What, billing, exchanging
stolen glances, and broken murmurs! Ah!

TONY

As for murmurs, mother, we grumble a little now and
then, to be sure. But there's no love lost between us.

MRS HARDCASTLE

A mere sprinkling, Tony, upon the flame, only to make it
burn brighter.

MISS NEVILLE

Cousin Tony promises to give us more of his company at
home. Indeed, he shan't leave us any more. It won't
leave us, cousin Tony, will it?

TONY

O! it's a pretty creature. No, I'd sooner leave my horse in
a pound, than leave you when you smile upon one so.
Your laugh makes you so becoming.

MISS NEVILLE

Agreeable cousin! Who can help admiring that natural
humour, that pleasant, broad, red, thoughtless [*patting his
cheek*] ah! it's a bold face.

MRS HARDCASTLE

Pretty innocence!

TONY

I'm sure I always loved cousin Con's hazel eyes, and her
pretty long fingers, that she twists this way and that, over
the haspicholls,[71] like a parcel of bobbins.

MRS HARDCASTLE

Ah, he would charm the bird from the tree. I was never
so happy before. My boy takes after his father, poor Mr
Lumpkin, exactly. The jewels, my dear Con, shall be yours
incontinently. You shall have them. Isn't he a sweet boy,
my dear? You shall be married tomorrow, and we'll put

off the rest of his education, like Dr Drowsy's sermons, to
a fitter opportunity.

[*Enter* DIGGORY.]

DIGGORY

Where's the 'Squire? I have got a letter for your worship.

TONY

Give it to my mamma. She reads all my letters first.

DIGGORY

I had orders to deliver it into your own hands.

TONY

Who does it come from?

DIGGORY

Your worship mun ask that o' the letter itself.

TONY

I could wish to know, though. [*Turning the letter, and
gazing on it.*]

MISS NEVILLE

[*Aside.*] Undone, undone. A letter to him from Hastings.
I know the hand. If my aunt sees it we are ruined for ever.
I'll keep her employed a little if I can. [*To* MRS HARD-
CASTLE.] But I have not told you, madam, of my cousin's
smart answer just now to Mr Marlow. We so laughed.—
You must know, madam—This way a little, for he must
not hear us. [*They confer.*]

TONY

[*Still gazing.*] A damned cramp piece of penmanship, as
ever I saw in my life. I can read your print-hand very well.
But here there are such handles, and shakes, and dashes,
that one can scarcely tell the head from the tail. 'To
Anthony Lumpkin, Esquire.' It's very odd, I can read the
outside of my letters, where my own name is, well enough.
But when I come to open it, it's all—buzz. That's hard,
very hard; for the inside of the letter is always the cream
of the correspondence.

MRS HARDCASTLE

Ha! ha! ha! Very well, very well. And so my son was too
hard for the philosopher.

MISS NEVILLE

Yes, madam; but you must hear the rest, madam. A little
more this way, or he may hear us. You'll hear how he
puzzled him again.

MRS HARDCASTLE

He seems strangely puzzled now himself, methinks.

TONY

[*Still gazing.*] A damned up and down hand, as if it was disguised in liquor. [*Reading.*] Dear Sir. Ay, that's that. Then there's an M, and a T, and an S, but whether the next be an izzard [72] or an R, confound me, I cannot tell.

MRS HARDCASTLE

What's that, my dear? Can I give you any assistance?

MISS NEVILLE

Pray, aunt, let me read it. Nobody reads a cramp hand better than I. [*Twitching the letter from her.*] Do you know who it is from?

TONY

Can't tell, except from Dick Ginger the feeder.

MISS NEVILLE

Ay, so it is. [*Pretending to read.*] Dear 'Squire, Hoping that you're in health, as I am, at this present. The gentlemen of the Shakebag club has cut the gentlemen of Goose-green quite out of feather. The odds—um—odd battle—um—long fighting—um, here, here, it's all about cocks, and fighting; it's of no consequence, here, put it up, put it up. [*Thrusting the crumpled letter upon him.*]

TONY

But I tell you, miss, it's of all the consequence in the world. I would not lose the rest of it for a guinea. Here, mother, do you make it out? Of no consequence!

[*Giving* MRS HARDCASTLE *the letter.*]

MRS HARDCASTLE

How's this! [*Reads.*] 'Dear 'Squire, I'm now waiting for Miss Neville, with a post-chaise and pair, at the bottom of the garden but I find my horses yet unable to perform the journey. I expect you'll assist us with a pair of fresh horses, as you promised. Dispatch is necessary, as the hag'—ay, the hag—'your mother, will otherwise suspect us. Yours, Hastings.' Grant me patience. I shall run distracted. My rage chokes me.

MISS NEVILLE

I hope, madam, you'll suspend your resentment for a few moments, and not impute to me any impertinence, or sinister design, that belongs to another.

MRS HARDCASTLE

[*Curtsying very low.*] Fine spoken, madam, you are most
miraculously polite and engaging, and quite the very pink
of courtesy and circumspection, madam. [*Changing her
tone.*] And you, you great ill-fashioned oaf, with scarce
sense enough to keep your mouth shut. Were you, too,
joined against me? But I'll defeat all your plots in a
moment. As for you, madam, since you have got a pair
of fresh horses ready, it would be cruel to disappoint them.
So, if you please, instead of running away with your spark,
prepare, this very moment, to run off with me. Your old
Aunt Pedigree will keep you secure, I'll warrant me. You
too, sir, may mount your horse, and guard us upon the
way. Here, Thomas, Roger, Diggory, I'll show you that I
wish you better than you do yourselves. [*Exit.*]

MISS NEVILLE

So now I'm completely ruined.

TONY

Ay, that's a sure thing.

MISS NEVILLE

What better could be expected from being connected with
such a stupid fool, and after all the nods and signs I made
him.

TONY

By the laws, miss, it was your own cleverness, and not my
stupidity, that did your business. You were so nice and so
busy with your Shake-bags and Goosegreens, that I thought
you could never be making believe.

[*Enter* HASTINGS.]

HASTINGS

So, sir, I find by my servant, that you have shown my
letter, and betrayed us. Was this well done, young gentleman?

TONY

Here's another. Ask Miss there who betrayed you. Ecod,
it was her doing, not mine.

[*Enter* MARLOW.]

MARLOW

So I have been finely used here among you. Rendered
contemptible, driven into ill manners, despised, insulted,
laughed at.

TONY

Here's another. We shall have old Bedlam broke loose presently.

MISS NEVILLE

And there, sir, is the gentleman to whom we all owe every obligation.

MARLOW

What can I say to him, a mere boy, an idiot, whose ignorance and age are a protection.

HASTINGS

A poor contemptible booby, that would but disgrace correction.

MISS NEVILLE

Yet with cunning and malice enough to make himself merry with all our embarrassments.

HASTINGS

An insensible cub.

MARLOW

Replete with tricks and mischief.

TONY

Baw! damme, but I'll fight you both one after the other— with baskets.[73]

MARLOW

As for him, he's below resentment. But your conduct, Mr Hastings, requires an explanation. You knew of my mistakes, yet would not undeceive me.

HASTINGS

Tortured as I am with my own disappointments, is this a time for explanations? It is not friendly, Mr Marlow.

MARLOW

But, sir—

MISS NEVILLE

Mr Marlow, we never kept on your mistake, till it was too late to undeceive you. Be pacified.

[*Enter* SERVANT.]

SERVANT

My mistress desires you'll get ready immediately, madam. The horses are putting to. Your hat and things are in the next room. We are to go thirty miles before morning. [*Exit* SERVANT.]

MISS NEVILLE

Well, well; I'll come presently.

MARLOW

[*To* HASTINGS.] Was it well done, sir, to assist in rendering me ridiculous? To hang me out for the scorn of all my acquaintance? Depend upon it, sir, I shall expect an explanation.

HASTINGS

Was it well done, sir, if you're upon that subject, to deliver what I entrusted to yourself, to the care of another, sir?

MISS NEVILLE

Mr Hastings, Mr Marlow. Why will you increase my distress by this groundless dispute? I implore, I entreat you—

[*Enter* SERVANT.]

SERVANT

Your cloak, madam. My mistress is impatient. [*Exit* SERVANT.]

MISS NEVILLE

I come. Pray be pacified. If I leave you thus, I shall die with apprehension!

[*Enter* SERVANT.]

SERVANT

Your fan, muff, and gloves, madam. The horses are waiting.

MISS NEVILLE

O, Mr Marlow! if you knew what a scene of constraint and ill-nature lies before me, I'm sure it would convert your resentment into pity.

MARLOW

I'm so distracted with a variety of passions, that I don't know what I do. Forgive me, madam. George, forgive me. You know my hasty temper, and should not exasperate it.

HASTINGS

The torture of my situation is my only excuse.

MISS NEVILLE

Well, my dear Hastings, if you have that esteem for me that I think, that I am sure you have, your constancy for three years will but increase the happiness of our future connexion. If—

MRS HARDCASTLE

[*Within.*] Miss Neville. Constance, why, Constance, I say.

MISS NEVILLE

I'm coming. Well, constancy. Remember, constancy is the word. [*Exit.*]

HASTINGS

My heart! How can I support this? To be so near happiness, and such happiness!

MARLOW

[*To* TONY.] You see now, young gentleman, the effects of your folly. What might be amusement to you, is here disappointment, and even distress.

TONY

[*From a reverie.*] Ecod, I have hit it. It's here. Your hands. Yours and yours, my poor Sulky. My boots there, ho! Meet me two hours hence at the bottom of the garden; and if you don't find Tony Lumpkin a more good-natur'd fellow than you thought for, I'll give you leave to take my best horse, and Bet Bouncer into the bargain. Come along. My boots, ho! [*Exeunt.*]

Act five.

[*Scene continues.*]

[*Enter* HASTINGS *and* SERVANT.]

HASTINGS
You saw the old lady and Miss Neville drive off, you say?

SERVANT
Yes, your honour. They went off in a post coach, and the young 'squire went on horseback. They're thirty miles off by this time.

HASTINGS
Then all my hopes are over.

SERVANT
Yes, sir. Old Sir Charles is arrived. He and the old gentleman of the house have been laughing at Mr Marlow's mistake this half-hour. They are coming this way.

HASTINGS
Then I must not be seen. So now to my fruitless appointment at the bottom of the garden. This is about the time.

[*Exit.* SIR CHARLES *and* HARDCASTLE.]

HARDCASTLE
Ha! ha! ha! The peremptory tone in which he sent forth his sublime commands.

SIR CHARLES
And the reserve with which I suppose he treated all your advances.

HARDCASTLE
And yet he might have seen something in me above a common innkeeper, too.

SIR CHARLES
Yes, Dick, but he mistook you for an uncommon innkeeper, ha! ha! ha!

HARDCASTLE

Well, I'm in too good spirits to think of anything but joy.
Yes, my dear friend, this union of our families will make
our personal friendships hereditary: and though my
daughter's fortune is but small—

SIR CHARLES

Why, Dick, will you talk of fortune to me? My son is
possessed of more than a competence already, and can
want nothing but a good and virtuous girl to share his
happiness and increase it. If they like each other, as you
say they do—

HARDCASTLE

If, man! I tell you they do like each other. My daughter
as good as told me so.

SIR CHARLES

But girls are apt to flatter themselves, you know.

HARDCASTLE

I saw him grasp her hand in the warmest manner myself;
and here he comes to put you out of your ifs, I warrant
him.

[*Enter* MARLOW.]

MARLOW

I come, sir, once more, to ask pardon for my strange
conduct. I can scarce reflect on my insolence without confusion.

HARDCASTLE

Tut, boy, a trifle. You take it too gravely. An hour or
two's laughing with my daughter will set all to rights again.
She'll never like you the worse for it.

MARLOW

Sir, I shall be always proud of her approbation.

HARDCASTLE

Approbation is but a cold word, Mr Marlow; if I am not
deceived, you have something more than approbation
thereabouts. You take me.

MARLOW

Really, sir, I have not that happiness.

HARDCASTLE

Come, boy, I'm an old fellow, and know what's what, as
well as you that are younger. I know what has past
between you; but mum.

MARLOW

Sure, sir, nothing has passed between us but the most
profound respect on my side, and the most distant reserve
on hers. You don't think, sir, that my impudence has been
passed upon all the rest of the family.

HARDCASTLE

Impudence! No, I don't say that—not quite impudence—
though girls like to be played with, and rumpled a little
too, sometimes. But she has told no tales, I assure you.

MARLOW

I never gave her the slightest cause.

HARDCASTLE

Well, well, I like modesty in its place well enough. But
this is over-acting, young gentleman. You may be open.
Your father and I will like you the better for it.

MARLOW

May I die, sir, if I ever—

HARDCASTLE

I tell you, she don't dislike you; and as I'm sure you like
her—

MARLOW

Dear sir—I protest, sir—

HARDCASTLE

I see no reason why you should not be joined as fast as
the parson can tie you.

MARLOW

But hear me, sir—

HARDCASTLE

Your father approves the match, I admire it, every
moment's delay will be doing mischief, so—

MARLOW

But why won't you hear me? By all that's just and true, I
never gave Miss Hardcastle the slightest mark of my attachment, or even the most distant hint to suspect me of
affection. We had but one interview, and that was formal,
modest, and uninteresting.

HARDCASTLE

[*Aside*.] This fellow's formal modest impudence is beyond bearing.

SIR CHARLES

And you never grasped her hand, or made any protestations!

MARLOW

As heaven is my witness, I came down in obedience to your commands. I saw the lady without emotion, and parted without reluctance. I hope you'll exact no further proofs of my duty, nor prevent me from leaving a house in which I suffer so many mortifications. [*Exit.*]

SIR CHARLES

I'm astonished at the air of sincerity with which he parted.

HARDCASTLE

And I'm astonished at the deliberate intrepidity of his assurance.

SIR CHARLES

I dare pledge my life and honour upon his truth.

HARDCASTLE

[*Looking out to right.*] Here comes my daughter, and I would stake my happiness upon her veracity.

[*Enter* MISS HARDCASTLE.]

HARDCASTLE

Kate, come hither, child. Answer us sincerely, and without reserve; has Mr Marlow made you any professions of love and affection?

MISS HARDCASTLE

The question is very abrupt, sir! But since you require unreserved sincerity, I think he has.

HARDCASTLE

[*To* SIR CHARLES.] You see.

SIR CHARLES

And pray, madam, have you and my son had more than one interview?

MISS HARDCASTLE

Yes, sir, several.

HARDCASTLE

[*To* SIR CHARLES.] You see.

SIR CHARLES

But did he profess any attachment?

MISS HARDCASTLE

A lasting one.

SIR CHARLES

Did he talk of love?

MISS HARDCASTLE
Much, sir.

SIR CHARLES
Amazing! And all this formally?

MISS HARDCASTLE
Formally.

HARDCASTLE
Now, my friend, I hope you are satisfied.

SIR CHARLES
And how did he behave, madam?

MISS HARDCASTLE
As most professed admirers do. Said some civil things of
my face, talked much of his want of merit, and the greatness of mine; mentioned his heart, gave a short tragedy
speech, and ended with pretended rapture.

SIR CHARLES
Now I'm perfectly convinced, indeed. I know his conversation among women to be modest and submissive. This
forward, canting, ranting manner by no means describes
him, and I am confident he never sat for the picture.

MISS HARDCASTLE
Then what, sir, if I should convince you to your face of
my sincerity? If you and my papa, in about half an hour,
will place yourselves behind that screen, you shall hear
him declare his passion to me in person.

SIR CHARLES
Agreed. And if I find him what you describe, all my happiness in him must have an end. [*Exit.*]

MISS HARDCASTLE
And if you don't find him what I describe—I fear my
happiness must never have a beginning. [*Exeunt.*]

   [*Scene changes to the back of the garden. Enter*
   HASTINGS.]

HASTINGS
What an idiot am I, to wait here for a fellow, who probably
takes a delight in mortifying me. He never intended to be
punctual, and I'll wait no longer. What do I see? It is he,
and perhaps with news of my Constance.

   [*Enter* TONY, *booted and spattered.*]

HASTINGS
My honest 'Squire! I now find you a man of your word.

This looks like friendship.

TONY

Ay, I'm your friend, and the best friend you have in the world, if you knew but all. This riding by night, by the by, is cursedly tiresome. It has shook me worse than the basket of a stage-coach.

HASTINGS

But how? Where did you leave your fellow-travellers? Are they in safety? Are they housed?

TONY

Five and twenty miles in two hours and a half is no such bad driving. The poor beasts have smoked for it: rabbit me, but I'd rather ride forty miles after a fox, than ten with such varmint.

HASTINGS

Well, but where have you left the ladies? I die with impatience.

TONY

Left them? Why, where should I leave them, but where I found them?

HASTINGS

This is a riddle.

TONY

Riddle me this, then. What's that goes round the house, and round the house, and never touches the house?

HASTINGS

I'm still astray.

TONY

Why, that's it, mon. I have led them astray. By jingo, there's not a pond or slough within five miles of the place but they can tell the taste of.

HASTINGS

Ha, ha, ha, I understand; you took them in a round, while they supposed themselves going forward. And so you have at last brought them home again.

TONY

You shall hear. I first took them down Feather-Bed Lane, where we stuck fast in the mud. I then rattled them crack over the stones of Up-and-Down Hill—I then introduced them to the gibbet on Heavy-Tree Heath, and from that, with a circumbendibus,[74] I fairly lodged them in the horse-pond at the bottom of the garden.

HASTINGS

But no accident, I hope.

TONY

No, no. Only mother is confoundedly frightened. She thinks herself forty miles off. She's sick of the journey, and the cattle can scarce crawl. So, if your own horses be ready, you may whip off with cousin, and I'll be bound that no soul here can budge a foot to follow you.

HASTINGS

My dear friend, how can I be grateful?

TONY

Ay, now it's dear friend, noble 'Squire. Just now, it was all idiot, cub, and run me through the guts. Damn your way of fighting, I say. After we take a knock in this part of the country, we kiss and be friends. But if you had run me through the guts, then I should be dead, and you might go to kiss the hangman.

HASTINGS

The rebuke is just. But I must hasten to relieve Miss Neville; if you keep the old lady employed, I promise to take care of the young one. [*Exit* HASTINGS.]

TONY

Never fear me. Here she comes. Vanish. She's got from the pond, and draggled up to the waist like a mermaid.

[*Enter* MRS HARDCASTLE.]

MRS HARDCASTLE

Oh, Tony, I'm killed. Shook. Battered to death. I shall never survive it. That last jolt that laid us against the quickset hedge has done my business.

TONY

Alack, mamma, it was all your own fault. You would be for running away by night, without knowing one inch of the way.

MRS HARDCASTLE

I wish we were at home again. I never met so many accidents in so short a journey. Drenched in the mud, overturned in a ditch, stuck fast in a slough, jolted to a jelly, and at last to lose our way. Whereabouts do you think we are, Tony?

TONY

By my guess we should be upon Crackskull Common, about forty miles from home.

MRS HARDCASTLE

O lud! O lud! the most notorious spot in all the country. We only want a robbery to make a complete night on't.

TONY

Don't be afraid, mamma, don't be afraid. Two of the five that kept [75] here are hanged, and the other three may not find us. Don't be afraid. Is that a man that's galloping behind us? No; it's only a tree. Don't be afraid.

MRS HARDCASTLE

The fright will certainly kill me.

TONY

Do you see anything like a black hat moving behind the thicket?

MRS HARDCASTLE

O death!

TONY

No, it's only a cow. Don't be afraid, mamma, don't be afraid.

MRS HARDCASTLE

As I'm alive, Tony, I see a man coming towards us. Ah! I'm sure on't. If he perceives us, we are undone.

TONY

[*Aside.*] Father-in-law, by all that's unlucky, come to take one of his night walks. [*To her.*] Ah, it's a highwayman, with pistols as long as my arm. A damned ill-looking fellow.

MRS HARDCASTLE

Good Heaven defend us! He approaches.

TONY

Do you hide yourself in that thicket and leave me to manage him. If there be any danger I'll cough and cry hem. When I cough be sure to keep close.

[MRS HARDCASTLE *hides behind a tree in the back scene. Enter* HARDCASTLE.]

HARDCASTLE

I'm mistaken, or I heard voices of people in want of help. Oh, Tony, is that you? I did not expect you so soon back. Are your mother and her charge in safety?

TONY

Very safe, sir, at my Aunt Pedigree's. Hem.

MRS HARDCASTLE

[*From behind.*] Ah! I find there's danger.

HARDCASTLE

Forty miles in three hours; sure, that's too much, my youngster.

TONY

Stout horses and willing minds make short journeys, as they say. Hem.

MRS HARDCASTLE

[*From behind.*] Sure he'll do the dear boy no harm.

HARDCASTLE

But I heard a voice here; I should be glad to know from whence it came?

TONY

It was I, sir, talking to myself, sir. I was saying that forty miles in four hours was very good going. Hem. As to be sure it was. Hem. I have got a sort of cold by being out in the air. We'll go in if you please. Hem.

HARDCASTLE

But if you talked to yourself, you did not answer yourself. I am certain I heard two voices, and am resolved [*raising his voice*] to find the other out.

MRS HARDCASTLE

[*From behind.*] Oh! he's coming to find me out. Oh!

TONY

What need you go, sir, if I tell you? Hem. I'll lay down my life for the truth—hem—I'll tell you all, sir. [*Detaining him.*]

HARDCASTLE

I tell you I will not be detained. I insist on seeing. It's in vain to expect I'll believe you.

MRS HARDCASTLE

[*Running forward from behind.*] O lud, he'll murder my poor boy, my darling. Here, good gentleman, whet your rage upon me. Take my money, my life, but spare that young gentleman, spare my child if you have any mercy.

HARDCASTLE

My wife! as I'm a Christian. From whence can she come, or what does she mean?

MRS HARDCASTLE

[*Kneeling.*] Take compassion on us, good Mr Highwayman. Take our money, our watches, all we have, but spare
our lives. We will never bring you to justice, indeed we
won't, good Mr Highwayman.

HARDCASTLE

I believe the woman's out of her senses. What, Dorothy,
don't you know me?

MRS HARDCASTLE

Mr Hardcastle, as I'm alive! My fears blinded me. But
who, my dear, could have expected to meet you here, in
this frightful place, so far from home. What has brought
you to follow us?

HARDCASTLE

Sure, Dorothy, you have not lost your wits. So far from
home, when you are within forty yards of your own
door! [*To him.*] This is one of your old tricks, you graceless rogue, you! [*To her.*] Don't you know the gate, and
the mulberry-tree; and don't you remember the horse-pond,
my dear?

MRS HARDCASTLE

Yes, I shall remember the horse-pond as long as I live; I
have caught my death in it. [*To* TONY.] And it is to you,
you graceless varlet, I owe all this? I'll teach you to abuse
your mother, I will.

TONY

Ecod, mother, all the parish says you have spoiled me, and
so you may take the fruits on't.

MRS HARDCASTLE

I'll spoil you, I will. [*Follows him off the stage.*]

HARDCASTLE

There's morality, however, in his reply. [*Exit. Enter*
HASTINGS *and* MISS NEVILLE.]

HASTINGS

My dear Constance, why will you deliberate thus? If we
delay a moment, all is lost for ever. Pluck up a little resolution, and we shall soon be out of the reach of her malignity.

MISS NEVILLE

I find it impossible. My spirits are so sunk with the
agitations I have suffered, that I am unable to face any
new danger. Two or three years' patience will at last crown

us with happiness.

HASTINGS

Such a tedious delay is worse than inconstancy. Let us fly, my charmer. Let us date our happiness from this very moment. Perish fortune. Love and content will increase what we possess beyond a monarch's revenue. Let me prevail.

MISS NEVILLE

No, Mr Hastings; no. Prudence once more comes to my relief, and I will obey its dictates. In the moment of passion, fortune may be despised, but it ever produces a lasting repentance. I'm resolved to apply to Mr Hardcastle's compassion and justice for redress.

HASTINGS

But though he had the will, he has not the power to relieve you.

MISS NEVILLE

But he has influence, and upon that I am resolved to rely.

HASTINGS

I have no hopes. But since you persist, I must reluctantly obey you. [*Exeunt.*]

[*Scene changes. Enter* SIR CHARLES *and* MISS HARD-CASTLE.]

SIR CHARLES

What a situation am I in. If what you say appears, I shall then find a guilty son. If what he says be true, I shall then lose one that, of all others, I most wished for a daughter.

MISS HARDCASTLE

I am proud of your approbation, and, to show I merit it, if you place yourselves as I directed, you shall hear his explicit declaration. But he comes.

SIR CHARLES

I'll to your father, and keep him to the appointment. [*Exit* SIR CHARLES. *Enter* MARLOW.]

MARLOW

Though prepared for setting out, I come once more to take leave, nor did I, till this moment, know the pain I feel in the separation.

MISS HARDCASTLE

[*In her own natural manner.*] I believe sufferings cannot be very great, sir, which you can so easily remove. A day or two longer, perhaps, might lessen your uneasiness, by showing the little value of what you think proper to regret.

MARLOW

[*Aside.*] This girl every moment improves upon me. [*To her.*] It must not be, madam. I have already trifled too long with my heart. My very pride begins to submit to my passion. The disparity of education and fortune, the anger of a parent, and the contempt of my equals, begin to lose their weight; and nothing can restore me to myself but this painful effort of resolution.

MISS HARDCASTLE

Then go, sir. I'll urge nothing more to detain you. Though my family be as good as hers you came down to visit, and my education, I hope, not inferior, what are these advantages without equal affluence? I must remain contented with the slight approbation of imputed merit; I must have only the mockery of your addresses, while all your serious aims are fixed on fortune.

[*Enter* HARDCASTLE *and* SIR CHARLES *from behind.*]

SIR CHARLES

Here, behind this screen.

HARDCASTLE

Ay, ay, make no noise. I'll engage my Kate covers him with confusion at last.

MARLOW

By heavens, madam, fortune was ever my smallest consideration. Your beauty at first caught my eye; for who could see that without emotion? But every moment that I converse with you, steals in some new grace, heightens the picture, and gives it stronger expression. What at first seemed rustic plainness, now appears refined simplicity. What seemed forward assurance, now strikes me as the result of courageous innocence, and conscious virtue.

SIR CHARLES

What can it mean! He amazes me!

HARDCASTLE

I told you how it would be. Hush!

MARLOW

I am now determined to stay, madam, and I have too good an opinion of my father's discernment, when he sees you, to doubt his approbation.

MISS HARDCASTLE

No, Mr Marlow, I will not, cannot detain you. Do you think I could suffer a connexion, in which there is the smallest room for repentance? Do you think I would take the mean advantage of a transient passion, to load you with confusion? Do you think I could ever relish that happiness, which was acquired by lessening yours!

MARLOW

By all that's good, I can have no happiness but what's in your power to grant me. Nor shall I ever feel repentance, but in not having seen your merits before. I will stay, even contrary to your wishes; and though you should persist to shun me, I will make my respectful assiduities atone for the levity of my past conduct.

MISS HARDCASTLE

Sir, I must entreat you'll desist. As our acquaintance began, so let it end, in indifference. I might have given an hour or two to levity; but, seriously, Mr Marlow, do you think I could ever submit to a connexion, where I must appear mercenary, and you imprudent? Do you think, I could ever catch at the confident addresses of a secure admirer?

MARLOW

[*Kneeling.*] Does this look like security? Does this look like confidence? No, madam, every moment that shows me your merit, only serves to increase my diffidence and confusion. Here let me continue—

SIR CHARLES

I can hold it no longer. Charles, Charles, how hast thou deceived me! Is this your indifference, your uninteresting conversation!

HARDCASTLE

Your cold contempt; your formal interview. What have you to say now?

MARLOW

That I'm all amazement! What can it mean!

HARDCASTLE

It means that you can say and unsay things at pleasure. That you can address a lady in private, and deny it in public; that you have one story for us, and another for my daughter!

MARLOW

Daughter! this lady your daughter!

HARDCASTLE

Yes, sir, my only daughter. My Kate, whose else should she be?

MARLOW

Oh, the devil!

MISS HARDCASTLE

Yes, sir, that very identical tall squinting lady you were pleased to take me for. [*Curtsying.*] She that you addressed as the mild, modest, sentimental man of gravity, and the bold, forward, agreeable Rattle of the Ladies' Club: ha, ha, ha.

MARLOW

Zounds, there's no bearing this; it's worse than death.

MISS HARDCASTLE

In which of your characters, sir, will you give us leave to address you? As the faltering gentleman, with looks on the ground, that speaks just to be heard, and hates hypocrisy: or the loud confident creature, that keeps it up with Mrs Mantrap, and old Miss Biddy Buckskin, till three in the morning; ha, ha, ha!

MARLOW

Oh, curse on my noisy head. I never attempted to be imprudent yet, that I was not taken down. I must be gone [*Going.*]

HARDCASTLE

By the hand of my body, but you shall not. I see it was all a mistake, and I am rejoiced to find it. You shall not, sir, I tell you. I know she'll forgive you. Won't you forgive him, Kate? We'll all forgive you. Take courage, man.

[*They retire, she tormenting him, to the back scene.*
Enter MRS HARDCASTLE, TONY.]

MRS HARDCASTLE

So, so, they're gone off. Let them go, I care not.

HARDCASTLE

Who gone?

MRS HARDCASTLE

My dutiful niece and her gentleman, Mr Hastings, from town. He who came down with our modest visitor here.

SIR CHARLES

Who, my honest George Hastings? As worthy a fellow as lives, and the girl could not have made a more prudent choice.

HARDCASTLE

Then, by the hand of my body, I'm proud of the connexion.

MRS HARDCASTLE

Well, if he has taken away the lady, he has not taken her fortune, that remains in this family to console us for her loss.

HARDCASTLE

Sure, Dorothy, you would not be so mercenary?

MRS HARDCASTLE

Ay, that's my affair, not yours.

HARDCASTLE

But you know, if your son, when of age, refuses to marry his cousin, her whole fortune is then at her own disposal.

MRS HARDCASTLE

Ah, but he's not of age, and she has not thought proper to wait for his refusal.

[*Enter* HASTINGS *and* MISS NEVILLE.]

MRS HARDCASTLE

[*Aside.*] What, returned so soon! I begin not to like it.

HASTINGS

[*To* HARDCASTLE.] For my late attempt to fly off with your niece, let my present confusion be my punishment. We are now come back to appeal from your justice to your humanity. By her father's consent, I first paid her my addresses, and our passions were first founded in duty.

MISS NEVILLE

Since his death, I have been obliged to stoop to dissimulation to avoid oppression. In an hour of levity, I was ready even to give up my fortune to secure my choice. But I'm now recovered from the delusion, and hope from your tenderness what is denied me from a nearer connexion.

MRS HARDCASTLE

Pshaw, pshaw, this is all but the whining end of a modern novel.

HARDCASTLE

Be it what it will, I'm glad they're come back to reclaim their due. Come hither, Tony boy. Do you refuse this lady's hand whom I now offer you?

TONY

What signifies my refusing? You know I can't refuse her till I'm of age, father.

HARDCASTLE

While I thought concealing your age, boy, was likely to conduce to your improvement, I concurred with your mother's desire to keep it secret. But since I find she turns it to a wrong use, I must now declare, you have been of age these three months.

TONY

Of age! Am I of age, father?

HARDCASTLE

Above three months.

TONY

Then you'll see the first use I'll make of my liberty. [*Taking* MISS NEVILLE'S *hand*.] Witness all men by these presents, that I, Anthony Lumpkin, Esquire, of BLANK place, refuse you, Constantia Neville, spinster, of no place at all, for my true and lawful wife. So Constance Neville may marry whom she pleases and Tony Lumpkin is his own man again!

SIR CHARLES

O brave 'squire!

HASTINGS

My worthy friend!

MRS HARDCASTLE

My undutiful offspring!

MARLOW

Joy, my dear George, I give you joy, sincerely. And could I prevail upon my little tyrant here to be less arbitrary, I should be the happiest man alive, if you would return me the favour.

HASTINGS

[*To* MISS HARDCASTLE.] Come, madam, you are now driven to the very last scene of all your contrivances. I know you like him, I'm sure he loves you, and you must and shall have him.

HARDCASTLE

[*Joining their hands*.] And I say so, too. And Mr Marlow, if she makes as good a wife as she has a daughter, I don't believe you'll ever repent your bargain. So now to supper. Tomorrow we shall gather all the poor of the parish about us, and the mistakes of the night shall be crowned with a merry morning; so boy, take her; and as you have been mistaken in the mistress, my wish is, that you may never be mistaken in the wife.

Epilogue

BY DR GOLDSMITH

[*Spoken by* MISS HARDCASTLE.]

Well, having stooped to conquer with success,
And gained a husband without aid from dress,
Still as a barmaid, I could wish it too,
As I have conquered him to conquer you:
And let me say, for all your resolution,
That pretty barmaids have done execution.
Our life is all a play, composed to please,
'We have our exits and our entrances.' [76]
The first act shows the simple country maid,
Harmless and young, of everything afraid;
Blushes when hired, and with unmeaning action,
'I hopes as how to give you satisfaction.'
Her second act displays a livelier scene,—
Th' unblushing barmaid of a country inn,
Who whisks about the house, at market caters,
Talks loud, coquets the guests, and scolds the waiters.
Next the scene shifts to town, and there she soars,
The chop-house toast of ogling connoisseurs.
On 'squires and cits [77] she there displays her arts,
And on the gridiron broils her lovers' hearts—
And as she smiles, her triumphs to complete,
Even common councilmen forget to eat.
The fourth act shows her wedded to the 'squire,
And madam now begins to hold it higher;
Pretends to taste, at Operas cries caro, [78]
And quits her Nancy Dawson, [79] for Che Faro. [80]
Doats upon dancing, and in all her pride,
Swims round the room, the Heinel of Cheapside: [81]
Ogles and leers with artificial skill,

Till having lost in age the power to kill,
She sits all night at cards, and ogles at spadille.[82]
Such, through our lives, the eventful history—
The fifth and last act still remains for me.
The barmaid now for your protection prays,
Turns female Barrister, and pleads for Bayes.[83]

Epilogue

BY J. CRADDOCK, ESQ.[84]

[*Spoken by* TONY LUMPKIN.]

Well—now all's ended—and my comrades gone,
Pray what becomes of mother's nonly son?
A hopeful blade!—in town I'll fix my station,
And try to make a bluster in the nation.
As for my cousin Neville, I renounce her,
Off—in a crack—I'll carry big Bet Bouncer.
Why should not I in the great world appear?
I soon shall have a thousand pounds a year;
No matter what a man may here inherit,
In London—'gad, they've some regard to spirit.
I see the horses prancing up the streets,
And big Bet Bouncer bobs to all she meets;
Then hoikes to jiggs and pastimes every night—
Not to the plays—they say it a'n't polite,
To Sadler's Wells perhaps, or operas go,
And once, by chance, to the roratorio.[85]
Thus here and there, for ever up and down,
We'll set the fashions, too, to half the town;
And then at auctions—money ne'er regard,
Buy pictures like the great, ten pounds a yard;
Zounds, we shall make these London gentry say,
We know what's damn'd genteel, as well as they.

THE RIVALS

by RICHARD BRINSLEY SHERIDAN

Dramatis Personæ

As acted at Covent Garden Theatre on January 17, 1775

SIR ANTHONY ABSOLUTE	*Mr Shuter*
CAPTAIN ABSOLUTE	*Mr Woodward*
FAULKLAND	*Mr Lewis*
ACRES	*Mr Quick*
SIR LUCIUS O'TRIGGER	*Mr Lee*
FAG	*Mr Lee Lewes*
DAVID	*Mr Dunstal*
THOMAS	*Mr Fearon*
MRS MALAPROP	*Mrs Green*
LYDIA LANGUISH	*Miss Barsanti*
JULIA	*Mrs Bulkley*
LUCY	*Mrs Lessingham*

Maid, Boy, Servants, &c.

SCENE—*Bath*

Time of Action—Five Hours

Prologue

[*Spoken by* MR WOODWARD *and* MR QUICK.]

[*Enter* SERJEANT-AT-LAW,[1] *and* ATTORNEY *following, and giving a paper.*]

SERJEANT
What's here!—a vile cramp hand! I cannot see
Without my spectacles.

ATTORNEY

              He means his fee.
Nay, Mr Serjeant, good sir, try again.   [*Gives money.*]

SERJEANT
The scrawl improves! [*More.*] O come, 'tis pretty plain.
Hey! how's this? Dibble!—sure it cannot be!
A poet's brief! a poet and a fee!

ATTORNEY
Yes, sir! though you without reward, I know,
Would gladly plead the Muse's cause.

SERJEANT

                    So!—So!

ATTORNEY
And if the fee offends, your wrath should fall
On me.

SERJEANT
Dear Dibble, no offence at all.

ATTORNEY
Some sons of Phœbus[2] in the courts we meet—

SERJEANT
And fifty sons of Phœbus in the Fleet![3]

ATTORNEY
Nor pleads he worse, who with a decent sprig
Of bays[4] adorns his legal waste of wig.

SERJEANT

Full-bottomed heroes[5] thus, on signs, unfurl
A leaf of laurel in a grove of curl!
Yet tell your client, that, in adverse days,
This wig is warmer than a bush of bays.

ATTORNEY

Do you, then, sir, my client's place supply,
Profuse of robe, and prodigal of tie—
Do you, with all those blushing powers of face,
And wonted bashful hesitating grace,
Rise in the court and flourish on the case. [*Exit*.]

SERJEANT

For practice then suppose—this brief will show it,—
Me, Serjeant Woodward,—counsel for the poet.
Used to the ground, I know 'tis hard to deal
With this dread court,[6] from whence there's no appeal;
No tricking here, to blunt the edge of law,
Or, damn'd in equity, escape by flaw:
But judgment given, your sentence must remain;
No writ of error lies—to Drury-lane![7]

   Yet when so kind you seem, 'tis past dispute
We gain some favour, if not costs of suit.
No spleen is here! I see no hoarded fury;—
I think I never faced a milder jury!
Sad else our plight! where frowns are transportation,[8]
A hiss the gallows, and a groan damnation!
But such the public candour, without fear
My client waives all right of challenge here.
No newsman from our session is dismiss'd,
Nor wit nor critic we scratch off the list;
His faults can never hurt another's ease,
His crime, at worst, a bad attempt to please:
Thus, all respecting, he appeals to all,
And by the general voice will stand or fall.

Prologue

[*Spoken on the tenth night, by* MRS BULKLEY.]

Granted our cause, our suit and trial o'er,
The worthy serjeant need appear no more:
In pleasing I a different client choose,
He served the Poet—I would serve the Muse.
Like him, I'll try to merit your applause,
A female counsel in a female's cause.

    Look on this form,°—where humour, quaint and sly,
Dimples the cheek, and points the beaming eye;
Where gay invention seems to boast its wiles
In amorous hint, and half-triumphant smiles;
While her light mask or covers satire's strokes,
Or hides the conscious blush her wit provokes.
Look on her well—does she seem form'd to teach?
Should you expect to hear this lady preach?
Is grey experience suited to her youth?
Do solemn sentiments become that mouth?
Bid her be grave, those lips should rebel prove
To every theme that slanders mirth or love.

    Yet, thus adorn'd with every graceful art
To charm the fancy and yet reach the heart—
Must we displace her, and instead advance
The goddess of the woful countenance—
The sentimental Muse?—Her emblems view,
The Pilgrim's Progress, and a sprig of rue!
View her—too chaste to look like flesh and blood—
Primly portray'd on emblematic wood!
There' fix'd in usurpation, should she stand,
She'll snatch the dagger from her sister's hand: ¹⁰
And having made her votaries weep a flood,

Good heaven! she'll end her comedies in blood—
Bid Harry Woodward break poor Dunstal's crown,
Imprison Quick, and knock Ned Shuter down;
While sad Barsanti, weeping o'er the scene,
Shall stab herself—or poison Mrs Green.[11]

   Such dire encroachments to prevent in time,
Demands the critic's voice—the poet's rhyme.
Can our light scenes add strength to holy laws!
Such puny patronage but hurts the cause:
Fair virtue scorns our feeble aid to ask;
And moral truth disdains the trickster's mask.
For here their favourite stands, whose brow, severe
And sad, claims youth's respect, and pity's tear;
Who, when oppress'd by foes her worth creates,
Can point a poniard at the guilt she hates.

Act one.

SCENE I

[*A street in Bath.*]

[*Enter* THOMAS; *he crosses the stage;* FAG *follows, looking after him.*]

FAG
What! Thomas! Sure 'tis he?—What! Thomas! Thomas!

THOMAS
Hey!—Odd's[12] life! Mr Fag—give us your hand, my old fellow-servant.

FAG
Excuse my glove, Thomas:—I'm devilish glad to see you, my lad. Why, my prince of charioteers, you look as hearty! —but who the deuce thought of seeing you in Bath?

THOMAS
Sure, master, Madam Julia, Harry, Mrs Kate, and the postilion, be all come.

FAG
Indeed!

THOMAS
Ay, master thought another fit of the gout was coming to make him a visit; so he'd a mind to gi't the slip, and whip! we were all off at an hour's warning.

FAG
Ay, ay, hasty in everything, or it would not be Sir Anthony Absolute!

THOMAS
But tell us, Mr Fag, how does young master? Odd! Sir Anthony will stare to see the captain here!

FAG
I do not serve Captain Absolute now.

THOMAS

Why sure!

FAG

At present I am employed by Ensign Beverley.

THOMAS

I doubt, Mr Fag, you ha'n't changed for the better.

FAG

I have not changed, Thomas.

THOMAS

No! Why didn't you say you had left young master?

FAG

No.—Well, honest Thomas, I must puzzle you no farther:
—briefly then—Captain Absolute and Ensign Beverley are
one and the same person.

THOMAS

The devil they are!

FAG

So it is indeed, Thomas; and the ensign half of my master
being on guard at present—the captain has nothing to do
with me.

THOMAS

So, so!—What, this is some freak, I warrant!—Do tell us,
Mr Fag, the meaning o't—you know I ha' trusted you.

FAG

You'll be secret, Thomas?

THOMAS

As a coach-horse.

FAG

Why then the cause of all this is—Love—Love, Thomas,
who (as you may get read to you) has been a masquerader
ever since the days of Jupiter.

THOMAS

Ay, ay;—I guessed there was a lady in the case:—but pray,
why does your master pass only for an ensign,—Now if
he had shammed general indeed—

FAG

Ah! Thomas, there lies the mystery o' the matter. Hark'ee,
Thomas, my master is in love with a lady of a very
singular taste: a lady who likes him better as a half-pay
ensign than if she knew he was son and heir to Sir Anthony Absolute, a baronet of three thousand a year.

THOMAS

That is an odd taste indeed!—But has she got the stuff, Mr Fag? Is she rich, hey?

FAG

Rich!—Why, I believe she owns half the stocks! Zounds! [13] Thomas, she could pay the national debt as easily as I could my washerwoman! She has a lap-dog that eats out of gold, —she feeds her parrot with small pearls,—and all her thread-papers[14] are made of banknotes!

THOMAS

Bravo, faith!—Odd! I warrant she has a set of thousands at least:—but does she draw kindly with the captain?

FAG

As fond as pigeons.

THOMAS

May one hear her name?

FAG

Miss Lydia Languish.—But there is an old tough aunt in the way; though, by-the-by, she has never seen my master —for we got acquainted with miss while on a visit in Gloucestershire.

THOMAS

Well—I wish they were once harnessed together in matrimony.—But pray, Mr Fag, what kind of a place is this Bath?—I ha' heard a deal of it—here's a mort [15] o' merrymaking, hey?

FAG

Pretty well, Thomas, pretty well—'tis a good lounge; in the morning we go to the pump-room[16] (though neither my master nor I drink the waters); after breakfast we saunter on the parades or play a game at billiards; at night we dance; but damn the place, I'm tired of it: their regular hours stupefy me—not a fiddle nor a card after eleven!— However Mr Faulkland's gentleman and I keep it up a little in private parties;—I'll introduce you there, Thomas —you'll like him much.

THOMAS

Sure I know Mr Du-Peigne—you know his master is to marry Madam Julia.

FAG

I had forgot.—But, Thomas, you must polish a little—

indeed you must.—Here now—this wig! [17] What the devil do
you do with a wig, Thomas?—None of the London whips of
any degree of *ton*[18] wear wigs now.

THOMAS

More's the pity! more's the pity! I say.—Odd's life! when
I heard how the lawyers and doctors had took to their
own hair, I thought how 'twould go next:—odd rabbit it!
when the fashion had got foot on the bar, I guessed
'twould mount to the box!—but 'tis all out of character,
believe me, Mr Fag: and look'ee, I'll never gi' up mine—
the lawyers and doctors may do as they will.

FAG

Well, Thomas, we'll not quarrel about that.

THOMAS

Why, bless you, gentlemen of the professions ben't all of
a mind—for in our village now, thoff [19] Jack Gauge, the
exciseman, has ta'en to his carrots,[20] there's little Dick the
farrier swears he'll never forsake his bob,[21] though all the
college should appear with their own heads!

FAG

Indeed! well said, Dick!—but hold—mark! mark! Thomas.

THOMAS

Zooks! 'tis the captain.—Is that the Lady with him?

FAG

No, no, that is Madam Lucy, my master's mistress's maid.
They lodge at that house—but I must after him to tell him
the news.

THOMAS

Odd! he's given her money!—Well, Mr Fag—

FAG

Good-bye, Thomas. I have an appointment in Gyde's
porch [22] this evening at eight; meet me there, and we'll make
a little party. [*Exeunt severally.*]

SCENE II

[*A Dressing-room in* MRS MALAPROP'S *lodgings.*]

[LYDIA *sitting on a sofa, with a book in her hand.* LUCY, *as just returned from a message.*]

LUCY
Indeed, ma'am, I traversed half the town in search of it! I don't believe there's a circulating library in Bath I hadn't been at.

LYDIA
And could not you get *The Reward of Constancy?*

LUCY
No, indeed, ma'am.

LYDIA
Nor *The Fatal Connection?*

LUCY
No, indeed, ma'am.

LYDIA
Nor *The Mistakes of the Heart?*

LUCY
Ma'am, as ill luck would have it, Mr Bull said Miss Sukey Saunter had just fetched it away.

LYDIA
Heigh-ho! Did you inquire for *The Delicate Distress?*

LUCY
Or, *The Memoirs of Lady Woodford?*²⁸ Yes, indeed, ma'am. I asked everywhere for it; and I might have brought it from Mr Frederick's, but Lady Slattern Lounger, who had just sent it home, had so soiled and dog's-eared it, it wa'n't fit for a Christian to read.

LYDIA
Heigh-ho! Yes, I always know when Lady Slattern has

been before me. She has a most observing thumb; and, I
believe, cherishes her nails for the convenience of making
marginal notes.—Well, child, what have you brought me?

LUCY

Oh! here, ma'am.—[*Taking books from under her cloak
and from her pockets.*] This is *The Gordian Knot*,—and
this *Peregrine Pickle*. Here are *The Tears of Sensibility*,
and *Humphrey Clinker*. This is *The Memoirs of a Lady of
Quality, written by Herself,* and here the second volume of
The Sentimental Journey. [24]

LYDIA

Heigh-ho!—What are those books by the glass?

LUCY

The great one is only *The Whole Duty of Man,* [25] where I
press a few blonds,[26] ma'am.

LYDIA

Very well—give me the *sal volatile.*[27]

LUCY

Is it in a blue cover, ma'am?

LYDIA

My smelling-bottle, you simpleton!

LUCY

Oh, the drops—here, ma'am.

LYDIA

Hold!—here's some one coming—quick! see who it is.—
[*Exit* LUCY.] Surely I heard my cousin Julia's voice.
   [*Reenter* LUCY.]

LUCY

Lud! ma'am, here is Miss Melville.

LYDIA

Is it possible?—
   [*Exit* LUCY. *Enter* JULIA.]

LYDIA

My dearest Julia, how delighted am I!—[*Embrace.*] How
unexpected was this happiness!

JULIA

True, Lydia—and our pleasure is the greater.—But what
has been the matter?—you were denied to me at first!

LYDIA

Ah, Julia, I have a thousand things to tell you!—But first

LYDIA

Well, Julia, you are your own mistress (though under the
protection of Sir Anthony), yet have you, for this long
year, been a slave to the caprice, the whim, the jealousy of
this ungrateful Faulkland, who will ever delay assuming
the right of a husband, while you suffer him to be equally
imperious as a lover.

JULIA

Nay, you are wrong entirely. We were contracted before
my father's death. That, and some consequent embarrassments, have delayed what I know to be my Faulkland's
most ardent wish. He is too generous to trifle on such a
point—and for his character, you wrong him there, too.
No, Lydia, he is too proud, too noble, to be jealous; if he is
captious, 'tis without dissembling; if fretful, without rudeness. Unused to the fopperies of love, he is negligent of the
little duties expected from a lover—but being unhackneyed
in the passion, his affection is ardent and sincere; and as
it engrosses his whole soul, he expects every thought and
emotion of his mistress to move in unison with his. Yet,
though his pride calls for this full return, his humility
makes him undervalue those qualities in him which would
entitle him to it; and not feeling why he should be loved to
the degree he wishes, he still suspects that he is not loved
enough. This temper, I must own, has cost me many unhappy hours; but I have learned to think myself his debtor,
for those imperfections which arise from the ardour of
his attachment.

LYDIA

Well, I cannot blame you for defending him. But tell me
candidly, Julia, had he never saved your life, do you think
you should have been attached to him as you are?—Believe
me, the rude blast that overset your boat was a prosperous
gale of love to him.

JULIA

Gratitude may have strengthened my attachment to Mr
Faulkland, but I loved him before he had preserved me;
yet surely that alone were an obligation sufficient.

LYDIA

Obligation! why a water spaniel would have done as much!
—Well, I should never think of giving my heart to a man

because he could swim.

JULIA

Come, Lydia, you are too inconsiderate.

LYDIA

Nay, I do but jest—What's here?

[*Reenter* LUCY *in a hurry.*]

LUCY

O ma'am, here is Sir Anthony Absolute just come home with your aunt.

LYDIA

They'll not come here.—Lucy, do you watch.

[*Exit* LUCY.]

JULIA

Yet I must go. Sir Anthony does not know I am here, and if we meet, he'll detain me, to show me the town. I'll take another opportunity of paying my respects to Mrs Malaprop, when she shall treat me, as long as she chooses, with her select words so ingeniously misapplied, without being mispronounced.

[*Reenter* LUCY.]

LUCY

O Lud! ma'am, they are both coming upstairs.

LYDIA

Well, I'll not detain you, coz.[30]—Adieu, my dear Julia. I'm sure you are in haste to send to Faulkland.—There, through my room you'll find another staircase.

JULIA

Adieu! [*Embraces* LYDIA, *and exit.*]

LYDIA

Here, my dear Lucy, hide these books. Quick quick!— Fling *Peregrine Pickle* under the toilet—throw *Roderick Random* into the closet—put *The Innocent Adultery* into *The Whole Duty of Man*—thrust *Lord Aimworth* under the sofa—cram *Ovid* behind the bolster—there—put *The Man of Feeling* into your pocket—so, so—now lay *Mrs Chapone* in sight, and leave *Fordyce's Sermons*[31] open on the table.

LUCY

O burn it, ma'am! the hair-dresser has torn away[32] as far as *Proper Pride*.

LYDIA

Never mind—open at *Sobriety*.—Fling me *Lord Chester-field's Letters*.[33] Now for 'em.

[*Exit* LUCY. *Enter* MRS MALAPROP *and* SIR ANTHONY ABSOLUTE.]

MRS MALAPROP

There, Sir Anthony, there sits the deliberate simpleton who wants to disgrace her family, and lavish herself on a fellow not worth a shilling.

LYDIA

Madam, I thought you once—

MRS MALAPROP

You thought, miss! I don't know any business you have to think at all—thought does not become a young woman. But the point we would request of you is, that you will promise to forget this fellow—to illiterate[34] him, I say, quite from your memory.

LYDIA

Ah, madam! our memories are independent of our wills. It is not so easy to forget.

MRS MALAPROP

But I say it is, miss; there is nothing on earth so easy as to forget, if a person chooses to set about it. I'm sure I have as much forgot your poor dear uncle as if he had never existed—and I thought it my duty so to do; and let me tell you, Lydia, these violent memories don't become a young woman.

SIR ANTHONY

Why sure she won't pretend to remember what she's ordered not!—ay, this comes of her reading!

LYDIA

What crime, madam, have I committed, to be treated thus?

MRS MALAPROP

Now don't attempt to extirpate yourself from the matter; you know I have proof controvertible of it.—But tell me, will you promise to do as you're bid? Will you take a husband of your friends' choosing?

LYDIA

Madam, I must tell you plainly, that had I no preference for any one else, the choice you have made would be my aversion.

MRS MALAPROP

What business have you, miss, with preference and aversion? They don't become a young woman; and you ought to know, that as both always wear off 'tis safest in matrimony to begin with a little aversion. I am sure I hated your poor dear uncle before marriage as if he'd been a blackamoor—and yet, miss, you are sensible what a wife I made!—and when it pleased Heaven to release me from him, 'tis unknown what tears I shed! But suppose we were going to give you another choice, will you promise us to give up this Beverley?

LYDIA

Could I belie my thoughts so far as to give that promise, my actions would certainly as far belie my words.

MRS MALAPROP

Take yourself to your room. You are fit company for nothing but your own ill-humours.

LYDIA

Willingly, ma'am—I cannot change for the worse. [*Exit.*]

MRS MALAPROP

There's a little intricate hussy for you!

SIR ANTHONY

It is not to be wondered at, ma'am,—all this is the natural consequence of teaching girls to read. Had I a thousand daughters, by Heaven! I'd as soon have them taught the black art [35] as their alphabet!

MRS MALAPROP

Nay, nay, Sir Anthony, you are an absolute misanthropy.

SIR ANTHONY

In my way hither, Mrs Malaprop, I observed your niece's maid coming forth from a circulating library!—She had a book in each hand—they were half-bound volumes, with marble covers!—From that moment I guessed how full of duty I should see her mistress!

MRS MALAPROP

Those are vile places, indeed!

SIR ANTHONY

Madam, a circulating library in a town is as an evergreen tree of diabolical knowledge! It blossoms through the year!—and depend on it, Mrs Malaprop, that they who are so fond of handling the leaves, will long for the fruit at last.

MRS MALAPROP

Fy, fy, Sir Anthony, you surely speak laconically.

SIR ANTHONY

Why, Mrs Malaprop, in moderation now, what would you
have a woman know?

MRS MALAPROP

Observe me, Sir Anthony. I would by no means wish a
daughter of mine to be a progeny of learning; I don't think
so much learning becomes a young woman; for instance, I
would never let her meddle with Greek, or Hebrew, or
algebra, or simony, or fluxions, or paradoxes, or such in-
flammatory branches of learning—neither would it be
necessary for her to handle any of your mathematical,
astronomical, diabolical instruments.—But, Sir Anthony, I
would send her, at nine years old, to a boarding-school, in
order to learn a little ingenuity and artifice. Then, sir, she
should have a supercilious knowledge in accounts;—and
as she grew up, I would have her instructed in geometry,
that she might know something of the contagious countries;
—but above all, Sir Anthony, she should be mistress of
orthodoxy, that she might not mis-spell, and mis-pronounce
words so shamefully as girls usually do; and likewise that
she might reprehend the true meaning of what she is saying. This, Sir Anthony, is what I would have a woman
know;—and I don't think there is a superstitious article in
it.

SIR ANTHONY

Well, well, Mrs Malaprop, I will dispute the point no
further with you; though I must confess that you are a
truly moderate and polite arguer, for almost every third
word you say is on my side of the question. But, Mrs
Malaprop, to the more important point in debate—you
say you have no objection to my proposal?

MRS MALAPROP

None, I assure you. I am under no positive engagement
with Mr Acres, and as Lydia is so obstinate against him,
perhaps your son may have better success.

SIR ANTHONY

Well, madam, I will write for the boy directly. He knows
not a syllable of this yet, though I have for some time had

the proposal in my head. He is at present with his regiment.

MRS MALAPROP

We have never seen your son, Sir Anthony; but I hope no objection on his side.

SIR ANTHONY

Objection!—let him object if he dare!—No, no, Mrs Malaprop, Jack knows that the least demur puts me in a frenzy directly. My process was always very simple—in their younger days, 'twas "Jack do this";—if he demurred, I knocked him down—and if he grumbled at that, I always sent him out of the room.

MRS MALAPROP

Ah, and the properest way, o' my conscience!—nothing is so conciliating to young people as severity.—Well, Sir Anthony, I shall give Mr Acres his discharge, and prepare Lydia to receive your son's invocations;—and I hope you will represent her to the captain as an object not altogether illegible.

SIR ANTHONY

Madam, I will handle the subject prudently.—Well, I must leave you; and let me beg you, Mrs Malaprop, to enforce this matter roundly to the girl.—Take my advice—keep a tight hand; if she rejects this proposal, clap her under lock and key; and if you were just to let the servants forget to bring her dinner for three or four days, you can't conceive how she'd come about. [*Exit.*]

MRS MALAPROP

Well, at any rate, I shall be glad to get her from under my intuition. She has somehow discovered my partiality for Sir Lucius O'Trigger—sure, Lucy can't have betrayed me! —No, the girl is such a simpleton, I should have made her confess it.—Lucy!—Lucy!—[*Calls.*] Had she been one of your artificial ones, I should never have trusted her.

[*Reenter* LUCY.]

LUCY

Did you call, ma'am?

MRS MALAPROP

Yes, girl.—Did you see Sir Lucius while you was out?

LUCY

No, indeed, ma'am, not a glimpse of him.

MRS MALAPROP
You are sure, Lucy, that you never mentioned—
LUCY
Oh, gemini! I'd sooner cut my tongue out.
MRS MALAPROP
Well, don't let your simplicity[36] be imposed on.
LUCY
No, ma'am.
MRS MALAPROP
So, come to me presently, and I'll give you another letter
to Sir Lucius; but mind, Lucy—if ever you betray what you
are entrusted with (unless it be other people's secrets to
me), you forfeit my malevolence for ever, and your being
a simpleton shall be no excuse for your locality. [*Exit.*]
LUCY
Ha! ha! ha!—So, my dear Simplicity, let me give you a
little respite.—[*Altering her manner.*] Let girls in my
station be as fond as they please of appearing expert, and
knowing in their trusts; commend me to a mask of silliness,
and a pair of sharp eyes for my own interest under it—Let
me see to what account have I turned my simplicity lately.
—[*Looks at a paper.*] For *abetting Miss Lydia Languish
in a design of running away with an ensign!—in money,
sundry times, twelve pound twelve; gowns, five; hats,
ruffles, caps, etc., etc., numberless!—From the said ensign,
within this last month, six guineas and a half.*—About a
quarter's pay!—Item, *from Mrs Malaprop, for betraying
the young people to her*—when I found matters were
likely to be discovered—*two guineas and a black paduasoy.*[37]—Item *from Mr Acres, for carrying divers letters*—
which I never delivered—*two guineas and a pair of
buckles*—Item, *from Sir Lucius O'Trigger, three crowns,
two gold pocket-pieces, and a silver snuff-box!*—Well done,
Simplicity!—Yet I was forced to make my Hibernian believe that he was corresponding, not with the aunt, but
with the niece; for though not over rich, I found he had
too much pride and delicacy to sacrifice the feelings of a
gentleman to the necessities of his fortune. [*Exit.*]

Act two.

[CAPTAIN ABSOLUTE'S *lodgings*.]

[CAPTAIN ABSOLUTE *and* FAG.]

FAG

Sir, while I was there, Sir Anthony came in: I told him you had sent me to inquire after his health, and to know if he was at leisure to see you.

ABSOLUTE

And what did he say, on hearing I was at Bath?

FAG

Sir, in my life I never saw an elderly gentleman more astonished! He started back two or three paces, rapped out a dozen interjectural oaths, and asked what the devil had brought you here.

ABSOLUTE

Well, sir, and what did you say?

FAG

Oh, I lied, sir—I forget the precise lie; but you may depend on't, he got no truth from me. Yet, with submission, for fear of blunders in future, I should be glad to fix what has brought us to Bath, in order that we may lie a little consistently. Sir Anthony's servants were curious, sir, very curious indeed.

ABSOLUTE

You have said nothing to them?

FAG

Oh, not a word, sir,—not a word! Mr Thomas, indeed, the coachman (whom I take to be the discreetest of whips)—

ABSOLUTE

'Sdeath!—you rascal! you have not trusted him!

FAG

Oh, no, sir—no—no—not a syllable, upon my veracity!—
He was, indeed, a little inquisitive; but I was sly, sir—
devilish sly! My master (said I), honest Thomas (you
know, sir, one says honest to one's inferiors), is come to
Bath to recruit.—Yes, sir, I said to recruit—and whether
for men, money, or constitution, you know, sir, is nothing
to him nor any one else.

ABSOLUTE

Well, recruit will do—let it be so.

FAG

Oh, sir, recruit will do surprisingly—indeed, to give the
thing an air, I told Thomas that your honour had already
enlisted five disbanded chairmen,⁸ seven minority waiters,⁹
and thirteen billiard-markers.

ABSOLUTE

You blockhead, never say more than is necessary.

FAG

I beg pardon, sir—I beg pardon—but, with submission, a
lie is nothing unless one supports it. Sir, whenever I draw
on my invention for a good current lie, I always forge
indorsements as well as the bill.

ABSOLUTE

Well, take care you don't hurt your credit by offering too
much security.—Is Mr Faulkland returned?

FAG

He is above, sir, changing his dress.

ABSOLUTE

Can you tell whether he has been informed of Sir Anthony
and Miss Melville's arrival?

FAG

I fancy not, sir; he has seen no one since he came in but
his gentleman, who was with him at Bristol.—I think, sir,
I hear Mr Faulkland coming down—

ABSOLUTE

Go tell him I am here.

FAG

Yes, sir.—[*Going.*] I beg pardon, sir, but should Sir Anthony call, you will do me the favour to remember that we are recruiting, if you please.

ABSOLUTE

Well, well.

FAG

And, in tenderness to my character, if your honour could bring in the chairmen and waiters, I should esteem it as an obligation; for though I never scruple a lie to serve my master, yet it hurts one's conscience to be found out. [*Exit.*]

ABSOLUTE

Now for my whimsical friend—if he does not know that his mistress is here, I'll tease him a little before I tell him—[*Enter* FAULKLAND.] Faulkland, you're welcome to Bath again; you are punctual in your return.

FAULKLAND

Yes; I had nothing to detain me when I had finished the business I went on. Well, what news since I left you? how stand matters between you and Lydia?

ABSOLUTE

Faith, much as they were; I have not seen her since our quarrel; however, I expect to be recalled every hour.

FAULKLAND

Why don't you persuade her to go off with you at once?

ABSOLUTE

What, and lose two-thirds of her fortune? You forget that, my friend.—No, no, I could have brought her to that long ago.

FAULKLAND

Nay, then, you trifle too long—if you are sure of her, propose to the aunt in your own character, and write to Sir Anthony for his consent.

ABSOLUTE

Softly, softly; for though I am convinced my little Lydia would elope with me as Ensign Beverley, yet am I by no means certain that she would take me with the impediment of our friends' consent, a regular humdrum wedding, and the reversion of a good fortune[40] on my side: no, no; I must prepare her gradually for the discovery, and make myself necessary to her, before I risk it.—Well, but Faulkland; you'll dine with us to-day at the hotel?

FAULKLAND

Indeed, I cannot; I am not in spirits to be of such a party.

ABSOLUTE

By heavens! I shall forswear your company. You are the most teasing, captious, incorrigible lover!—Do love like a man.

FAULKLAND

I own I am unfit for company.

ABSOLUTE

Am I not a lover; ay, and a romantic one too? Yet do I carry everywhere with me such a confounded farrago[a] of doubts, fears, hopes, wishes, and all the flimsy furniture of a country miss's brain!

FAULKLAND

Ah! Jack, your heart and soul are not, like mine, fixed immutably on one only object. You throw for a large stake, but losing, you could stake and throw again:—but I have set my sum of happiness on this cast, and not to succeed were to be stripped of all.

ABSOLUTE

But, for heaven's sake! what grounds for apprehension can your whimsical brain conjure up at present?

FAULKLAND

What grounds for apprehension, did you say? Heavens! are there not a thousand! I fear for her spirits—her health— her life!—My absence may fret her; her anxiety for my return, her fears for me, may oppress her gentle temper: and for her health, does not every hour bring me cause to be alarmed? If it rains, some shower may even then have chilled her delicate frame. If the wind be keen, some rude blast may have affected her! The heat of noon, the dews of evening, may endanger the life of her for whom only I value mine. O Jack! when delicate and feeling souls are separated, there is not a feature in the sky, not a movement of the elements, not an aspiration of the breeze, but hints some cause for a lover's apprehension!

ABSOLUTE

Ay, but we may choose whether we will take the hint or not.—So, then, Faulkland, if you were convinced that Julia were well and in spirits, you would be entirely content?

FAULKLAND

I should be happy beyond measure—I am anxious only for that.

ABSOLUTE

Then to cure your anxiety at once—Miss Melville is in perfect health, and is at this moment in Bath.

FAULKLAND

Nay, Jack—don't trifle with me.

ABSOLUTE

She is arrived here with my father within this hour.

FAULKLAND

Can you be serious?

ABSOLUTE

I thought you knew Sir Anthony better than to be surprised at a sudden whim of this kind.—Seriously, then, it is as I tell you—upon my honour.

FAULKLAND

My dear friend!—Hollo, Du-Peigne! my hat.—My dear Jack—now nothing on earth can give me a moment's uneasiness.

    [*Reenter* FAG.]

FAG

Sir, Mr Acres, just arrived, is below.

ABSOLUTE

Stay, Faulkland, this Acres lives within a mile of Sir Anthony, and he shall tell you how your mistress has been ever since you left her. Fag, show this gentleman up.

    [*Exit* FAG.]

FAULKLAND

What, is he much acquainted in the family?

ABSOLUTE

Oh, very intimate: I insist on your not going: besides, his character will divert you.

FAULKLAND

Well, I should like to ask him a few questions.

ABSOLUTE

He is likewise a rival of mine—that is, of my other self's, for he does not think his friend Captain Absolute ever saw the lady in question; and it is ridiculous enough to hear him complain to me of one Beverley, a concealed skulking rival, who—

FAULKLAND
Hush!—he's here.
  [*Enter* ACRES.]
ACRES
Ha! my dear friend, noble captain, and honest Jack, how do'st thou? just arrived, faith, as you see.—Sir, your humble servant. Warm work on the roads, Jack!—Odds whips and wheels! I've travelled like a comet, with a tail of dust all the way as long as the Mall.
ABSOLUTE
Ah! Bob, you are indeed an eccentric planet,[42] but we know your attraction hither.—Give me leave to introduce Mr Faulkland to you; Mr Faulkland, Mr Acres.
ACRES
Sir, I am most heartily glad to see you: sir, I solicit your connections.—Hey, Jack—what, this is Mr Faulkland, who—
ABSOLUTE
Ay, Bob, Miss Melville's Mr Faulkland.
ACRES
Odso! she and your father can be but just arrived before me?—I suppose you have seen them. Ah! Mr Faulkland, you are indeed a happy man.
FAULKLAND
I have not seen Miss Melville yet, sir;—I hope she enjoyed full health and spirits in Devonshire?
ACRES
Never knew her better in my life, sir,—never better. Odds blushes and blooms! she has been as healthy as the German Spa.
FAULKLAND
Indeed! I did hear that she had been a little indisposed.
ACRES
False, false, sir—only said to vex you: quite the reverse, I assure you.
FAULKLAND
There, Jack, you see she has the advantage of me; I had almost fretted myself ill.
ABSOLUTE
Now are you angry with your mistress for not having been sick?

FAULKLAND

No, no, you misunderstand me: yet surely a little trifling indisposition is not an unnatural consequence of absence from those we love.—Now confess—isn't there something unkind in this violent, robust, unfeeling health?

ABSOLUTE

Oh, it was very unkind of her to be well in your absence, to be sure!

ACRES

Good apartments, Jack.

FAULKLAND

Well, sir, but you were saying that Miss Melville has been so exceedingly well—what then she has been merry and gay, I suppose?—Always in spirits—hey?

ACRES

Merry, odds crickets! she has been the belle and spirit of the company wherever she has been—so lively and entertaining! so full of wit and humour!

FAULKLAND

There, Jack, there.—Oh, by my soul! there is an innate levity in woman that nothing can overcome.—What! happy, and I away!

ABSOLUTE

Have done!—How foolish this is! just now you were only apprehensive for your mistress' spirits.

FAULKLAND

Why, Jack, have I been the joy and spirit of the company?

ABSOLUTE

No, indeed, you have not.

FAULKLAND

Have I been lively and entertaining?

ABSOLUTE

Oh, upon my word, I acquit you.

FAULKLAND

Have I been full of wit and humour?

ABSOLUTE

No, faith, to do you justice, you have been confoundedly stupid indeed.

ACRES

What's the matter with the gentleman?

ABSOLUTE

He is only expressing his great satisfaction at hearing that
Julia has been so well and happy—that's all—hey, Faulkland?

FAULKLAND

Oh! I am rejoiced to hear it—yes, yes, she has a happy disposition!

ACRES

That she has indeed—then she is so accomplished—so
sweet a voice—so expert at her harpsichord—such a mistress of flat and sharp, squallante, rumblante, and quiverante!—There was this time month—odds minums and
crotches! [43] how she did chirrup at Mrs Piano's concert!

FAULKLAND

There again, what say you to this? you see she has been all
mirth and song—not a thought of me!

ABSOLUTE

Pho! man, is not music the food of love?

FAULKLAND

Well, well, it may be so.—Pray, Mr.———, what's his
damned name?—Do you remember what songs Miss Melville sung?

ACRES

Not I indeed.

ABSOLUTE

Stay, now, they were some pretty melancholy purling-
stream airs, I warrant; perhaps you may recollect;—did she
sing, *When absent from my soul's delight*?

ACRES

No, that wa'n't it.

ABSOLUTE

[*Sings.*] *Or Go, gentle gales!*

ACRES

Oh, no! nothing like it. Odds! now I recollect one of them
—[*Sings.*] *My heart's my own, my will is free.* [44]

FAULKLAND

Fool! fool that I am! to fix all my happiness on such a
trifler! 'Sdeath! to make herself the pipe and ballad-monger
of a circle to soothe her light heart with catches and
glees!—What can you say to this, sir?

ABSOLUTE

Why, that I should be glad to hear my mistress had been so merry, sir.

FAULKLAND

Nay, nay, nay—I'm not sorry that she has been happy—no, no, I am glad of that—I would not have had her sad or sick—yet surely a sympathetic heart would have shown itself even in the choice of a song—she might have been temperately healthy, and somehow, plaintively gay;—but she has been dancing too, I doubt not!

ACRES

What does the gentleman say about dancing?

ABSOLUTE

He says the lady we speak of dances as well as she sings.

ACRES

Ay, truly, does she—there was at our last race ball [45]—

FAULKLAND

Hell and the devil!—There!—there—I told you so! I told you so! Oh! she thrives in my absence!—Dancing! But her whole feelings have been in opposition with mine;—I have been anxious, silent, pensive, sedentary—my days have been hours of care, my nights of watchfulness.[46]—She has been all health! spirit! laugh! song! dance!—Oh! damned, damned levity!

ABSOLUTE

For heaven's sake, Faulkland, don't expose yourself so!—Suppose she has danced, what then?—does not the ceremony of society often oblige—

FAULKLAND

Well, well, I'll contain myself—perhaps as you say—for form sake.—What, Mr Acres, you were praising Miss Melville's manner of dancing a minuet—hey?

ACRES

Oh, I dare insure her for that—but what I was going to speak of was her country dancing. Odds swimmings! she has such an air with her!

FAULKLAND

Now disappointment on her!—Defend this, Absolute; why don't you defend this?—Country-dances! jigs and reels! am I to blame now? A minuet I could have forgiven—I should not have minded that—I say I should not have regarded

a minuet—but country-dances!—Zounds! had she made
one in a cotillon—I believe I could have forgiven even that
—but to be monkey-led for a night!—to run the gauntlet
through a string of amorous palming puppies!—to show
paces like a managed filly!—Oh, Jack, there never can be
but one man in the world whom a truly modest and
delicate woman ought to pair with in a country-dance; and,
even then, the rest of the couples should be her great-
uncles and aunts!

ABSOLUTE

Ay, to be sure!—grandfathers and grandmothers!

FAULKLAND

If there be but one vicious mind in the set, 'twill spread
like a contagion—the action of their pulse beats to the
lascivious movement of the jig—their quivering, warm-
breathed sighs impregnate the very air—the atmosphere
becomes electrical to love, and each amorous spark darts
through every link of the chain!—I must leave you—I
own I am somewhat flurried—and that confounded looby[47]
has perceived it. [*Going.*]

ABSOLUTE

Nay, but stay, Faulkland, and thank Mr Acres for his
good news.

FAULKLAND

Damn his news! [*Exit.*]

ABSOLUTE

Ha! ha! ha! poor Faulkland. Five minutes since—"nothing
on earth could give him a moment's uneasiness!"

ACRES

The gentleman wa'n't angry at my praising his mistress,
was he?

ABSOLUTE

A little jealous, I believe, Bob.

ACRES

You don't say so? Ha! ha! jealous of me—that's a good
joke.

ABSOLUTE

There's nothing strange in that, Bob! let me tell you, that
sprightly grace and insinuating manner of yours will do
some mischief among the girls here.

ACRES

Ah! you joke—ha! ha! mischief—ha! ha! but you know I
am not my own property, my dear Lydia has forestalled
me. She could never abide me in the country, because I
used to dress so badly—but odds frogs and tambours! [48] I
shan't take matters so here, now ancient madam has no
voice in it: I'll make my old clothes know who's master. I
shall straightway cashier [49] the hunting-frock, and render
my leather breeches incapable. My hair has been in training
some time.

ABSOLUTE

Indeed!

ACRES

Ay—and tho'ff the side curls are a little restive, my hind-
part takes it very kindly.

ABSOLUTE

Oh, you'll polish, I doubt not.

ACRES

Absolutely I propose so—then if I can find out this
Ensign Beverley, odds triggers and flints! I'll make him
know the difference o't.

ABSOLUTE

Spoke like a man! But pray, Bob, I observe you have got
an odd kind of a new method of swearing—

ACRES

Ha! ha! you've taken notice of it—'tis genteel, isn't it!—
I didn't invent it myself though; but a commander in our
militia, a great scholar, I assure you, says that there is no
meaning in the common oaths, and that nothing but their
antiquity makes them respectable; because, he says, the
ancients would never stick to an oath or two, but would
say, by Jove! or by Bacchus! or by Mars! or by Venus! or
by Pallas, according to the sentiment: so that to swear with
propriety, says my little major, the oath should be an echo
to the sense; and this we call the *oath referential*, or
sentimental swearing—ha! ha! 'tis genteel, isn't it.

ABSOLUTE

Very genteel, and very new, indeed!—and I dare say will
supplant all other figures of imprecation.

ACRES

Ay, ay, the best terms will grow obsolete.—Damns have

had their day.

[*Reenter* FAG.]

FAG

Sir, there is a gentleman below desires to see you.—shall I show him into the parlour?

ABSOLUTE

Ay—you may.

ACRES

Well, I must be gone—

ABSOLUTE

Stay; who is it, Fag?

FAG

Your father, sir.

ABSOLUTE

You puppy, why didn't you show him up directly? [*Exit* FAG.]

ACRES

You have business with Sir Anthony.—I expect a message from Mrs Malaprop at my lodgings. I have sent also to my dear friend, Sir Lucius O'Trigger. Adieu, Jack! we must meet at night, when you shall give me a dozen bumpers to little Lydia.

ABSOLUTE

That I will with all my heart.—[*Exit* ACRES.] Now for a parental lecture—I hope he has heard nothing of the business that brought me here—I wish the gout had held him fast in Devonshire, with all my soul! [*Enter* SIR ANTHONY ABSOLUTE.] Sir, I am delighted to see you here; looking so well! your sudden arrival at Bath made me apprehensive for your health.

SIR ANTHONY

Very apprehensive, I dare say, Jack.—What, you are re-cruiting here, hey?

ABSOLUTE

Yes, sir, I am on duty.

SIR ANTHONY

Well, Jack, I am glad to see you, though I did not expect it, for I was going to write to you on a little matter of business.—Jack, I have been considering that I grow old and infirm, and shall probably not trouble you long.

ABSOLUTE

Pardon me, sir, I never saw you look more strong and
hearty; and I pray frequently that you may continue so.

SIR ANTHONY

I hope your prayers may be heard, with all my heart. Well,
then, Jack, I have been considering that I am so strong
and hearty I may continue to plague you a long time. Now,
Jack, I am sensible that the income of your commission,
and what I have hitherto allowed you, is but a small pit-
tance for a lad of your spirit.

ABSOLUTE

Sir, you are very good.

SIR ANTHONY

And it is my wish, while yet I live, to have my boy make
some figure in the world. I have resolved, therefore, to fix
you at once in a noble independence.

ABSOLUTE

Sir, your kindness overpowers me—such generosity makes
the gratitude of reason more lively than the sensations even
of filial affection.

SIR ANTHONY

I am glad you are so sensible of my attention—and you
shall be master of a large estate in a few weeks.

ABSOLUTE

Let my future life, sir, speak my gratitude; I cannot express
the sense I have of your munificence.—Yet, sir, I presume
you would not wish me to quit the army?

SIR ANTHONY

Oh, that shall be as your wife chooses.

ABSOLUTE

My wife, sir!

SIR ANTHONY

Ay, ay, settle that between you—settle that between you.

ABSOLUTE

A wife, sir, did you say?

SIR ANTHONY

Ay, a wife—why, did not I mention her before?

ABSOLUTE

Not a word of her, sir.

SIR ANTHONY

Odd so!—I mus'n't forget her though.—Yes, Jack, the

independence I was talking of is by marriage—the fortune is saddled with a wife—but I suppose that makes no difference.

ABSOLUTE

Sir! sir!—you amaze me!

SIR ANTHONY

Why, what the devil's the matter with the fool? Just now you were all gratitude and duty.

ABSOLUTE

I was, sir—you talked to me of independence and a fortune, but not a word of a wife.

SIR ANTHONY

Why—what difference does that make? Odds life, sir! if you have the estate, you must take it with the live stock on it, as it stands.

ABSOLUTE

If my happiness is to be the price, I must beg leave to decline the purchase.—Pray, sir, who is the lady?

SIR ANTHONY

What's that to you, sir?—Come, give me your promise to love, and to marry her directly.

ABSOLUTE

Sure, sir, this is not very reasonable, to summon my affections for a lady I know nothing of!

SIR ANTHONY

I am sure, sir, 'tis more unreasonable in you to object to a lady you know nothing of.

ABSOLUTE

Then, sir, I must tell you plainly that my inclinations are fixed on another—my heart is engaged to an angel.

SIR ANTHONY

Then pray let it send an excuse. It is very sorry—but business prevents its waiting on her.

ABSOLUTE

But my vows are pledged to her.

SIR ANTHONY

Let her foreclose, Jack; let her foreclose; they are not worth redeeming; besides, you have the angel's vows in exchange, I suppose; so there can be no loss there.

ABSOLUTE

You must excuse me, sir, if I tell you, once for all, that in this point I cannot obey you.

SIR ANTHONY

Hark'ee, Jack;—I have heard you for some time with
patience—I have been cool—quite cool; but take care—
you know I am compliance itself—when I am not
thwarted;—no one more easily led—when I have my own
way;—but don't put me in a frenzy.

ABSOLUTE

Sir, I must repeat—in this I cannot obey you.

SIR ANTHONY

Now damn me! if ever I call you Jack again while I live!

ABSOLUTE

Nay, sir, but hear me.

SIR ANTHONY

Sir, I won't hear a word—not a word! not one word! so
give me your promise by a nod—and I'll tell you what,
Jack—I mean, you dog—if you don't, by—

ABSOLUTE

What, sir, promise to link myself to some mass of ugliness!
to—

SIR ANTHONY

Zounds! sirrah! the lady shall be as ugly as I choose: she
shall have a hump on each shoulder; she shall be as
crooked as the crescent; her one eye shall roll like the
bull's in Cox's Museum; [60] she shall have a skin like a
mummy, and the beard of a Jew—she shall be all this,
sirrah!—yet I will make you ogle her all day, and sit up all
night to write sonnets on her beauty.

ABSOLUTE

This is reason and moderation indeed!

SIR ANTHONY

None of your sneering, puppy! no grinning, jackanapes!

ABSOLUTE

Indeed, sir, I never was in a worse humour for mirth in my
life.

SIR ANTHONY

'Tis false, sir. I know you are laughing in your sleeve; I
know you'll grin when I'm gone, sirrah!

ABSOLUTE

Sir, I hope I know my duty better.

SIR ANTHONY

None of your passion, sir! none of your violence, if you please!—It won't do with me, I promise you.

ABSOLUTE

Indeed, sir, I never was cooler in my life.

SIR ANTHONY

'Tis a confounded lie!—I know you are in a passion in your heart; I know you are, you hypocritical young dog! but it won't do.

ABSOLUTE

Nay, sir, upon my word—

SIR ANTHONY

So you will fly out! can't you be cool like me? What the devil good can passion do?—Passion is of no service, you impudent, insolent, overbearing reprobate!—There, you sneer again! don't provoke me!—but you rely upon the mildness of my temper—you do, you dog! you play upon the meekness of my disposition!—Yet take care—the patience of a saint may be overcome at last!—but mark! I give you six hours and a half to consider of this: if you then agree, without any condition, to do everything on earth that I choose, why—confound you! I may in time forgive you.—If not, zounds! don't enter the same hemisphere with me! don't dare to breathe the same air, or use the same light with me; but get an atmosphere and a sun of your own! I'll strip you of your commission; I'll lodge a five-and-threepence in the hands of trustees,[51] and you shall live on the interest.—I'll disown you, I'll disinherit you, I'll unget you! and damn me! if ever I call you Jack again! [*Exit* SIR ANTHONY.]

ABSOLUTE

Mild, gentle, considerate father—I kiss your hands!— What a tender method of giving his opinion in these matters Sir Anthony has! I dare not trust him with the truth.—I wonder what old wealthy hag it is that he wants to bestow on me!—Yet he married himself for love! and was in his youth a bold intriguer, and a gay companion!

[*Reenter* FAG.]

FAG

Assuredly, sir, your father is wrath to a degree; he comes down stairs eight or ten steps at a time—muttering, growl-

ing, and thumping the banisters all the way: I and the
cook's dog stand bowing at the door—rap! he gives me a
stroke on the head with his cane; bids me carry that to my
master; then kicking the poor turnspit into the area,
damns us all, for a puppy triumvirate!—Upon my credit,
sir, were I in your place, and found my father such very
bad company, I should certainly drop his acquaintance.

ABSOLUTE

Cease your impertinence, sir, at present.—Did you come
in for nothing more?—Stand out of the way! [*Pushes
him aside, and exit.*]

FAG

So! Sir Anthony trims my master; he is afraid to reply to
his father—then vents his spleen on poor Fag!—When one
is vexed by one person, to revenge one's self on another,
who happens to come in the way, is the vilest injustice!
Ah! it shows the worst temper—the basest—

    [*Enter* BOY.]

BOY

Mr Fag! Mr Fag! your master calls you.

FAG

Well, you little dirty puppy, you need not bawl so!—The
meanest disposition! the—

BOY

Quick, quick, Mr. Fag—

FAG

Quick! quick! you impudent jackanapes! am I to be commanded by you too? you little, impertinent, insolent,
kitchen-bred—[*Exit kicking and beating him.*]

SCENE II

    [*The North Parade.*]

    [*Enter* LUCY.]

LUCY

So—I shall have another rival to add to my mistress's list—

Captain Absolute. However, I shall not enter his name till my purse has received notice in form. Poor Acres is dismissed!—Well, I have done him a last friendly office, in letting him know that Beverley was here before him.—Sir Lucius is generally more punctual, when he expects to hear from his *dear Dalia,* as he calls her: I wonder he's not here!—I have a little scruple of conscience from this deceit; though I should not be paid so well, if my hero knew that Delia was near fifty, and her own mistress.

[*Enter* SIR LUCIUS O'TRIGGER.]

SIR LUCIUS
Ha! my little ambassadress—upon my conscience, I have been looking for you; I have been on the South Parade this half hour.

LUCY
[*Speaking simply.*] O gemini! and I have been waiting for your lordship here on the North.

SIR LUCIUS
Faith!—may be that was the reason we did not meet; and it is very comical too, how you could go out and I not see you—for I was only taking a nap at the Parade Coffeehouse, and I chose the window on purpose that I might not miss you.

LUCY
My stars! Now I'd wager a sixpence I went by while you were asleep.

SIR LUCIUS
Sure enough it must have been so—and I never dreamt it was so late, till I waked. Well, but my little girl, have you got nothing for me?

LUCY
Yes, but I have—I've got a letter for you in my pocket.

SIR LUCIUS
O faith! I guessed you weren't come empty-handed—Well —let me see what the dear creature says.

LUCY
There, Sir Lucius. [*Gives him a letter.*]

SIR LUCIUS
[Reads.] *Sir—there is often a sudden incentive impulse in love, that has a greater induction than years of domestic combination: such was the commotion I felt at the first*

superfluous view of Sir Lucius O'Trigger.—Very pretty, upon my word.—*Female punctuation forbids me to say more; yet let me add, that it will give me joy infallible to find Sir Lucius worthy the last criterion of my affections.* —DELIA.

Upon my conscience! Lucy, your lady is a great mistress of language. Faith, she's quite the queen of the dictionary! —for the devil a word dare refuse coming at her call— though one would think it was quite out of hearing.

LUCY

Ay, sir, a lady of her experience—

SIR LUCIUS

Experience! what, at seventeen?

LUCY

O true, sir—but then she reads so—my stars! how she will read off hand!

SIR LUCIUS

Faith, she must be very deep read to write this way— though she is rather an arbitrary writer too—for here are a great many poor words pressed into the service of this note, that would get their *habeas corpus*[52] from any court in Christendom.

LUCY

Ah! Sir Lucius, if you were to hear how she talks of you!

SIR LUCIUS

Oh, tell her I'll make her the best husband in the world, and Lady O'Trigger into the bargain!—But we must get the old gentlewoman's consent—and do everything fairly.

LUCY

Nay, Sir Lucius, I thought you wa'n't rich enough to be so nice.

SIR LUCIUS

Upon my word, young woman, you have hit it:—I am so poor, that I can't afford to do a dirty action.—If I did not want money, I'd steal your mistress and her fortune with a great deal of pleasure.—However, my pretty girl [*gives her money*], here's a little something to buy you a ribbon; and meet me in the evening, and I'll give you an answer to this. So, hussy, take a kiss beforehand to put you in mind. [*Kisses her.*]

LUCY

O Lud! Sir Lucius—I never seed such a gemman! My lady won't like you if you're so impudent.

SIR LUCIUS

Faith she will, Lucy!—That same—pho! what's the name of it?—modesty—is a quality in a lover more praised by the women than liked; so, if your mistress asks you whether Sir Lucius ever gave you a kiss, tell her fifty—my dear.

LUCY

What, would you have me tell her a lie?

SIR LUCIUS

Ah, then, you baggage! I'll make it a truth presently.

LUCY

For shame now! here is some one coming.

SIR LUCIUS

Oh, faith, I'll quiet your conscience! [*Exit humming a tune. Enter* FAG.]

FAG

So, so, ma'am! I humbly beg pardon.

LUCY

O Lud! now, Mr Fag, you flurry one so.

FAG

Come, come, Lucy, here's no one by—so a little less simplicity, with a grain or two more sincerity, if you please. —You play false with us, madam.—I saw you give the baronet a letter.—My master shall know this—and if he don't call him out, I will.

LUCY

Ha! ha! ha! you gentlemen's gentlemen are so hasty. That letter was from Mrs Malaprop, simpleton.—She is taken with Sir Lucius's address.[53]

FAG

How! what tastes some people have!—Why, I suppose I have walked by her window a hundred times.—But what says our young lady? any message to my master?

LUCY

Sad news, Mr Fag.—A worse rival than Acres! Sir Anthony Absolute has proposed his son.

FAG

What, Captain Absolute?

LUCY

Even so—I overheard it all.

FAG

Ha! ha! ha! very good, faith. Good bye, Lucy, I must away with the news.

LUCY

Well, you may laugh—but it is true, I assure you.— [*Going.*] But, Mr Fag, tell your master not to be cast down by this.

FAG

Oh, he'll be so disconsolate!

LUCY

And charge him not to think of quarrelling with young Absolute.

FAG

Never fear! never fear!

LUCY

Be sure—bid him keep up his spirits.

FAG

We will—we will. [*Exeunt severally.*]

Act three.

[*The North Parade.*]

[*Enter* CAPTAIN ABSOLUTE.]

ABSOLUTE

'Tis just as Fag told me, indeed. Whimsical enough, faith. My father wants to force me to marry the very girl I am plotting to run away with! He must not know of my connection with her yet awhile. He has too summary a method of proceeding in these matters. However, I'll read my recantation instantly. My conversion is something sudden, indeed—but I can assure him it is very sincere. So, so— here he comes. He looks plaguy gruff. [*Steps aside. Enter* SIR ANTHONY ABSOLUTE.]

SIR ANTHONY

No—I'll die sooner than forgive him. Die, did I say? I'll live these fifty years to plague him. At our last meeting, his impudence had almost put me out of temper. An obstinate, passionate, self-willed boy! Who can he take after? This is my return for getting him before all his brothers and sisters!—for putting him, at twelve years old, into a marching regiment, and allowing him fifty pounds a year, besides his pay, ever since! But I have done with him; he's anybody's son for me. I never will see him more, never— never—never.

ABSOLUTE

[*Aside, coming forward.*] Now for a penitential face.

SIR ANTHONY

Fellow, get out of my way.

ABSOLUTE

Sir, you see a penitent before you.

SIR ANTHONY

I see an impudent scoundrel before me.

ABSOLUTE

A sincere penitent. I am come, sir, to acknowledge my error, and to submit entirely to your will.

SIR ANTHONY

What's that?

ABSOLUTE

I have been revolving, and reflecting, and considering on your past goodness, and kindness, and condescension to me.

SIR ANTHONY

Well, sir?

ABSOLUTE

I have been likewise weighing and balancing what you were pleased to mention concerning duty, and obedience, and authority.

SIR ANTHONY

Well, puppy?

ABSOLUTE

Why, then, sir, the result of my reflections is—a resolution to sacrifice every inclination of my own to your satisfaction.

SIR ANTHONY

Why now you talk sense—absolute sense.—I never heard anything more sensible in my life. Confound you! you shall be Jack again.

ABSOLUTE

I am happy in the appellation.

SIR ANTHONY

Why, then, Jack, my dear Jack, I will now inform you who the lady really is. Nothing but your passion and violence, you silly fellow, prevented my telling you at first. Prepare, Jack, for wonder and rapture—prepare. What think you of Miss Lydia Languish?

ABSOLUTE

Languish! What the Languishes of Worcestershire?

SIR ANTHONY

Worcestershire! no. Did you ever meet Mrs Malaprop and her niece, Miss Languish, who came into our country just before you were last ordered to your regiment.

ABSOLUTE

Malaprop! Languish! I don't remember ever to have heard the names before. Yet stay—I think I do recollect something. Languish! Languish! She squints, don't she? A little red-haired girl?

SIR ANTHONY

Squints! A red-haired girl! Zounds! no.

ABSOLUTE

Then I must have forgot; it can't be the same person.

SIR ANTHONY

Jack! Jack! what think you of blooming, love-breathing seventeen?

ABSOLUTE

As to that, sir, I am quite indifferent. If I can please you in the matter, 'tis all I desire.

SIR ANTHONY

Nay, but, Jack, such eyes! such eyes! so innocently wild! so bashfully irresolute! not a glance but speaks and kindles some thought of love! Then, Jack, her cheeks! her cheeks, Jack! so deeply blushing, at the insinuations of her tell-tale eyes! Then, Jack, her lips! O, Jack, lips smiling at their own discretion; and if not smiling, more sweetly pouting; more lovely in sullenness.

ABSOLUTE

That's she, indeed. [*Aside.*] Well done, old gentleman.

SIR ANTHONY

Then, Jack, her neck! O Jack! Jack!

ABSOLUTE

And which is to be mine, sir; the niece or the aunt?

SIR ANTHONY

Why, you unfeeling, insensible puppy, I despise you! When I was your age, such a description would have made me fly like a rocket! The aunt, indeed! Odds life! when I ran away with your mother, I would not have touched anything old or ugly to gain an empire.

ABSOLUTE

Not to please your father, sir?

SIR ANTHONY

To please my father! zounds! not to please—Oh, my father—odd so!—yes—yes; if my father indeed had desired

—that's quite another matter. Though he wa'n't the indulgent father that I am, Jack.

SIR ANTHONY

I dare say not, sir.

SIR ANTHONY

But, Jack, you are not sorry to find your mistress is so beautiful?

ABSOLUTE

Sir, I repeat it—if I please you in this affair, 'tis all I desire. Not that I think a woman the worse for being handsome; but, sir, if you please to recollect, you before hinted something about a hump or two, one eye, and a few more graces of that kind—now, without being very nice, I own I should rather choose a wife of mine to have the usual number of limbs, and a limited quantity of back: and though one eye may be very agreeable, yet as the prejudice has always run in favour of two, I would not wish to affect a singularity in that article.

SIR ANTHONY

What a phlegmatic sot it is! Why, sirrah, you're an anchorite! [54]—a vile, insensible stock. You a soldier!—you're a walking block, fit only to dust the company's regimentals on! Odds life! I have a great mind to marry the girl myself!

ABSOLUTE

I am entirely at your disposal, sir: if you should think of addressing Miss Languish yourself, I suppose you would have me marry the aunt; or if you should change your mind, and take the old lady—'tis the same to me—I'll marry the niece.

SIR ANTHONY

Upon my word, Jack, thou'rt either a very great hypocrite, or—but, come, I know your indifference on such a subject must be all a lie—I'm sure it must—come, now—damn your demure face!—come, confess, Jack—you have been lying, ha'n't you? You have been playing the hypocrite, hey!—I'll never forgive you, if you ha'n't been lying and playing the hypocrite.

ABSOLUTE

I'm sorry, sir, that the respect and duty which I bear to you should be so mistaken.

SIR ANTHONY

Hang your respect and duty! But come along with me, I'll
write a note to Mrs Malaprop, and you shall visit the
lady directly. Her eyes shall be the Promethean torch [55] to
you—come along, I'll never forgive you, if you don't come
back stark mad with rapture and impatience—if you don't,
egad, I will marry the girl myself! [*Exeunt.*]

SCENE II

[JULIA'S *dressing-room.*]

[FAULKLAND *discovered alone.*]

FAULKLAND

They told me Julia would return directly; I wonder she is
not yet come! How mean does this captious, unsatisfied
temper of mine appear to my cooler judgment! Yet I know
not that I indulge it in any other point: but on this one
subject, and to this one subject, whom I think I love
beyond my life, I am ever ungenerously fretful and madly
capricious! I am conscious of it—yet I cannot correct
myself! What tender honest joy sparkled in her eyes when
we met! how delicate was the warmth of her expression! I
was ashamed to appear less happy—though I had come
resolved to wear a face of coolness and upbraiding. Sir
Anthony's presence prevented my proposed expostulations:
yet I must be satisfied that she has not been so very happy
in my absence. She is coming! Yes!—I know the nimbleness
of her tread, when she thinks her impatient Faulkland
counts the moments of her stay.

[*Enter* JULIA.]

JULIA

I had not hoped to see you again so soon.

FAULKLAND

Could I, Julia, be contented with my first welcome—restrained as we were by the presence of a third person?

JULIA

O Faulkland, when your kindness can make me thus happy, let me not think that I discovered something of coldness in your first salutation.

FAULKLAND

'Twas but your fancy, Julia. I was rejoiced to see you—to see you in such health. Sure I had no cause for coldness?

JULIA

Nay, then, I see you have taken something ill. You must not conceal from me what it is.

FAULKLAND

Well, then—shall I own to you that my joy at hearing of your health and arrival here, by your neighbour Acres, was somewhat dampened by his dwelling much on the high spirits you had enjoyed in Devonshire—on your mirth—your singing—dancing, and I know not what! For such is my temper, Julia, that I should regard every mirthful moment in your absence as a treason to constancy. The mutual tear that steals down the cheek of parting lovers is a compact, that no smile shall live there till they meet again.

JULIA

Must I never cease to tax my Faulkland with this teasing minute caprice? Can the idle reports of a silly boor weigh in your breast against my tried affections?

FAULKLAND

They have no weight with me, Julia: No, no—I am happy if you have been so—yet only say, that you did not sing with mirth—say that you thought of Faulkland in the dance.

JULIA

I never can be happy in your absence. If I wear a countenance of content, it is to show that my mind holds no doubt of my Faulkland's truth. If I seemed sad, it were to make malice triumph; and say, that I fixed my heart on one, who left me to lament his roving, and my own credulity. Believe me, Faulkland, I mean not to upbraid you, when I say, that I have often dressed sorrow in smiles, lest my friends should guess whose unkindness had caused my tears.

FAULKLAND

You were ever all goodness to me. Oh, I am a brute, when I but admit a doubt of your true constancy!

JULIA

If ever without such cause from you, as I will not suppose possible, you find my affections veering but a point, may I become a proverbial scoff for levity and base ingratitude.

FAULKLAND

Ah! Julia, that last word is grating to me. I would I had no title of your gratitude! Search your heart, Julia; perhaps what you have mistaken for love, is but the warm effusion of a too thankful heart.

JULIA

For what quality must I love you?

FAULKLAND

For no quality! To regard me for any quality of mind or understanding, were only to esteem me. And for person— I have often wished myself deformed, to be convinced that I owe no obligation there for any part of your affection.

JULIA

Where nature has bestowed a show of nice attention in the features of a man, he should laugh at it as misplaced. I have seen men, who in this vain article, perhaps, might rank above you; but my heart has never asked my eyes if it were so or not.

FAULKLAND

Now this is not well from you, Julia—I despise person[56] in a man—yet if you loved me as I wish, though I were an Æthiop, you'd think none so fair.

JULIA

I see you are determined to be unkind! The contract which my poor father bound us in gives you more than a lover's privilege.

FAULKLAND

Again, Julia, you raise ideas that feed and justify my doubts. I would not have been more free—no—I am proud of my restraint. Yet—yet—perhaps your high respect alone for this solemn compact has fettered your inclinations, which else had made a worthier choice. How shall I be sure, had you remained unbound in thought and promise, that I should still have been the object of your persevering love?

JULIA

Then try me now. Let us be free as strangers as to what is past: my heart will not feel more liberty!

FAULKLAND

There now! so hasty, Julia! so anxious to be free! If your love for me were fixed and ardent, you would not lose your hold, even though I wished it!

JULIA

Oh! you torture me to the heart! I cannot bear it.

FAULKLAND

I do not mean to distress you. If I loved you less I should never give you an uneasy moment. But hear me. All my fretful doubts arise from this. Women are not used to weigh and separate the motives of their affections: the cold dictates of prudence, gratitude, or filial duty, may sometimes be mistaken for the pleadings of the heart. I would not boast—yet let me say, that I have neither age, person, nor character, to found dislike on; my fortune such as few ladies could be charged with indiscretion in the match. O Julia! when love receives such countenance from prudence, nice minds will be suspicious of its birth.

JULIA

I know not whither your insinuations would tend:—but as they seem pressing to insult me, I will spare you the regret of having done so.—I have given you no cause for this! [*Exit in tears.*]

FAULKLAND

In tears! Stay, Julia: stay but for a moment.—The door is fastened!—Julia!—my soul—but for one moment!—I hear her sobbing!—'Sdeath! what a brute am I to use her thus! Yet stay! Ay—she is coming now:—how little resolution there is in a woman!—how a few soft words can turn them!—No, faith!—she is not coming either.—Why, Julia—my love—say but that you forgive me—come but to tell me that—now this is being too resentful. Stay! she is coming too—I thought she would—no steadiness in anything: her going away must have been a mere trick then—she sha'n't see that I was hurt by it—I'll affect indifference—[*Hums a tune; then listens.*] No—zounds! she's not coming!—nor don't intend it, I suppose.—This is not steadiness, but obstinacy! Yet I deserve it.—What, after so long an absence to quarrel with her tenderness!—'twas barbarous and unmanly!—I should be ashamed to see her now.—I'll wait till her just resentment is abated—and when I distress her so again, may I lose her for ever! and be linked instead to some antique virago[57] whose gnawing passions, and long hoarded spleen, shall make me curse my folly half the day and all the night. [*Exit.*]

SCENE III

[MRS MALAPROP'S *lodgings.*]

[MRS MALAPROP, *with a letter in her hand, and* CAPTAIN ABSOLUTE.]

MRS MALAPROP

Your being Sir Anthony's son, captain, would itself be a sufficient accommodation; but from the ingenuity of your appearance, I am convinced you deserve the character here given of you.

ABSOLUTE

Permit me to say, madam, that as I never yet have had the pleasure of seeing Miss Languish, my principal inducement in this affair at present is the honour of being allied to Mrs Malaprop; of whose intellectual accomplishments, elegant manners, and unaffected learning, no tongue is silent.

MRS MALAPROP

Sir, you do me infinite honour! I beg, captain, you'll be seated.—[*They sit.*] Ah! few gentlemen, now-a-days, know how to value the ineffectual qualities in a woman!—few think how a little knowledge becomes a gentlewoman.—Men have no sense now but for the worthless flower of beauty!

ABSOLUTE

It is but too true, indeed, ma'am;—yet I fear our ladies

should share the blame—they think our admiration of
beauty so great, that knowledge in them would be superfluous. Thus, like garden-trees, they seldom show fruit,
till time has robbed them of more specious blossom.—Few,
like Mrs Malaprop and the orange-tree, are rich in both
at once!

MRS MALAPROP

Sir, you overpower me with good-breeding.—He is the
very pine-apple of politeness!—You are not ignorant, captain, that this giddy girl has somehow contrived to fix her
affections on a beggarly, strolling, eavesdropping ensign,
whom none of us have seen, and nobody knows anything
of.

ABSOLUTE

Oh, I have heard the silly affair before.—I'm not at all
prejudiced against her on that account.

MRS MALAPROP

You are very good and very considerate, captain. I am
sure I have done everything in my power since I exploded
the affair; long ago I laid my positive conjunctions on her,
never to think on the fellow again;—I have since laid Sir
Anthony's preposition before her; but, I am sorry to say,
she seems resolved to decline every particle that I enjoin
her.

ABSOLUTE

It must be very distressing, indeed, ma'am.

MRS MALAPROP

Oh! it gives me the hydrostatics to such a degree.—I
thought she had persisted from corresponding with him;
but, behold, this very day, I have interceded another letter
from the fellow; I believe I have it in my pocket.

ABSOLUTE

[*Aside.*] Oh, the devil, my last note.

MRS MALAPROP

Ay, here it is.

ABSOLUTE

[*Aside.*] Ay, my note indeed! Oh, the little traitress Lucy.

MRS MALAPROP

There, perhaps you may know the writting. [*Gives him the
letter.*]

ABSOLUTE

I think I have seen the hand before—yes, I certainly must
have seen this hand before—

MRS MALAPROP

Nay, but read it, captain.

ABSOLUTE

[*Reads.*] *My soul's idol, my adored Lydia!*—Very tender,
indeed!

MRS MALAPROP

Tender, ay, and profane too, o' my conscience.

ABSOLUTE

[*Reads.*] *I am excessively alarmed at the intelligence you
send me, the more so as my new rival*—

MRS MALAPROP

That's you, sir.

ABSOLUTE

[*Reads.*] *Has universally the character of being an accomplished gentleman and a man of honour.*—Well, that's
handsome enough.

MRS MALAPROP

Oh, the fellow has some design in writing so.

ABSOLUTE

That he had, I'll answer for him, ma'am.

MRS MALAPROP

But go on, sir—you'll see presently.

ABSOLUTE

[*Reads.*] *As for the old weather-beaten she-dragon who
guards you.*—Who can he mean by that?

MRS MALAPROP

Me, sir!—me!—he means me!—There—what do you think
now?—but go on a little further.

ABSOLUTE

Impudent scoundrel!—[*Reads.*] *it shall go hard but I will
elude her vigilance, as I am told that the same ridiculous
vanity, which makes her dress up her coarse features, and
deck her dull chat with hard words which she don't understand*—

MRS MALAPROP

There, sir, an attack upon my language! what do you think
of that?—an aspersion upon my parts of speech! was ever
such a brute! Sure, if I reprehend any thing in this world it

is the use of my oracular tongue, and a nice derangement
of epitaphs!

ABSOLUTE

He deserves to be hanged and quartered! let me see—
[*Reads.*] *Same ridiculous vanity*—

MRS MALAPROP

You need not read it again, sir.

ABSOLUTE

I beg pardon, ma'am.—[*Reads.*] *does also lay her open to
the grossest deceptions from flattery and pretended admiration*—an impudent coxcomb!—*so that I have a scheme to
see you shortly with the old harridan's consent, and even
to make her a go-between in our interview.*—Was ever such
assurance!

MRS MALAPROP

Did you ever hear anything like it?—he'll elude my
vigilance, will he?—Yes, yes! ha! ha! he's very likely to
enter these doors;—we'll try who can plot best!

ABSOLUTE

So we will, ma'am—so we will! Ha! ha! ha! a conceited
puppy, ha! ha! ha—Well, but, Mrs Malaprop, as the girl
seems so infatuated by this fellow, suppose you were to
wink at her corresponding with him for a little time—let
her even plot an elopement with him—then do you connive
at her escape—while I, just in the nick, will have the
fellow laid by the heels, and fairly contrive to carry her
off in his stead.

MRS MALAPROP

I am delighted with the scheme; never was anything better
perpetrated!

ABSOLUTE

But, pray, could not I see the lady for a few minutes now?
—I should like to try her temper a little.

MRS MALAPROP

Why, I don't know—I doubt she is not prepared for a
visit of this kind. There is a decorum in these matters.

ABSOLUTE

O Lord! she won't mind me—only tell her Beverley—

MRS MALAPROP

Sir!

ABSOLUTE

[*Aside.*] Gently, good tongue.

MRS MALAPROP

What did you say of Beverley?

ABSOLUTE

Oh, I was going to propose that you should tell her, by way of jest, that it was Beverley who was below; she'd come down fast enough then—ha! ha! ha!

MRS MALAPROP

'Twould be a trick she well deserves; besides, you know the fellow tells her he'll get my consent to see her—ha! ha! Let him if he can, I say again. Lydia, come down here!—[*Calling.*] He'll make me a go-between in their interviews! —ha! ha! ha! Come down, I say, Lydia! I don't wonder at your laughing, ha! ha! ha! his impudence is truly ridiculous.

ABSOLUTE

'Tis very ridiculous, upon my soul, ma'am, ha! ha! ha!

MRS MALAPROP

The little hussy won't hear. Well, I'll go and tell her at once who it is—she shall know that Captain Absolute is come to wait on her. And I'll make her behave as becomes a young woman.

ABSOLUTE

As you please, madam.

MRS MALAPROP

For the present, captain, your servant. Ah! you've not done laughing yet, I see—elude my vigilance; yes, yes; ha! ha! ha! [*Exit.*]

ABSOLUTE

Ha! ha! ha! one would think now that I might throw off all disguise at once, and seize my prize with security; but such is Lydia's caprice, that to undeceive were probably to lose her. I'll see whether she knows me. [*Walks aside, and seems engaged in looking at the pictures. Enter* LYDIA.]

LYDIA

What a scene am I now to go through! surely nothing can be more dreadful than to be obliged to listen to the loathsome addresses of a stranger to one's heart. I have heard of girls persecuted as I am, who have appealed in behalf of their favoured lover to the generosity of his rival; suppose I were to try it—there stands the hated rival—an officer too;—but oh, how unlike my Beverley! I wonder he don't begin—truly he seems a very negligent wooer!— quite at his ease, upon my word! I'll speak first—Mr Absolute.

ABSOLUTE

[*Turns round.*] Ma'am.

LYDIA

O heavens! Beverley!

ABSOLUTE

Hush;—hush, my life! softly! be not surprised!

LYDIA

I am so astonished! and so terrified! and so everjoyed!— for Heaven's sake! how came you here?

ABSOLUTE

Briefly, I have deceived your aunt—I was informed that my new rival was to visit here this evening, and contriving to have him kept away, have passed myself on her for Captain Absolute.

LYDIA

O charming! And she really takes you for young Absolute.

ABSOLUTE

Oh, she's convinced of it.

LYDIA

Ha! ha! ha! I can't forbear laughing to think how her sagacity is overreached!

ABSOLUTE

But we trifle with our precious moments—such another opportunity may not occur; then let me conjure my kind, my condescending angel, to fix the time when I may rescue her from undeserving persecution, and with a licensed warmth plead for my reward.

LYDIA

Will you then, Beverley, consent to forfeit that portion of my paltry wealth?—that burden on the wings of love?

ABSOLUTE

Oh, come to me—rich only thus—in loveliness! Bring no portion to me but thy love—'twill be generous in you, Lydia,—for well you know it is the only dower your poor Beverley can repay.

LYDIA

[*Aside.*] How persuasive are his words!—how charming

will poverty be with him!

ABSOLUTE

Ah! my soul, what a life will we then live! Love shall be
our idol and support! we will worship him with a monastic
strictness; adjuring all worldly toys, to centre every thought
and action there. Proud of calamity, we will enjoy the
wreck of wealth; while the surrounding gloom of adversity
shall make the flame of our pure love show doubly bright.
By Heavens! I would fling all goods of fortune from me
with a prodigal hand, to enjoy the scene where I might
clasp my Lydia to my bosom, and say, the world affords
no smile to me but here—[*Embracing her. Aside.*] If she
holds out now, the devil is in it.

LYDIA

[*Aside.*] Now could I fly with him to the antipodes! [58] *but*
my persecution is not yet come to a crisis.

    [*Reenter* MRS MALAPROP, *listening.*]

MRS MALAPROP

[*Aside.*] I am impatient to know how the little hussy de-
ports herself.

ABSOLUTE

So pensive, Lydia!—is then your warmth abated?

MRS MALAPROP

[*Aside.*] Warmth abated!—so!—she has been in a passion, I
suppose.

LYDIA

No—nor ever can while I have life.

MRS MALAPROP

[*Aside.*] An ill-tempered little devil! She'll be in a passion
all her life—will she?

LYDIA

Think not the idle threats of my ridiculous aunt can ever
have any weight with me.

MRS MALAPROP

[*Aside.*] Very dutiful, upon my word!

LYDIA

Let her choice be Captain Absolute, but Beverley is mine.

MRS MALAPROP

[*Aside.*] I am astonished at her assurance!—to his face—
this is to his face.

ABSOLUTE

Thus then let me enforce my suit. [*Kneeling.*]

MRS MALAPROP

[*Aside.*] Ay, poor young man!—down on his knees entreating for pity!—I can contain no longer.—[*Coming forward.*] Why, thou vixen!—I have overheard you.

ABSOLUTE

[*Aside.*] Oh, confound her vigilance!

MRS MALAPROP

Captain Absolute, I know not how to apologize for her shocking rudeness.

ABSOLUTE

[*Aside.*] So all's safe, I find.—[*Aloud.*] I have hopes, madam, that time will bring the young lady—

MRS MALAPROP

Oh, there's nothing to be hoped for from her! she's as headstrong as an allegory on the banks of Nile.

LYDIA

Nay, madam, what do you charge me with now?

MRS MALAPROP

Why, thou unblushing rebel—didn't you tell this gentleman to his face that you loved another better?—didn't you say you never would be his?

LYDIA

No, madam—I did not.

MRS MALAPROP

Good heavens! what assurance!—Lydia, Lydia, you ought to know that lying don't become a young woman!—Didn't you boast that Beverley, that stroller Beverley, possessed your heart?—Tell me that, I say.

LYDIA

'Tis true, ma'am, and none but Beverley—

MRS MALAPROP

Hold!—Hold, Assurance!—you shall not be so rude.

ABSOLUTE

Nay, pray, Mrs Malaprop, don't stop the young lady's speech: she's very welcome to talk thus—it does not hurt me in the least, I assure you.

MRS MALAPROP

You are too good, captain—too amiably patient—but come with me, miss.—Let us see you again soon, captain—remember what we have fixed.

ABSOLUTE

I shall, ma'am.

MRS MALAPROP

Come, take a graceful leave of the gentleman.

LYDIA

May every blessing wait on my Beverley, my loved Bev—

MRS MALAPROP

Hussy! I'll choke the word in your throat!—come along—
come along. [*Exeunt severally;* CAPTAIN ABSOLUTE *kissing
his hand to* LYDIA—MRS MALAPROP *stopping her from
speaking.*]

SCENE IV

[ACRES' *lodgings.*]

[ACRES, *as just dressed, and* DAVID.]

ACRES

Indeed, David—do you think I become it so?

DAVID

You are quite another creature, believe me, master, by
the mass! an' we've any luck we shall see the Devon
monkeyrony[59] in all the print-shops in Bath!

ACRES

Dress does make a difference, David.

DAVID

'Tis all in all, I think.—Difference! why, an' you were to go
now to Clod Hall, I am certain the old lady wouldn't
know you: Master Butler wouldn't believe his own eyes,
and Mrs Pickle would cry, Lard presarve me! our dairy-
maid would come giggling to the door, and I warrant
Dolly Tester, your honour's favourite, would blush like my
waistcoat.—Oons! I'll hold a gallon, there an't a dog in the
house but would bark, and I question whether Phillis would
wag a hair of her tail!

ACRES

Ay, David, there's nothing like polishing.

DAVID

So I says of your honour's boots; but the boy never heeds me!

ACRES

But, David, has Mr De-la-grace been here? I must rub up my balancing, and chasing, and boring.[60]

DAVID

I'll call again, sir.

ACRES

Do—and see if there are any letters for me at the post-office.

DAVID

I will.—By the mass, I can't help looking at your head!—if I hadn't been by at the cooking, I wish I may die if I should have known the dish again myself. [*Exit.*]

ACRES

[*Practising a dancing-step.*] Sink, slide—coupee.—Confound the first inventors of cotillons![61] say I—they are as bad as algebra to us country gentlemen.—I can walk a minuet easy enough when I am forced!—and I have been accounted a good stick in a country-dance.—Odds, jigs and tabors! I never valued your cross-over to couple—figure in—right and left—and I'd foot it with e'er a captain in the county!—but these outlandish heathen allemandes[62] and cotillons are quite beyond me!—I shall never prosper at 'em, that's sure—mine are true-born English legs—they don't understand their curst French lingo!—their *pas*[63] this, and *pas* that, and *pas* t'other!—damn me!—my feet don't like to be called paws! no, 'tis certain I have most Anti-gallican[64] toes!

[*Enter* SERVANT.]

SERVANT

Here is Sir Lucius O'Trigger to wait on you, sir.

ACRES

Show him in.

[*Exit* SERVANT. *Enter* SIR LUCIUS O'TRIGGER.]

SIR LUCIUS

Mr Acres, I am delighted to embrace you.

ACRES

My dear Sir Lucius, I kiss your hands.

SIR LUCIUS

Pray, my friend, what has brought you so suddenly to Bath?

ACRES

Faith! I have followed Cupid's Jack-a-lantern, and find myself in a quagmire at last.—In short, I have been very ill-used, Sir Lucius.—I don't choose to mention names, but look on me as on a very ill-used gentleman.

SIR LUCIUS

Pray what is the case?—I ask no names.

ACRES

Mark me, Sir Lucius, I fall as deep as need be in love with a young lady—her friends take my part—I follow her to Bath—send word of my arrival; and receive answer, that the lady is to be otherwise disposed of—This, Sir Lucius, I call being ill-used.

SIR LUCIUS

Very ill, upon my conscience.—Pray, can you divine the cause of it?

ACRES

Why, there's the matter; she has another lover, one Beverley, who, I am told, is now in Bath.—Odds slanders and lies! he must be at the bottom of it.

SIR LUCIUS

A rival in the case, is there?—and you think he has supplanted you unfairly?

ACRES

Unfairly! to be sure he has. He never could have done it fairly.

SIR LUCIUS

Then sure you know what is to be done!

ACRES

Not I, upon my soul!

SIR LUCIUS

We wear no swords here,[65] but you understand me.

ACRES

What! fight him.

SIR LUCIUS

Ay, to be sure: what can I mean else?

ACRES

But he has given me no provocation.

SIR LUCIUS

Now, I think he has given you the greatest provocation in the world. Can a man commit a more heinous offence against another man than to fall in love with the same woman? Oh, by my soul! it is the most unpardonable breach of friendship.

ACRES

Breach of friendship! ay, ay! but I have no acquaintance with this man. I never saw him in my life.

SIR LUCIUS

That's no argument at all—he has the less right than to take such a liberty.

ACRES

Gad, that's true—I grow full of anger, Sir Lucius!—I fire apace! Odds hilts and blades! I find a man may have a deal of valour in him, and not know it! But couldn't I contrive to have a little right on my side?

SIR LUCIUS

What the devil signifies right, when your honour is concerned? Do you think Achilles, or my little Alexander the Great, ever inquired where the right lay? No, by my soul, they drew their broad-swords, and left the lazy sons of peace to settle the justice of it.

ACRES

Your words are a grenadier's march to my heart! I believe courage must be catching! I certainly do feel a kind of valour rising as it were—a kind of courage, as I may say. —Odds flints, pans, and triggers! I'll challenge him directly.

SIR LUCIUS

Ah, my little friend, if I had Blunderbuss Hall here, I could show you a range of ancestry, in the old O'Trigger line, that would furnish the new room; every one of whom had killed his man!—For though the mansion-house and dirty acres have slipped through my fingers, I thank heaven our honour and the family-pictures are as fresh as ever.

ACRES

O Sir Lucius! I have had ancestors too!—every man of 'em colonel or captain in the militia!—Odds balls and barrels! say no more—I'm braced for it. The thunder of your words has soured the milk of human kindness in my breast:—Zounds! as the man in the play[66] says, *I could do such deeds!*

SIR LUCIUS

Come, come, there must be no passion at all in the case— these things should always be done civilly.

ACRES

I must be in a passion, Sir Lucius—I must be in a rage.— Dear Sir Lucius, let me be in a rage, if you love me. Come, here's pen and paper.—[*Sits down to write.*] I would the ink were red!—Indite, I say, indite!—How shall I begin? Odds bullets and blades! I'll write a good bold hand, however.

SIR LUCIUS

Pray compose yourself.

ACRES

Come—now, shall I begin with an oath? Do, Sir Lucius, let me begin with a damme.

SIR LUCIUS

Pho! pho! do the thing decently, and like a Christian. Begin now—*Sir*—

ACRES

That's too civil by half.

SIR LUCIUS

To prevent the confusion that might arise—

ACRES

Well—

SIR LUCIUS

From our both addressing the same lady—

ACRES

Ay, there's the reason—*same lady*—well—

SIR LUCIUS

I shall expect the honour of your company—

ACRES

Zounds! I'm not asking him to dinner.

SIR LUCIUS

Pray be easy.

ACRES

Well, then, *honour of your company*—

SIR LUCIUS
To settle our pretensions—

ACRES
Well.

SIR LUCIUS
Let me see, ay, King's-Mead-Fields will do—*in King's-Mead-Fields.*

ACRES
So, that's done—Well, I'll fold it up presently; my own crest—a hand and dagger shall be the seal.

SIR LUCIUS
You see now this little explanation will put a stop at once to all confusion or misunderstanding that might arise between you.

ACRES
Ay, we fight to prevent any misunderstanding.

SIR LUCIUS
Now, I'll leave you to fix your own time.—Take my advice, and you'll decide it this evening if you can; then let the worst come of it, 'twill be off your mind tomorrow.

ACRES
Very true.

SIR LUCIUS
So I shall see nothing of you, unless it be by letter, till the evening.—I would do myself the honour to carry your message; but, to tell you a secret, I believe I shall have just another affair on my own hands. There is a gay captain here, who put a jest on me lately, at the expense of my country, and I only want to fall in with the gentleman, to call him out.

ACRES
By my valour, I should like to see you fight first! Odds life! I should like to see you kill him, if it was only to get a little lesson.

SIR LUCIUS
I shall be very proud of instructing you. Well for the present—but remember now, when you meet your antagonist, do every thing in a mild and agreeable manner.— Let your courage be as keen, but at the same time as polished, as your sword. [*Exeunt severally.*]

Act four.

SCENE I

[ACRES' *lodgings*.]

[ACRES *and* DAVID.]

DAVID

Then, by the mass, sir! I would do no such thing—ne'er a Sir Lucius O'Trigger in the kingdom should make me fight, when I wasn't so minded. Oons! what will the old lady say, when she hears o't?

ACRES

Ah! David, if you had heard Sir Lucius!—Odds sparks and flames! he would have roused your valour.

DAVID

Not he, indeed, I hates such bloodthirsty cormorants.[67] Look'ee, master, if you wanted a bout at boxing, quarter-staff, or short-staff, I should never be the man to bid you cry off: but for your curst sharps and snaps;[68] I never knew any good come of 'em.

ACRES

But my honour, David, my honour! I must be very careful of my honour.

DAVID

Ay, by the mass! and I would be very careful of it; and I think in return my honour couldn't do less than to be very careful of me.

ACRES

Odds blades! David, no gentleman will ever risk the loss of his honour!

DAVID

I say then, it would be but civil in honour never to risk the

loss of a gentleman.—Look'ee, master, this honour seems
to me to be a marvellous false friend: ay, truly, a very
courtier-like servant.—Put the case, I was a gentleman
(which, thank God, no one can say of me); well—my
honour makes me quarrel with another gentleman of my
acquaintance.—So—we fight. (Pleasant enough that!)
Boh;—I kill him—(the more's my luck!) now, pray who
gets the profit of it?—Why, my honour. But put the case
that he kills me!—by the mass! I go to the worms, and my
honour whips over to my enemy.

ACRES

No, David—in that case!—odds crowns and laurels! your
honour follows you to the grave.

DAVID

Now, that's just the place where I could make a shift to do
without it.

ACRES

Zounds! David, you are a coward!—It doesn't become my
valour to listen to you.—What, shall I disgrace my ancestors?—Think of that, David—think what it would be to
disgrace my ancestors!

DAVID

Under favour, the surest way of not disgracing them, is to
keep as long as you can out of their company. Look'ee
now, master, to go to them in such haste—with an ounce
of lead in your brains—I should think might as well be
let alone. Our ancestors are very good kind of folks; but
they are the last people I should choose to have a visiting
acquaintance with.

ACRES

But, David, now, you don't think there is such very, very,
very great danger, hey?—Odds life! people often fight
without any mischief done!

DAVID

By the mass, I think 'tis ten to one against you!—Oons!
here to meet some lion-hearted fellow, I warrant, with his
damned double-barrelled swords, and cut-and-thrust pistols!
Lord bless us! it makes me tremble to think o't—Those be
such desperate bloody-minded weapons! Well, I never
could abide 'em!—from a child I never could fancy 'em!—
I suppose there an't been so merciless a beast in the world

as your loaded pistol!

ACRES

Zounds! I won't be afraid!—Odds fire and fury! you shan't make me afraid.—Here is the challenge, and I have sent for my dear friend Jack Absolute to carry it for me.

DAVID

Ay, i' the name of mischief, let him be the messenger.— For my part I wouldn't lend a hand to it for the best horse in your stable. By the mass! it don't look like another letter! It is, as I may say, a designing and malicious-looking letter; and I warrant smells of gun-powder like a soldier's pouch!—Oons! I wouldn't swear it mayn't go off!

ACRES

Out, you poltroon! you han't the valour of a grasshopper.

DAVID

Well, I say no more—'twill be sad news, to be sure, at Clod Hall! but I ha' done. How Phillis will howl when she hears of it!—Ah, poor bitch, she little thinks what shooting her master's going after! And I warrant old Crop, who has carried your honour, field and road, these ten years, will curse the hour he was born. [*Whimpering.*]

ACRES

It won't do, David—I am determined to fight—so get along, you coward, while I'm in the mind.

[*Enter* SERVANT.]

SERVANT

Captain Absolute, sir.

ACRES

Oh! show him up.

[*Exit* SERVANT.]

DAVID

Well, Heaven send we be all alive this time tomorrow.

ACRES

What's that?—Don't provoke me, David!

DAVID

Good-bye, master. [*Whimpering.*]

ACRES

Get along, you cowardly, dastardly, croaking raven!

[*Exit* DAVID. *Enter* CAPTAIN ABSOLUTE.]

ABSOLUTE

What's the matter, Bob?

ACRES

A vile, sheep-hearted blockhead! If I hadn't the valour of
St. George and the dragon to boot—

ABSOLUTE

But what did you want with me, Bob?

ACRES

Oh!—There—[*Gives him the challenge.*]

ABSOLUTE

[*Aside to* ENSIGN BEVERLEY.] So, what's going on now?—
Well, what's this?

ACRES

A challenge!

ABSOLUTE

Indeed! Why, you won't fight him; will you, Bob?

ACRES

Egad, but I will, Jack. Sir Lucius has wrought me to it.
He has left me full of rage—and I'll fight this evening,
that so much good passion mayn't be wasted.

ABSOLUTE

But what have I to do with this?

ACRES

Why, as I think you know something of this fellow, I want
you to find him out for me, and give him this mortal
defiance.

ABSOLUTE

Well, give it to me, and trust me he gets it.

ACRES

Thank you, my dear friend, my dear Jack; but it is giving
you a great deal of trouble.

ABSOLUTE

Not in the least—I beg you won't mention it.—No trouble
in the world, I assure you.

ACRES

You are very kind.—What it is to have a friend!—You
couldn't be my second, could you, Jack?

ABSOLUTE

Why no, Bob—not in this affair—it would not be quite
so proper.

ACRES

Well, then, I must get my friend Sir Lucius. I shall have
your good wishes, however, Jack?

ABSOLUTE

Whenever he meets you, believe me.

[*Reenter* SERVANT.]

SERVANT

Sir Anthony Absolute is below, inquiring for the captain.

ABSOLUTE

I'll come instantly.—[*Exit* SERVANT.] Well, my little hero, success attend you. [*Going.*]

ACRES

Stay—stay, Jack.—If Beverley should ask you what kind of a man your friend Acres is, do tell him I am a devil of a fellow—will you, Jack?

ABSOLUTE

To be sure I shall. I'll say you are a determined dog—hey, Bob?

ACRES

Ah, do, do—and if that frightens him, egad, perhaps he mayn't come. So tell him I generally kill a man a week; will you, Jack?

ABSOLUTE

I will, I will; I'll say you are called in the country Fighting Bob.

ACRES

Right—right—'tis all to prevent mischief; for I don't want to take his life if I clear my honour.

ABSOLUTE

No!—that's very kind of you.

ACRES

Why, you don't wish me to kill him—do you, Jack?

ABSOLUTE

No, upon my soul, I do not. But a devil of a fellow, hey? [*Going.*]

ACRES

True, true—but stay—stay, Jack,—you may add, that you never saw me in such a rage before—a most devouring rage!

ABSOLUTE

I will, I will.

ACRES

Remember, Jack—a determined dog!

ABSOLUTE
Ay, ay, Fighting Bob! [*Exeunt severally.*]

SCENE II

[MRS MALAPROP'S *lodgings.*]

[MRS MALAPROP *and* LYDIA.]

MRS MALAPROP
Why, thou perverse one!—tell me what you can object to
him? Isn't he a handsome man?—tell me that. A genteel
man? a pretty figure of a man?

LYDIA
[*Aside.*] She little thinks whom she is praising!—[*Aloud.*]
So is Beverley, ma'am.

MRS MALAPROP
No caparisons, miss, if you please. Caparisons don't become a young woman. No! Captain Absolute is indeed a
fine gentleman!

LYDIA
[*Aside.*] Ay, the Captain Absolute you have seen.

MRS MALAPROP
Then he's so well bred;—so full of alacrity, and adulation!
—and has so much to say for himself:—in such good
language, too! His physiognomy so grammatical! Then
his presence is so noble! I protest, when I saw him, I
thought of what Hamlet says in the play: ⁰⁰—

"Hesperian curls—the front of Job himself!—
    An eye, like March, to threaten at command!—
    A station, like Harry Mercury, new—"

Something about kissing—on a hill—however, the simili-
tude struck me directly.

LYDIA
[*Aside.*] How enraged she'll be presently, when she dis-

covers her mistake!

[*Enter* SERVANT.]

SERVANT

Sir Anthony and Captain Absolute are below, ma'am.

MRS MALAPROP

Show them up here.—[*Exit* SERVANT.] Now Lydia, I insist
on your behaving as becomes a young woman. Show your
good breeding, at least, though you have forgot your duty.

LYDIA

Madam, I have told you my resolution!—I shall not only
give him no encouragement, but I won't even speak to, or
look at him. [*Flings herself into a chair, with her face
from the door. Enter* SIR ANTHONY ABSOLUTE *and* CAPTAIN
ABSOLUTE.]

SIR ANTHONY

Here we are, Mrs Malaprop; come to mitigate the frowns
of unrelenting beauty,—and difficulty enough I had to
bring this fellow.—I don't know what's the matter; but if
I had not held him by force, he'd have given me the slip.

MRS MALAPROP

You have infinite trouble, Sir Anthony, in the affair. I
am ashamed for the cause!—[*Aside to* LYDIA.] Lydia,
Lydia, rise, I beseech you!—pay your respects!

SIR ANTHONY

I hope, madam, that Miss Languish has reflected on the
worth of this gentleman, and the regard due to her aunt's
choice, and my alliance.—[*Aside to* CAPTAIN ABSOLUTE.]
Now, Jack, speak to her.

ABSOLUTE

[*Aside.*] What the devil shall I do!—[*Aside to* SIR AN-
THONY.] You see, sir, she won't even look at me whilst
you are here. I knew she wouldn't! I told you so. Let me
entreat you, sir, to leave us together! [*Seems to expostulate
with his father.*]

LYDIA

[*Aside.*] I wonder I han't heard my aunt exclaim yet! sure
she can't have looked at him!—perhaps the regimentals
are alike, and she is something blind.

SIR ANTHONY

I say, sir, I won't stir a foot yet!

MRS MALAPROP

I am sorry to say, Sir Anthony, that my affluence over my
niece is very small.—[*Aside to* LYDIA.] Turn round, Lydia:
I blush for you!

SIR ANTHONY

May I not flatter myself, that Miss Languish will assign
what cause of dislike she can have to my son!—[*Aside to*
CAPTAIN ABSOLUTE.] Why don't you begin, Jack?—Speak,
you puppy—speak!

MRS MALAPROP

It is impossible, Sir Anthony, she can have any. She will
not say she has.—[*Aside to* LYDIA.] Answer, hussy! why
don't you answer?

SIR ANTHONY

Then, madam, I trust that a childish and hasty predilection
will be no bar to Jack's happiness.—[*Aside to* CAPTAIN
ABSOLUTE.] Zounds! sirrah! why don't you speak?

LYDIA

[*Aside.*] I think my lover seems as little inclined to conversation as myself.—How strangely blind my aunt must
be!

ABSOLUTE

Hem! hem! madam—hem!—[*Attempts to speak, then returns to* SIR ANTHONY.] Faith! sir, I am so confounded!—
and—so—so—confused!—I told you I should be so, sir—
I knew it.—The—the—tremor of my passion entirely takes
away my presence of mind.

SIR ANTHONY

But it don't take away your voice, fool, does it?—Go up,
and speak to her directly!

[CAPTAIN ABSOLUTE *makes signs to* MRS MALAPROP *to
leave them together.*]

MRS MALAPROP

Sir Anthony, shall we leave them together?—[*Aside to*
LYDIA.] Ah! you stubborn little vixen!

SIR ANTHONY

Not yet, ma'am, not yet!—[*Aside to* CAPTAIN ABSOLUTE.]
What the devil are you at? unlock your jaws, sirrah, or—

ABSOLUTE

[*Aside.*] Now Heaven send she may be too sullen to look
round!—I must disguise my voice.—[*Draws near* LYDIA,

and speaks in a low hoarse tone.] Will not Miss Languish lend an ear to the mild accents of true love? Will not—

SIR ANTHONY

What the devil ails the fellow? why don't you speak out?—not stand croaking like a frog in a quinsy! [70]

ABSOLUTE

The—the—excess of my awe, and my—my—modesty quite choke me!

SIR ANTHONY

Ah! your modesty again!—I'll tell you what, Jack, if you don't speak out directly, and glibly too, I shall be in such a rage!—Mrs Malaprop, I wish the lady would favour us with something more than a side-front. [71]

[MRS MALAPROP *seems to chide* LYDIA.]

ABSOLUTE

[*Aside.*] So all will out, I see!—[*Goes up to* LYDIA, *speaks softly.*] Be not surprised, my Lydia, suppress all surprise at present.

LYDIA

[*Aside.*] Heavens! 'tis Beverley's voice! Sure he can't have imposed on Sir Anthony too!—[*Looks round by degrees, then starts up.*] Is this possible?—my Beverley!—how can this be?—my Beverley?

ABSOLUTE

[*Aside.*] Ah! 'tis all over.

SIR ANTHONY

Beverley!—the devil—Beverley!—What can the girl mean? —this is my son, Jack Absolute.

MRS MALAPROP

For shame, hussy! for shame! your head runs so on that fellow, that you have him always in your eyes!—beg Captain Absolute's pardon directly.

LYDIA

I see no Captain Absolute, but my loved Beverley!

SIR ANTHONY

Zounds! the girl's mad!—her brain's turned by reading.

MRS MALAPROP

O' my conscience, I believe so!—What do you mean by Beverley, hussy?—You saw Captain Absolute before to-day; there he is—your husband that shall be.

LYDIA

With all my soul, ma'am—when I refuse my Beverley—

SIR ANTHONY

Oh! she's as mad as Bedlam! [72]—or has this fellow been playing us a rogue's trick!—Come here, sirrah, who the devil are you?

ABSOLUTE

Faith, sir, I am not quite clear myself; but I'll endeavour to recollect.

SIR ANTHONY

Are you my son or not?—answer for your mother, you dog, if you won't for me.

MRS MALAPROP

Ay, sir, who are you? O mercy! I begin to suspect!—

ABSOLUTE

[*Aside.*] Ye powers of impudence, befriend me!—[*Aloud.*] Sir Anthony, most assuredly I am your wife's son; and I sincerely believe myself to be yours also, I hope my duty has always shown.—Mrs Malaprop, I am your most respectful admirer, and shall be proud to add affectionate nephew.—I need not tell my Lydia, that she sees her faithful Beverley, who, knowing the singular generosity of her temper, assumed that name and station, which has proved a test of the most disinterested love, which he now hopes to enjoy in a more elevated character.

LYDIA

[*Sullenly.*] So!—there will be no elopement after all!

SIR ANTHONY

Upon my soul, Jack, thou art a very impudent fellow! to do you justice, I think I never saw a piece of more consummate assurance!

ABSOLUTE

Oh, you flatter me, sir—you compliment—'tis my modesty, you know, sir—my modesty that has stood in my way.

SIR ANTHONY

Well, I am glad you are not the dull, insensible varlet you pretended to be, however!—I'm glad you have made a fool of your father, you dog—I am. So this was your *penitence,* your *duty* and *obedience!*—I thought it was damned sudden!—*You never heard their names before,* not you!—*what, the Languishes of Worcestershire,* hey?—*if you could please me in the affair it was all you desired!*—Ah! you dissembling villain!—What!—[*Pointing to* LYDIA.] *she squints don't she?*—*a little red-haired girl!*—hey?—Why, you hypocritical young rascal!—I wonder you a'n't ashamed to hold up your head!

ABSOLUTE

'Tis with difficulty, sir.—I am confused—very much confused, as you must perceive.

MRS MALAPROP

O Lud! Sir Anthony!—a new light breaks in upon me!— hey!—how! what! captain, did you write the letters then?— What—am I to thank you for the elegant compilation of *an old weather-beaten she-dragon*—hey?—O mercy!— was it you that reflected on my parts of speech?

ABSOLUTE

Dear sir! my modesty will be overpowered at last, if you don't assist me.—I shall certainly not be able to stand it!

SIR ANTHONY

Come, come, Mrs Malaprop, we must forget and forgive; —odds life! matters have taken so clever a turn all of a sudden, that I could find in my heart to be so good-humoured! and so gallant! hey! Mrs Malaprop!

MRS MALAPROP

Well, Sir Anthony, since you desire it, we will not anticipate the past!—so mind, young people—our retrospection will be all to the future.

SIR ANTHONY

Come, we must leave them together; Mrs Malaprop, they long to fly into each other's arms, I warrant!—Jack, isn't the cheek as I said, hey?—and the eye, you rogue?—and the lip—hey? Come, Mrs Malaprop, we'll not disturb their tenderness—theirs is the time of life for happiness!— [*Sings.*] *Youth's the season made for joy*[73]—hey!—Odds life! I'm in such spirits,—I don't know what I could not do!—Permit me, ma'am—[*Gives his hand to* MRS MALAPROP.] Tol-de-rol—'gad, I should like to have a little fooling myself- Tol-de-rol! de-rol. [*Exit, singing and handing* MRS MALAPROP.—LYDIA *sits sullenly in her chair.*]

ABSOLUTE

[*Aside.*] So much thought bodes me no good.—[*Aloud.*] So grave, Lydia!

LYDIA

Sir!

ABSOLUTE

[*Aside.*] So!—egad! I thought as much!—that damned
monosyllable has froze me!—[*Aloud.*] What, Lydia, now
that we are as happy in our friends' consent, as in our
mutual vows—

LYDIA

[*Peevishly.*] Friends' consent indeed!

ABSOLUTE

Come, come, we must lay aside some of our romance—a
little wealth and comfort may be endured after all. And for
your fortune, the lawyers shall make such settlements as—

LYDIA

Lawyers! I hate lawyers!

ABSOLUTE

Nay, then, we will not wait for their lingering forms, but
instantly procure the license, and—

LYDIA

The license!—I hate license!

ABSOLUTE

[*Kneeling.*] Oh, my love! be not so unkind!—thus let me
entreat—

LYDIA

Psha!—what signifies kneeling, when you know I must
have you?

ABSOLUTE

[*Rising.*] Nay, madam, there shall be no constraint upon
your inclinations, I promise you.—If I have lost your
heart—I resign the rest—[*Aside.*] 'Gad, I must try what
a little spirit will do.

LYDIA

[*Rising.*] Then, sir, let me tell you, the interest you had
there was acquired by a mean, unmanly imposition, and
deserves the punishment of fraud.—What, you have been
treating me like a child!—humouring my romance! and
laughing, I suppose, at your success!

ABSOLUTE

You wrong me, Lydia, you wrong me—only hear—

LYDIA

So, while I fondly imagined we were deceiving my relations, and flattered myself that I should outwit and incense them all—behold my hopes are to be crushed at once, by my aunt's consent and approbation—and I am myself the only dupe at last!—[*Walking about in a heat.*] But here, sir, here is the picture—Beverley's picture! [*taking a miniature from her bosom*] which I have worn, night and day, in spite of threats and entreaties!—There, sir; [*Flings it to him.*] and be assured I throw the original from my heart as easily.

ABSOLUTE

Nay, nay, ma'am, we will not differ as to that.—Here, [*taking out a picture*] here is Miss Lydia Languish.—What a difference!—ay, there is the heavenly assenting smile that first gave soul and spirit to my hopes!—those are the lips which sealed a vow, as yet scarce dry in Cupid's calendar! and there the half-resentful blush, that would have checked the ardour of my thanks!—Well, all that's past?—all over indeed!—There, madam—in beauty, that copy is not equal to you, but in my mind its merit over the original, in being still the same, is such—that—I cannot find in my heart to part with it. [*Puts it up again.*]

LYDIA

[*Softening.*] 'Tis your own doing, sir—I, I, I suppose you are perfectly satisfied.

ABSOLUTE

O, most certainly—sure, now, this is much better than being in love!—ha! ha! ha!—there's some spirit in this!—What signifies breaking some scores of solemn promises: —all that's of no consequence, you know. To be sure people will say, that miss don't know her own mind but never mind that! Or, perhaps, they may be ill-natured enough to hint, that the gentleman grew tired of the lady and forsook her—but don't let that fret you.

LYDIA

There is no bearing his insolence. [*Bursts into tears. Re-enter* MRS MALAPROP *and* SIR ANTHONY ABSOLUTE.]

MRS MALAPROP

Come, we must interrupt your billing and cooing awhile.

LYDIA

[*Sobbing.*] This is worse than your treachery and deceit, you base ingrate!

SIR ANTHONY

What the devil's the matter now?—Zounds! Mrs Malaprop, this is the oddest billing and cooing I ever heard!—but what the deuce is the meaning of it?—I am quite astonished!

ABSOLUTE

Ask the lady, sir.

MRS MALAPROP

O mercy!—I'm quite analyzed, for my part!—Why, Lydia, what is the reason of this?

LYDIA

Ask the gentleman, ma'am.

SIR ANTHONY

Zounds! I shall be in a frenzy!—Why, Jack, you are not come out to be any one else, are you?

MRS MALAPROP

Ay, sir, there's no more trick, is there?—you are not like Cerberus,⁷⁴ three gentlemen at once, are you?

ABSOLUTE

You'll not let me speak—I say the lady can account for this much better than I can.

LYDIA

Ma'am, you once commanded me never to think of Beverley again—there is the man—I now obey you: for, from this moment, I renounce him for ever. [*Exit.*]

MRS MALAPROP

O mercy! and miracles! what a turn here is—why, sure, captain, you haven't behaved disrespectfully to my niece?

SIR ANTHONY

Ha! ha! ha!—ha! ha! ha!—now I see it. Ha! ha! ha!—now I see it—you have been too lively, Jack.

ABSOLUTE

Nay, sir, upon my word—

SIR ANTHONY

Come, no lying, Jack—I'm sure 'twas so.

MRS MALAPROP

O Lud! Sir Anthony!—O fy, captain!

ABSOLUTE

Upon my soul, ma'am—

SIR ANTHONY

Come, no excuse, Jack! why, your father, you rogue, was

so before you!—the blood of the Absolutes was always impatient.—Ha! ha! ha! poor little Lydia! why, you've frightened her, you dog, you have.

ABSOLUTE

By all that's good, sir—

SIR ANTHONY

Zounds! say no more, I tell you, Mrs Malaprop shall make your peace. You must make his peace, Mrs Malaprop:—you must tell her 'tis Jack's way—tell her 'tis all our ways—it runs in the blood of our family! Come away, Jack. Ha! ha! ha!—Mrs Malaprop—a young villain. [*Pushing him out.*]

MRS MALAPROP

O! Sir Anthony!—O fy, captain! [*Exeunt severally.*]

SCENE III

[*The North Parade.*]

[*Enter* SIR LUCIUS O'TRIGGER.]

LUCIUS

I wonder where this Captain Absolute hides himself! Upon my conscience! these officers are always in one's way in love affairs:—I remember I might have married Lady Dorothy Carmine, if it had not been for a little rogue of a major, who ran away with her before she could get a sight of me! And I wonder too what it is the ladies can see in them to be so fond of them—unless it be a touch of the old serpent in 'em, that makes the little creatures be caught, like vipers, with a bit of red cloth. Ha! isn't this the captain coming?—faith it is!—There is a probability of succeeding about that fellow, that is mighty provoking! Who the devil is he talking to? [*Steps aside. Enter* CAPTAIN ABSOLUTE.]

ABSOLUTE

[*Aside.*] To what fine purpose I have been plotting! a noble

reward for all my schemes, upon my soul!—a little gypsy!
—I did not think her romance could have made her so
damned absurd either. 'Sdeath, I never was in a worse
humour in my life!—I could cut my own throat, or any
other person's with the greatest pleasure in the world!

SIR LUCIUS

Oh, faith! I'm in the luck of it. I never could have found
him in a sweeter temper for my purpose—to be sure I'm
just come in the nick! Now to enter into conversation with
him, and so quarrel genteelly.—[*Goes up to* CAPTAIN
ABSOLUTE.] With regard to that matter, captain, I must beg
leave to differ in opinion with you.

ABSOLUTE

Upon my word, then, you must be a very subtle disputant:
—because, sir, I happened just then to be giving no opinion
at all.

SIR LUCIUS

That's no reason. For give me leave to tell you, a man may
think an untruth as well as speak one.

ABSOLUTE

Very true, sir; but if a man never utters his thoughts, I
should think they might stand a chance of escaping con-
troversy.

SIR LUCIUS

Then, sir, you differ in opinon with me, which amounts to
the same thing.

ABSOLUTE

Hark'ee, Sir Lucius; if I had not before known you to be
a gentleman, upon my soul, I should not have discovered
it at this interview: for what you can drive at, unless you
mean to quarrel with me, I cannot conceive!

SIR LUCIUS

I humbly thank you, sir, for the quickness of your apprehension.—[*Bowing.*] You have named the very thing
I would be at.

ABSOLUTE

Very well, sir; I shall certainly not balk your inclinations.
—But I should be glad you would be pleased to explain
your motives.

SIR LUCIUS

Pray, sir, be easy; the quarrel is a very pretty quarrel as it

stands; we should only spoil it by trying to explain it.
However, your memory is very short, or you could not
have forgot an affront you passed on me within this week.
So, no more, but name your time and place.

ABSOLUTE

Well, sir, since you are so bent on it, the sooner the better;
let it be this evening—here, by the Spring Gardens: We
shall scarcely be interrupted.

SIR LUCIUS

Faith! that same interruption in affairs of this nature shows
very great ill-breeding. I don't know what's the reason, but
in England if a thing of this kind gets wind, people make
such a pother, that a gentleman can never fight in peace
and quietness. However, if it's the same to you, I should
take it as a particular kindness if you'd let us meet in
King's-Mead-Fields, as a little business will call me there
about six o'clock, and I may despatch both matters at
once.

ABSOLUTE

'Tis the same to me exactly. A little after six, then, we
will discuss this matter more seriously.

SIR LUCIUS

If you please, sir; there will be very pretty small-sword
light, though it won't do for a long shot. So that matter's
settled, and my mind's at ease! [*Exit. Enter* FAULKLAND.]

ABSOLUTE

Well met! I was going to look for you. O Faulkland! all the
demons of spite and disappointment have conspired against
me! I'm so vex'd, that if I had not the prospect of a resource in being knocked o' the head by-and-by, I should
scarce have spirits to tell you the cause.

FAULKLAND

What can you mean?—Has Lydia changed her mind?—I
should have thought her duty and inclination would now
have pointed to the same object.

ABSOLUTE

Ay, just as the eyes do of a person who squints: when her
love-eye was fixed on me, t'other, her eye of duty, was
finely obliqued: but when duty bid her point that the
same way, off t'other turned on a swivel, and secured its
retreat with a frown!

FAULKLAND

But what's the resource you—

ABSOLUTE

Oh, to wind up the whole, a good-natured Irishman here
has—[*mimicking* SIR LUCIUS] begged leave to have the
pleasure of cutting my throat; and I mean to indulge him
—that's all.

FAULKLAND

Prithee, be serious!

ABSOLUTE

'Tis fact, upon my soul! Sir Lucius O'Trigger—you know
him by sight—for some affront, which I am sure I never
intended, has obliged me to meet him this evening at
six o'clock: 'tis on that account I wished to see you; you
must go with me.

FAULKLAND

Nay, there must be some mistake, sure. Sir Lucius shall
explain himself, and I dare say matters may be accommo-
dated. But this evening did you say? I wish it had been any
other time.

ABSOLUTE

Why? there will be light enough: there will (as Sir Lucius
says) be very pretty small-sword light, though it will not
do for a long shot. Confound his long shots.

FAULKLAND

But I am myself a good deal ruffled by a difference I have
had with Julia. My vile tormenting temper has made me
treat her so cruelly, that I shall not be myself till we are
reconciled.

ABSOLUTE

By heavens! Faulkland, you don't deserve her!

[*Enter* SERVANT, *gives* FAULKLAND *a letter, and exit.*]

FAULKLAND

Oh, Jack! this is from Julia. I dread to open it! I fear it
may be to take a last leave!—perhaps to bid me return her
letters, and restore—Oh, how I suffer for my folly!

ABSOLUTE

Here, let me see.—[*Takes the letter and opens it.*] Ay, a
final sentence, indeed!—'tis all over with you, faith!

FAULKLAND

Nay, Jack, don't keep me in suspense!

ABSOLUTE

Hear then—[*Reads.*] *As I am convinced that my dear Faulkland's own reflections have already upbraided him for his last unkindness to me, I will not add a word on the subject. I wish to speak with you as soon as possible. Yours ever and truly,* JULIA. There's stubbornness and resentment for you!—[*Gives him the letter.*] Why, man, you don't seem one whit happier at this!

FAULKLAND

O yes, I am; but—but—

ABSOLUTE

Confound your buts! you never hear anything that would make another man bless himself, but you immediately damn it with a but!

FAULKLAND

Now, Jack, as you are my friend, own honestly—don't you think there is something forward, something indelicate, in this haste to forgive? Women should never sue for reconciliation: that should always come from us. They should retain their coldness till wooed to kindness; and their pardon, like their love, should "not unsought be won." [75]

ABSOLUTE

I have not patience to listen to you! thou'rt incorrigible! so say no more on the subject. I must go to settle a few matters. Let me see you before six, remember, at my lodgings. A poor industrious devil like me, who have toiled, and drudged, and plotted to gain my ends, and am at last disappointed by other people's folly, may in pity be allowed to swear and grumble a little; but a captious sceptic in love, a slave to fretfulness and whim, who has no difficulties but of his own creating, is a subject more fit for ridicule than compassion! [*Exit.*]

FAULKLAND

I feel his reproaches; yet I would not change this too exquisite nicety for the gross content with which he tramples on the thorns of love! His engaging me in this duel has started an idea in my head, which I will instantly pursue. I'll use it as the touch-stone of Julia's sincerity and disinterestedness. If her love proves pure and sterling ore, my name will rest on it with honour; and once I've stamped it there, I lay aside my doubts for ever! But if the dross of selfishness, the alloy of pride, predominate, 'twill be best to leave her as a toy for some less cautious fool to sigh for! [*Exit.*]

Act five.

SCENE I

[JULIA'S *dressing-room.*]

[JULIA *discovered alone.*]

JULIA

How this message has alarmed me! what dreadful accident can he mean? why such charge to be alone?— O Faulkland!—how many unhappy moments—how many tears have you cost me.

[*Enter* FAULKLAND.]

JULIA

What means this?—why this caution, Faulkland?

FAULKLAND

Alas! Julia, I am come to take a long farewell.

JULIA

Heavens! what do you mean?

FAULKLAND

You see before you a wretch, whose life is forfeited. Nay, start not!—the infirmity of my temper has drawn all this misery on me. I left you fretful and passionate—an ontoward accident drew me into a quarrel—the event is, that I must fly this kingdom instantly. O Julia, had I been so fortunate as to have called you mine entirely, before this mischance had fallen on me, I should not so deeply dread my banishment!

JULIA

My soul is opprest with sorrow at the nature of your misfortune: had these adverse circumstances arisen from a less fatal cause I should have felt strong comfort in the thought I could now chase from your bosom every doubt of the warm sincerity of my love. My heart has long known no other guardian—I now entrust my person to your honour—we will fly together. When safe from pursuit, my father's will may be fulfilled—and I receive a legal claim to be the partner of your sorrows, and tenderest comforter. Then on the bosom of your wedded Julia, you may lull your keen regret to slumbering, while virtuous love, with a cherub's hand, shall smoothe the brow of upbraiding thought, and pluck the thorn from compunction.

FAULKLAND

O Julia! I am bankrupt in gratitude! but the time is so pressing, it calls on you for so hasty a resolution.—Would you not wish some hours to weigh the advantages you forego, and what little compensation poor Faulkland can make you beside his solitary love?

JULIA

I ask not a moment. No, Faulkland, I have loved you for yourself: and if I now, more than ever, prize the solemn engagement which so long has pledged us to each other, it is because it leaves no room for hard aspersions on my fame, and puts the seal of duty to an act of love. But let us not linger. Perhaps this delay—

FAULKLAND

'Twill be better I should not venture out again till dark. Yet am I grieved to think what numberless distresses will press heavy on your gentle disposition!

JULIA

Perhaps your fortune may be forfeited by this unhappy act.—I know not whether 'tis so; but sure that alone can never make us unhappy. The little I have will be sufficient to support us; and exile never should be splendid.

FAULKLAND

Ay, but in such an abject state of life, my wounded pride perhaps may increase the natural fretfulness of my temper, till I become a rude, morose companion, beyond your patience to endure. Perhaps the recollection of a deed my conscience cannot justify may haunt me in such gloomy and unsocial fits, that I shall hate the tenderness that would relieve me, break from your arms, and quarrel with your fondness!

JULIA

If your thoughts should assume so unhappy a bent, you will the more want some mild and affectionate spirit to watch over and console you! one who, by bearing your infirmities with gentleness and resignation, may teach you so to bear the evils of your fortune.

FAULKLAND

Julia, I have proved you to the quick! and with this useless device I throw away all my doubts. How shall I plead to be forgiven this last unworthy effect of my restless, unsatisfied disposition?

JULIA

Has no such disaster happened as you related?

FAULKLAND

I am ashamed to own that it was pretended; yet in pity, Julia, do not kill me with resenting a fault which never can be repeated: but sealing, this once, my pardon, let me to-morrow, in the face of Heaven, receive my future guide and monitress, and expiate my past folly by years of tender adoration.

JULIA

Hold, Faulkland!—that you are free from a crime, which I before feared to name, Heaven knows how sincerely I rejoice! These are tears of thankfulness for that! But that your cruel doubts should have urged you to an imposition that has wrung my heart, gives me now a pang more keen than I can express.

FAULKLAND

By Heavens! Julia—

JULIA

Yet hear me.—My father loved you, Faulkland! and you preserved the life that tender parent gave me; in his presence I pledged my hand—joyfully pledged it—where before I had given my heart. When, soon after, I lost that parent, it seemed to me that Providence had, in Faulkland, shown me whither to transfer without a pause, my grateful duty, as well as my affection; hence I have been content to bear from you what pride and delicacy would have forbid me from another. I will not upbraid you, by repeating how you have trifled with my sincerity—

FAULKLAND
I confess it all! yet hear—

JULIA
After such a year of trial, I might have flattered myself
that I should not have been insulted with a new probation
of my sincerity, as cruel as unnecessary! I now see it is not
in your nature to be content or confident in love. With this
conviction—I never will be yours. While I had hopes that
my persevering attention, and unreproaching kindness,
might in time reform your temper, I should have been
happy to have gained a dearer influence over you; but I
will not furnish you with a licensed power to keep alive an
incorrigible fault, at the expense of one who never would
contend with you.

FAULKLAND
Nay, but, Julia, by my soul and honour, if after this—

JULIA
But one word more.—As my faith has once been given to
you, I never will barter it with another.—I shall pray for
your happiness with the truest sincerity; and the dearest
blessing I can ask of Heaven to send you will be to charm
you from that unhappy temper, which alone has prevented
the performance of our solemn engagement. All I request
of you is, that you will yourself reflect upon this infirmity,
and when you number up the many true delights it has
deprived you of, let it not be your least regret, that it lost
you the love of one who would have followed you in
beggary through the world. [*Exit*.]

FAULKLAND
She's gone—for ever!—There was an awful resolution in
her manner, that riveted me to my place.—O fool!—dolt!
—barbarian! Cursed as I am, with more imperfections than
my fellow-wretches, kind Fortune sent a heaven-gifted
cherub to my aid, and, like a ruffian, I have driven her
from my side!—I must now haste to my appointment. Well,
my mind is tuned for such a scene. I shall wish only to
become a principal in it, and reverse the tale my cursed
folly put me upon forging here.—O Love!—tormentor!—
fiend!—whose influence, like the moon's, acting on men
of dull souls, makes idiots of them, but meeting subtler
spirits, betrays their course, and urges sensibility to mad-

ness! [*Exit. Enter* LYDIA *and* MAID.]

MAID

My mistress, ma'am, I know, was here just now—perhaps she is only in the next room. [*Exit.*]

LYDIA

Heigh-ho! Though he has used me so, this fellow runs strangely in my head. I believe one lecture from my grave cousin will make me recall him. [*Reenter* JULIA.] O Julia, I have come to you with such an appetite for consolation. —Lud! child, what's the matter with you? You have been crying!—I'll be hanged if that Faulkland has not been tormenting you.

JULIA

You mistake the cause of my uneasiness!—Something has flurried me a little. Nothing that you can guess at.— [*Aside.*] I would not accuse Faulkland to a sister!

LYDIA

Ah! whatever vexations you may have, I can assure you mine surpass them. You know who Beverley proves to be?

JULIA

I will now own to you, Lydia, that Mr Faulkland had before informed me of the whole affair. Had young Absolute been the person you took him for, I should not have accepted your confidence on the subject, without a serious endeavour to counteract your caprice.

LYDIA

So, then, I see I have been deceived by every one! But I don't care—I'll never have him.

JULIA

Nay, Lydia—

LYDIA

Why, is it not provoking? when I thought we were coming to the prettiest distress imaginable, to find myself made a mere Smithfield bargain[76] of at last! There, had I projected one of the most sentimental elopements!—so becoming a disguise!—so amiable a ladder of ropes!—Conscious moon —four horses—Scotch parson[77]—with such surprise to Mrs Malaprop—and such paragraphs in the newspapers!—Oh, I shall die with disappointment!

JULIA

I don't wonder at it!

LYDIA

Now—sad reverse!—what have I to expect, but, after a
deal of flimsy preparation, with a bishop's license, and my
aunt's blessing, to go simpering up to the altar; or perhaps
be cried three times in a country church, and have an unmannerly fat clerk ask the consent of every butcher in the
parish to join John Absolute and Lydia Languish, spinster!
Oh that I should live to hear myself called spinster!

JULIA

Melancholy, indeed!

LYDIA

How mortifying, to remember the dear delicious shifts I
used to be put to, to gain half a minute's conversation
with this fellow! How often have I stole forth, in the
coldest night in January, and found him in the garden,
stuck like a dripping statue! There would he kneel to me
in the snow, and sneeze and cough so pathetically! he
shivering with cold and I with apprehension! and while the
freezing blast numbed our joints, how warmly would he
press me to pity his flame, and glow with mutual ardour!
—Ah, Julia, that was something like being in love.

JULIA

If I were in spirits, Lydia, I should chide you only by
laughing heartily at you; but it suits more the situation of
my mind, at present, earnestly to entreat you not to let a
man, who loves you with sincerity, suffer that unhappiness
from your caprice, which I know too well caprice can
inflict.

LYDIA

O Lud! what has brought my aunt here?

[*Enter* MRS MALAPROP, FAG, *and* DAVID.]

MRS MALAPROP

So! so! here's fine work!—here's fine suicide, parricide, and
simulation, going on in the fields! and Sir Anthony not to
be found to prevent the antistrophe!

JULIA

For Heaven's sake, madam, what's the meaning of this?

MRS MALAPROP

That gentleman can tell you—'twas he enveloped the
affair to me.

LYDIA

[*To* FAG.] Do, sir, will you, inform us?

FAG

Ma'am, I should hold myself very deficient in every requisite that forms the man of breeding, if I delayed a moment to give all the information in my power to a lady so deeply interested in the affair as you are.

LYDIA

But quick! quick, sir!

FAG

True, ma'am, as you say, one should be quick in divulging matters of this nature; for should we be tedious, perhaps while we are flourishing on the subject, two or three lives may be lost!

LYDIA

O patience!—do, ma'am, for Heaven's sake! tell us what is the matter?

MRS MALAPROP

Why, murder's the matter! slaughter's the matter! killing's the matter!—but he can tell you the perpendiculars.

LYDIA

Then, prithee, sir, be brief.

FAG

Why, then, ma'am, as to murder—I cannot take upon me to say—and as to slaughter, or manslaughter, that will be as the jury finds it.

LYDIA

But who, sir—who are engaged in this?

FAG

Faith, ma'am, one is a young gentleman whom I should be very sorry anything was to happen to—a very pretty behaved gentleman! We have lived much together, and always on terms.

LYDIA

But who is this? who? who? who?

FAG

My master, ma'am—my master—I speak of my master.

LYDIA

Heavens! What, Captain Absolute!

MRS MALAPROP

Oh, to be sure, you are frightened now!

JULIA

But who are with him, sir?

FAG

As to the rest, ma'am, this gentleman can inform you better than I?

JULIA

[*To* DAVID.] Do speak, friend.

DAVID

Look'ee, my lady—by the mass! there's mischief going on. Folks don't use to meet for amusement with firearms, firelocks, fire-engines, fire-screens, fire-office,[78] and the devil knows what other crackers beside!—This, my lady, I say, has an angry savour.

JULIA

But who is there beside Captain Absolute, friend?

DAVID

My poor master—under favour for mentioning him first. You know me, my lady—I am David—and my master of course is, or was, Squire Acres. Then comes Squire Faulkland.

JULIA

Do, ma'am, let us instantly endeavour to prevent mischief.

MRS MALAPROP

O fy! it would be very inelegant in us:—we should only participate things.

DAVID

Ah! do, Mrs Aunt, save a few lives—they are desperately given, believe me.—Above all, there is that bloodthirsty Philistine, Sir Lucius O'Trigger.

MRS MALAPROP

Sir Lucius O'Trigger? O mercy! have they drawn poor little dear Sir Lucius into the scrape? Why how you stand, girl! you have no more feeling than one of the Derbyshire petrifactions! [79]

LYDIA

What are we to do, madam?

MRS MALAPROP

Why, fly with the utmost felicity, to be sure, to prevent mischief!—Here, friend, you can show us the place?

FAG

If you please, ma'am, I will conduct you.—David, do you

look for Sir Anthony.

   [*Exit* DAVID.]

MRS MALAPROP

Come, girls! this gentleman will exhort us.—Come, sir,
you're our envoy—lead the way, and we'll precede.

FAG

Not a step before the ladies for the world!

MRS MALAPROP

You're sure you know the spot?

FAG

I think I can find it, ma'am; and one good thing is, we
shall hear the report of the pistols as we draw near, so we
can't miss them;—never fear, ma'am, never fear. [*Exeunt,
he talking.*]

SCENE II

   [*The South Parade.*]

   [*Enter* CAPTAIN ABSOLUTE, *putting his sword under his
great-coat.*]

ABSOLUTE

A sword seen in the streets of Bath would raise as great
an alarm as a mad dog.—How provoking this is in Faulkland!—never punctual! I shall be obliged to go without
him at last.—Oh, the devil! here's Sir Anthony! how shall
I escape him? [*Muffles up his face, and takes a circle to
go off. Enter* SIR ANTHONY ABSOLUTE.]

SIR ANTHONY

How one may be deceived at a little distance! Only that I
see he don't know me, I could have sworn that was Jack!
—Hey! Gad's life! it is.—Why, Jack, what are you afraid
of? hey—sure I'm right. Why Jack, Jack Absolute! [*Goes
up to him.*]

ABSOLUTE

Really, sir, you have the advantage of me:—I don't re-

member ever to have had the honour—my name is Saunderson, at your service.

SIR ANTHONY

Sir, I beg your pardon—I took you—hey?—why, zounds!
it is—Stay—[*Looks up to his face.*] So, so—your humble
servant, Mr Saunderson! Why, you scoundrel, what tricks
are you after now?

ABSOLUTE

Oh, a joke, sir, a joke! I came here on purpose to look for
you, sir.

SIR ANTHONY

You did! well, I am glad you were so lucky:—but what are
you muffled up so for?—what's this for?—hey?

ABSOLUTE

'Tis cool, sir, isn't it?—rather chilly somehow:—but I shall
be late—I have a particular engagement.

SIR ANTHONY

Stay!—Why, I thought you were looking for me?—Pray,
Jack, where is't you are going?

ABSOLUTE

Going, sir?

SIR ANTHONY

Ay, where are you going?

ABSOLUTE

Where am I going?

SIR ANTHONY

You unmannerly puppy!

ABSOLUTE

I was going, sir, to—to—to—to—Lydia—sir, to Lydia—
to make matters up if I could; and I was looking for you,
sir, to—to—

SIR ANTHONY

To go with you, I suppose.—Well, come along.

ABSOLUTE

Oh! zounds! no, sir, not for the world!—I wished to meet
with you, sir,—to—to—to—You find it cool, I'm sure,
sir—you'd better not stay out.

SIR ANTHONY

Cool!—not at all.—Well, Jack—and what will you say to
Lydia?

ABSOLUTE

Oh, sir, beg her pardon, humour her—promise and vow: but I detain you, sir—consider the cold air on your gout.

SIR ANTHONY

Oh, not at all!—not at all! I'm in no hurry.—Ah! Jack, you youngsters, when once you are wounded here. [*Putting his hand to* CAPTAIN ABSOLUTE'S *breast*.] Hey! what the deuce have you got here?

ABSOLUTE

Nothing, sir—nothing.

SIR ANTHONY

What's this?—here's something damned hard.

ABSOLUTE

Oh, trinkets, sir! trinkets!—a bauble for Lydia.

SIR ANTHONY

Nay, let me see your taste.—[*Pulls his coat open, the sword falls*.] Trinkets! a bauble for Lydia!—Zounds! sirrah, you are not going to cut her throat, are you?

ABSOLUTE

Ha! ha! ha!—I thought it would divert you, sir, though I didn't mean to tell you till afterwards.

SIR ANTHONY

You didn't?—Yes, this is a very diverting trinket, truly!

ABSOLUTE

Sir, I'll explain to you.—You know, sir, Lydia is romantic, devilish romantic, and very absurd of course: now, sir, I intend, if she refuses to forgive me, to unsheath this sword, and swear—I'll fall upon its point, and expire at her feet!

SIR ANTHONY

Fall upon a fiddlestick's end!—why, I suppose it is the very thing that would please her.—Get along, you fool!

ABSOLUTE

Well, sir, you shall hear of my success—you shall hear.— *O Lydia!—forgive me, or this pointed steel*—says I.

SIR ANTHONY

O, booby! stab away and welcome—says she.—Get along! and damn your trinkets!

[*Exit* CAPTAIN ABSOLUTE. *Enter* DAVID, *running*.]

DAVID

Stop him! stop him! Murder! Thief! Fire!—Stop fire! Stop fire!—O Sir Anthony—call! call! bid'm stop! Murder!

Fire!

SIR ANTHONY

Fire! Murder!—Where?

DAVID

Oons! he's out of sight! and I'm out of breath for my part!
O Sir Anthony, why didn't you stop him? why didn't you
stop him?

SIR ANTHONY

Zounds! the fellow's mad!—Stop whom? stop Jack?

DAVID

Ay, the captain, sir!—there's murder and slaughter—

SIR ANTHONY

Murder!

DAVID

Ay, please you, Sir Anthony, there's all kinds of murder,
all sorts of slaughter to be seen in the fields: there's fighting going on, sir—bloody sword-and-gun fighting!

SIR ANTHONY

Who are going to fight, dunce?

DAVID

Everybody that I know of, Sir Anthony:—everybody is
going to fight, my poor master, Sir Lucius O'Trigger, your
son, the captain—

SIR ANTHONY

Oh, the dog! I see his tricks.—Do you know the place?

DAVID

King's-Mead-Fields.

SIR ANTHONY

You know the way?

DAVID

Not an inch; but I'll call the mayor—aldermen—constables
—churchwardens—and beadles—we can't be too many to
part them.

SIR ANTHONY

Come along—give me your shoulder! we'll get assistance
as we go—the lying villain!—Well, I shall be in such a
frenzy!—So—this was the history of his trinkets! I'll
bauble him! [*Exeunt.*]

SCENE III

[*King's-Mead-Fields.*]

[*Enter* SIR LUCIUS O'TRIGGER *and* ACRES, *with pistols.*]

ACRES

By my valour! then, Sir Lucius, forty yards is a good distance. Odds levels and aims!—I say it is the good distance.

SIR LUCIUS

Is it for muskets or small field-pieces? Upon my conscience, Mr Acres, you must leave those things to me.—Stay now—I'll show you.—[*Measures paces along the stage.*] There now, that is a very pretty distance—a pretty gentleman's distance.

ACRES

Zounds! we might as well fight in a sentry-box! I tell you, Sir Lucius, the farther he is off, the cooler I shall take my aim.

SIR LUCIUS

Faith! then I suppose you would aim at him best of all if he was out of sight!

ACRES

No, Sir Lucius; but I should think forty or eight and thirty yards—

SIR LUCIUS

Pho! pho! nonsense! three or four feet between the mouths of your pistols is as good as a mile.

ACRES

Odds bullets, no!—by my valour! there is no merit in killing him so near; do, my dear Sir Lucius, let me bring him down at a long shot—a long shot, Sir Lucius, if you love me.

SIR LUCIUS

Well, the gentleman's friend and I must settle that.—But tell me now, Mr Acres, in case of an accident, is there any little will or commission I could execute for you?

ACRES

I am much obliged to you, Sir Lucius, but I don't understand—

SIR LUCIUS

Why, you may think there's no being shot at without a
little risk—and if an unlucky bullet should carry a
quietus[80] with it—I say it will be no time then to be bother-
ing you about family matters.

ACRES

A quietus!

SIR LUCIUS

For instance, now—if that should be the case—would you
choose to be pickled and sent home?—or would it be the
same to you to lie here in the Abbey? I'm told there is very
snug lying in the Abbey.

ACRES

Pickled—Snug lying in the Abbey!—Odds tremors! Sir
Lucius, don't talk so!

SIR LUCIUS

I suppose, Mr Acres, you never were engaged in an affair
of this kind before?

ACRES

No, Sir Lucius, never before.

SIR LUCIUS

Ah! that's a pity!—there's nothing like being used to a
thing. Pray now, how would you receive the gentleman's
shot?

ACRES

Odds files!—I've practised that—there, Sir Lucius—there.
[*Puts himself in an attitude.*] A side-front, hey? Odd! I'll
make myself small enough? I'll stand edgeways.

SIR LUCIUS

Now—you're quite out—for if you stand so when I take
my aim—[*Levelling at him.*]

ACRES

Zounds! Sir Lucius—are you sure it is not cocked?

SIR LUCIUS

Never fear.

ACRES

But—but—you don't know—it may go off of its own

head!

SIR LUCIUS

Pho! be easy.—Well, now if I hit you in the body, my bullet has a double chance—for if it misses a vital part of your right side, 'twill be very hard if it don't succeed on the left!

ACRES

A vital part.

SIR LUCIUS

But, there—fix yourself so—[*placing him*]—let him see the broad-side of your full front—there—now a ball or two may pass clean through your body, and never do any harm at all.

ACRES

Clean through me!—a ball or two clean through me!

SIR LUCIUS

Ay—may they—and it is much the genteelest attitude into the bargain.

ACRES

Look'ee! Sir Lucius—I'd just as lieve be shot in an awkward posture as a genteel one; so, by my valour! I will stand edgeways.

SIR LUCIUS

[*Looking at his watch.*] Sure they don't mean to disappoint us—Hah!—no, faith—I think I see them coming.

ACRES

Hey!—what!—coming!—

SIR LUCIUS

Ay.—Who are those yonder getting over the stile?

ACRES

There are two of them indeed!—well—let them come—hey, Sir Lucius!—we—we—we—we—won't run.

SIR LUCIUS

Run!

ACRES

No—I say—we won't run, by my valour!

SIR LUCIUS

What the devil's the matter with you?

ACRES

Nothing—nothing—my dear friend—my dear Sir Lucius—but I—I—I don't feel quite so bold, somehow, as I did.

SIR LUCIUS

O fy!—consider your honour.

ACRES

Ay—true—my honour. Do, Sir Lucius, edge in a word or two every now and then about my honour.

SIR LUCIUS

[*Looking.*] Well, here they're coming.

ACRES

Sir Lucius—if I wa'n't with you, I should almost think I was afraid.—If my valour should leave me! Valour will come and go.

SIR LUCIUS

Then pray keep it fast, while you have it.

ACRES

Sir Lucius—I doubt it is going—yes—my valour is certainly going!—it is sneaking off!—I feel it oozing out as it were at the palms of my hands!

SIR LUCIUS

Your honour—your honour.—Here they are.

ACRES

O mercy!—now—that I was safe at Clod Hall! or could be shot before I was aware!

[*Enter* FAULKLAND *and* CAPTAIN ABSOLUTE.]

SIR LUCIUS

Gentlemen, your most obedient.—Hah!—what, Captain Absolute!—So, I suppose, sir, you are come here, just like myself—to do a kind office, first for your friend—then to proceed to business on your own account.

ACRES

What, Jack!—my dear Jack!—my dear friend!

ABSOLUTE

Hark'ee, Bob, Beverley's at hand.

SIR LUCIUS

Well, Mr Acres—I don't blame your saluting the gentleman civilly.—[*To* FAULKLAND.] So, Mr Beverley, if you'll choose your weapons, the captain and I will measure the ground.

FAULKLAND

My weapons, sir!

ACRES

Odds life! Sir Lucius, I'm not going to fight Mr Faulkland;

these are my particular friends.

SIR LUCIUS

What, sir, did you not come here to fight Mr Acres?

FAULKLAND

Not I, upon my word, sir.

SIR LUCIUS

Well, now, that's mighty provoking! But I hope, Mr Faulkland, as there are three of us come on purpose for the
game, you won't be so cantankerous as to spoil the party
by sitting out.

ABSOLUTE

O pray, Faulkland, fight to oblige Sir Lucius.

FAULKLAND

Nay, if Mr Acres is so bent on the matter—

ACRES

No, no, Mr Faulkland;—I'll bear my disappointment like a
Christian.—Look'ee, Sir Lucius, there's no occasion at all
for me to fight; and if it is the same to you, I'd as lieve let
it alone.

SIR LUCIUS

Observe me, Mr Acres—I must not be trifled with. You
have certainly challenged somebody—and you came here
to fight him. Now, if that gentleman is willing to represent
him—I can't see, for my soul, why it isn't just the same
thing.

ACRES

Why no—Sir Lucius—I tell you, 'tis one Beverley I've
challenged—a fellow, you see, that dare not show his face!
—if he were here, I'd make him give up his pretensions
directly!

ABSOLUTE

Hold, Bob—let me set you right—there is no such man as
Beverley in the case.—The person who assumed that name
is before you; and as his pretensions are the same in both
characters, he is ready to support them in whatever way you
please.

SIR LUCIUS

Well, this is lucky.—Now you have an opportunity—

ACRES

What, quarrel with my dear friend, Jack Absolute?—not
if he were fifty Beverleys! Zounds! Sir Lucius, you would

not have me so unnatural.

SIR LUCIUS

Upon my conscience, Mr Acres, your valour has oozed away with a vengeance!

ACRES

Not in the least! Odds backs and abettors! I'll be your second with all my heart—and if you should get a quietus, you may command me entirely. I'll get you snug lying in the Abbey here; or pickle you, and send you over to Blunderbuss-hall, or anything of the kind, with the greatest pleasure.

SIR LUCIUS

Pho! pho! you are little better than a coward.

ACRES

Mind, gentlemen, he calls me a coward; coward was the word, by my valour!

SIR LUCIUS

Well, sir?

ACRES

Look'ee, Sir Lucius, 'tisn't that I mind the word coward—coward may be said in joke.—But if you had called me a poltroon, odds daggers and balls—

SIR LUCIUS

Well, sir?

ACRES

I should have thought you a very ill-bred man.

SIR LUCIUS

Pho! you are beneath my notice.

ABSOLUTE

Nay, Sir Lucius, you can't have a better second than my friend Acres.—He is a most determined dog—called in the country, Fighting Bob.—He generally kills a man a week —don't you, Bob?

ACRES

Ay—at home!

SIR LUCIUS

Well, then, captain, 'tis we must begin—so come out, my little counsellor—[*draws his sword*]—and ask the gentleman, whether he will resign the lady, without forcing you to proceed against him?

ABSOLUTE

Come on them, sir—[*draws*]; since you won't let it be an amicable suit, here's my reply.

[*Enter* SIR ANTHONY ABSOLUTE, DAVID, MRS MALAPROP,
LYDIA, *and* JULIA.]

DAVID

Knock 'em all down, sweet Sir Anthony; knock down my master in particular; and bind his hands over to their good behaviour!

SIR ANTHONY

Put up, Jack, put up, or I shall be in a frenzy—how came you in a duel, sir?

ABSOLUTE

Faith, sir, that gentleman can tell you better than I; 'twas he called on me, and you know, sir, I serve his majesty.

SIR ANTHONY

Here's a pretty fellow; I catch him going to cut a man's throat, and he tells me he serves his majesty!—Zounds! sirrah, then how durst you draw the king's sword against one of his subjects?

ABSOLUTE

Sir! I tell you, that gentleman called me out, without explaining his reasons.

SIR ANTHONY

Gad! sir, how came you to call my son out without explaining your reasons?

SIR LUCIUS

Your son, sir, insulted me in a manner which my honour could not brook.

SIR ANTHONY

Zounds! Jack, how durst you insult the gentleman in a manner which his honour could not brook?

MRS MALAPROP

Come, come, let's have no honour before ladies—Captain Absolute, come here—How could you intimidate us so?— Here's Lydia has been terrified to death for you.

ABSOLUTE

For fear I should be killed, or escape, ma'am?

MRS MALAPROP

Nay, no delusions to the past—Lydia is convinced; speak, child.

SIR LUCIUS

With your leave, ma'am, I must put in a word, here: I believe I could interpret the young lady's silence. Now mark—

LYDIA

What is it you mean, sir?

SIR LUCIUS

Come, come, Delia, we must be serious now—this is no time for trifling.

LYDIA

'Tis true, sir; and your reproof bids me offer this gentleman my hand, and solicit the return of his affections.

ABSOLUTE

O! my little angel, say you so?—Sir Lucius, I perceive there must be some mistake here, with regard to the affront which you affirm I have given you. I can only say that it could not have been intentional. And as you must be convinced, that I should not fear to support a real injury— you shall now see that I am not ashamed to atone for an inadvertency—I ask your pardon.—But for this lady, while honoured with her approbation, I will support my claim against any man whatever.

SIR ANTHONY

Well said, Jack, and I'll stand by you, my boy.

ACRES

Mind, I give up all my claim—I make no pretensions to any thing in the world; and if I can't get a wife without fighting for her, by my valour! I'll live a bachelor.

SIR LUCIUS

Captain, give me your hand: an affront handsomely acknowledged becomes an obligation; and as for the lady, if she chooses to deny her own handwriting, here—[*Takes out letters.*]

MRS MALAPROP

O, he will dissolve my mystery!—Sir Lucius, perhaps there's some mistake—perhaps I can illuminate—

SIR LUCIUS

Pray, old gentlewoman, don't interfere where you have no business.—Miss Languish, are you my Delia or not?

LYDIA

Indeed, Sir Lucius, I am not. [*Walks aside with* CAPTAIN

ABSOLUTE.]

MRS MALAPROP

Sir Lucius O'Trigger—ungrateful as you are—I own the soft impeachment—pardon my blushes, I am Delia.

SIR LUCIUS

You Delia—pho! pho! be easy.

MRS MALAPROP

Why, thou barbarous vandyke—those letters are mine.— When you are more sensible of my benignity—perhaps I may be brought to encourage your addresses.

SIR LUCIUS

Mrs Malaprop, I am extremely sensible of your condescension; and whether you or Lucy have put this trick on me, I am equally beholden to you.—And, to show you I am not ungrateful, Captain Absolute, since you have taken that lady from me, I'll give you my Delia into the bargain.

ABSOLUTE

I am much obliged to you, Sir Lucius; but here's my friend, Fighting Bob, unprovided for.

SIR LUCIUS

Ha! little Valour—here, will you make your fortune?

ACRES

Odds wrinkles! No.—But give me your hand, Sir Lucius, forget and forgive; but if ever I give you a chance of pickling me again, say Bob Acres is a dunce, that's all.

SIR ANTHONY

Come, Mrs Malaprop, don't be cast down—you are in your bloom yet.

MRS MALAPROP

O Sir Anthony—men are all barbarians.

[*All retire but* JULIA *and* FAULKLAND.]

JULIA

[*Aside.*] He seems dejected and unhappy—not sullen; there was some foundation, however, for the tale he told me—O woman! how true should be your judgment, when your resolution is so weak!

FAULKLAND

Julia!—how can I sue for what I so little deserve? I dare not presume—yet Hope is the child of Penitence.

JULIA

Oh! Faulkland, you have not been more faulty in your unkind treatment of me than I am now in wanting inclination to resent it. As my heart honestly bids me place my weakness to the account of love, I should be ungenerous not to admit the same plea for yours.

FAULKLAND

Now I shall be blest indeed.

SIR ANTHONY

[*Coming forward.*] What's going on here?—So you have been quarrelling too, I warrant? Come, Julia, I never interfered before; but let me have a hand in the matter at last.—All the faults I have ever seen in my friend Faulkland seemed to proceed from what he calls the delicacy and warmth of his affection for you.—There, marry him directly, Julia; you'll find he'll mend surprisingly!

[*The rest come forward.*]

SIR LUCIUS

Come, now, I hope there is no dissatisfied person, but what is content; for as I have been disappointed myself, it will be very hard if I have not the satisfaction of seeing other people succeed better.

ACRES

You are right, Sir Lucius.—So, Jack, I wish you joy.— Mr Faulkland the same.—Ladies,—come now, to show you I'm neither vexed nor angry, odds tabors and pipes! I'll order the fiddles in half an hour to the New Rooms— and I insist on your all meeting me there.

SIR ANTHONY

'Gad! sir, I like your spirit; and at night we single lads will drink a health to the young couples, and a husband to Mrs Malaprop.

FAULKLAND

Our partners are stolen from us, Jack—I hope to be congratulated by each other—yours for having checked in time the errors of an ill-directed imagination, which might have betrayed an innocent heart; and mine, for having, by her gentleness and candour, reformed the unhappy temper of one, who by it made wretched whom he loved most, and tortured the heart he ought to have adored.

ABSOLUTE

Well, Jack, we have both tasted the bitters, as well as the

sweets of love; with this difference only, that you always
prepared the bitter cup for yourself, while I—

LYDIA

Was always obliged to me for it, hey! Mr Modesty?—But
come, no more of that—our happiness is now as unalloyed
as general.

JULIA

Then let us study to preserve it so: and while Hope pictures
to us a flattering scene of future bliss, let us deny its
pencil those colours which are too bright to be lasting.—
When hearts deserving happiness would unite their for-
tunes, Virtue would crown them with an unfading garland
of modest hurtless flowers; but ill-judging Passion will
force the gaudier rose into the wreath, whose thorn offends
them when its leaves are dropped! [*Exeunt omnes.*]

Epilogue

By the Author

[*Spoken by* MRS BULKLEY.]

Ladies, for you—I heard our poet say—
He'd try to coax some moral from his play:
"One moral's plain," cried I, "without more fuss;
Man's social happiness all rests on us:
Through all the drama—whether damn'd or not—
Love gilds the scene, and women guide the plot.
From every rank obedience is our due—
D'ye doubt?—The world's great stage shall prove it true."
    The cit,[51] well skill'd to shun domestic strife,
Will sup abroad! but first he'll ask his wife:
John Trot, his friend, for once will do the same,
But then—he'll just step home to tell his dame.
    The surly squire at noon resolves to rule,
And half the day—Zounds! madam is a fool!
Convinced at night, the vanquished victor says,
Ah, Kate! you women have such coaxing ways.
    The jolly toper chides each tardy blade,
Till reeling Bacchus calls on Love for aid:
Then with each toast he sees fair bumpers swim,
And kisses Chloe on the sparkling brim!
    Nay, I have heard that statemen—great and wise—
Will sometimes counsel with a lady's eyes!
The servile suitors watch her various face,
She smiles preferment, or she frowns disgrace,
Curtsies a pension here—there nods a place.
    Nor with less awe, in scenes of humbler life,
Is view'd the mistress, or is heard the wife.
The poorest peasant of the poorest soil,
The child of poverty, and heir to toil,

Early from radiant Love's impartial light
Steals one small spark to cheer this world of night:
Dear spark! that oft through winter's chilling woes
Is all the warmth his little cottage knows!
    The wandering tar, who not for years has press'd,
The widow'd partner of his day of rest,
On the cold deck, far from her arms removed,
Still hums the ditty which his Susan loved;
And while around the cadence rude is blown,
The boatswain whistles in a softer tone.
    The soldier, fairly proud of wounds and toil,
Pants for the triumph of his Nancy's smile!
But ere the battle should he list her cries,
The lover trembles—and the hero dies!
That heart, by war and honour steel'd to fear,
Droops on a sigh, and sickens at a tear!
    But ye more cautious, ye nice-judging few,
Who give to beauty only beauty's due,
Though friends to love—ye view with deep regret
Our conquests marr'd, our triumphs incomplete,
Till polish'd wit more lasting charms disclose,
And judgment fix the darts which beauty throws!
In female breasts did sense and merit rule,
The lover's mind would ask no other school;
Shamed into sense, the scholars of our eyes,
Our beaux from gallantry would soon be wise;
Would gladly light, their homage to improve,
The lamp of knowledge at the torch of love!

THE SCHOOL FOR SCANDAL

by RICHARD BRINSLEY SHERIDAN

Dramatis Personae

As originally acted at Drury Lane Theatre in 1777

SIR PETER TEAZLE	*Mr King*
SIR OLIVER SURFACE	*Mr Yates*
SIR TOBY BUMPER	*Mr Gaudry*
SIR BENJAMIN BACKBITE	*Mr Dodd*
JOSEPH SURFACE	*Mr Palmer*
CHARLES SURFACE	*Mr Smith*
CARELESS	*Mr Farren*
SNAKE	*Mr Packer*
CRABTREE	*Mr Parsons*
ROWLEY	*Mr Aickin*
MOSES	*Mr Baddeley*
TRIP	*Mr LaMash*
LADY TEAZLE	*Mrs Abingdon*
LADY SNEERWELL	*Miss Sherry*
MRS CANDOUR	*Miss Pope*
MARIA	*Miss P. Hopkins*

Gentlemen, Maid, and Servants

SCENE—*London*

A Portrait

Addressed to Mrs Crewe,[1] with the comedy of The School For Scandal

Tell me, ye prim adepts in Scandal's school,
Who rail by precept, and detract by rule,
Lives there no character, so tried, so known,
So decked with grace, and so unlike your own,
That even you assist her fame to raise,
Approve by envy, and by silence praise!
Attend!—a model shall attract your view—
Daughters of calumny, I summon you!
You shall decide if this a portrait prove,
Or fond creation of the Muse and Love.
Attend, ye virgin critics, shrewd and sage,
Ye matron censors of this childish age,
Whose peering eye and wrinkled front declare
A fixed antipathy to young and fair;
By cunning, cautious; or by nature, cold,
In maiden madness, virulently bold!
Attend, ye skilled to coin the precious tale,
Creating proof, where innuendos fail!
Whose practised memories, cruelly exact,
Omit no circumstance, except the fact!—
Attend, all ye who boast,—or old or young,—
The living libel of a slanderous tongue!
So shall my theme as far contrasted be,
As saints by fiends or hymns by calumny.
Come, gentle Amoret [2] (for 'neath that name
In worthier verse is sung thy beauty's fame),
Come—for but thee who seeks the Muse? and while
Celestial blushes check thy conscious smile,

With timid grace and hesitating eye,
The perfect model which I boast supply:—
Vain Muse! couldst thou the humblest sketch create
Of her, or slightest charm couldst imitate—
Could thy blest strain in kindred colors trace
The faintest wonder of her form and face—
Poets would study the immortal line,
And Reynolds' own *his* art subdued by thine;
That art, which well might added lustre give
To nature's best and heaven's superlative:
On Granby's cheek ' might bid new glories rise,
Or point a purer beam from Devon's eyes! '
Hard is the task to shape that beauty's praise,
Whose judgment scorns the homage flattery pays?
But praising Amoret we cannot err,
No tongue o'ervalues heaven, or flatters her!
Yet she by fate's perverseness—she alone
Would doubt our truth, nor deem such praise her own!
Adorning fashion, unadorned by dress,
Simple from taste, and not from carelessness;
Discreet in gesture, in deportment mild,
Not stiff with prudence, nor uncouthly wild:
No state has Amoret; no studied mien;
She frowns no *goddess*, and she moves no *queen*,
The softer charm that in her manner lies
Is framed to captivate, yet not surprise;
It justly suits th' expression of her face,—
'Tis less than dignity, and more than grace!
On her pure cheek the native hue is such,
That, formed by heaven to be admired so much,
The hand divine, with a less partial care,
Might well have fixed a fainter crimson there,
And bade the gentle inmate of her breast—
Inshrinèd Modesty—supply the rest.
But who the peril of her lips shall paint?
Strip them of smiles—still, still all words are faint!
But moving Love himself appears to teach
Their action, though denied to rule her speech;
And thou who seest her speak, and dost not hear,
Mourn not her distant accents 'scape thine ear;
Viewing those lips, thou still may'st make pretense

To judge of what she says, and swear 'tis sense:
Clothed with such grace, with such expression fraught,
They move in meaning, and they pause in thought!
But dost thou farther watch, with charmed surprise,
The mild irresolution of her eyes,
Curious to mark how frequent they repose,
In brief eclipse and momentary close—
Ah! seest thou not an ambushed Cupid there,
Too tim'rous of his charge, with jealous care
Veils and unveils those beams of heav'nly light,
Too full, too fatal else, for mortal sight?
Nor yet, such pleasing vengeance fond to meet,
In pard'ning dimples hope a safe retreat.
What though her peaceful breast should ne'er allow
Subduing frowns to arm her altered brow,
By Love, I swear, and by his gentle wiles,
More fatal still the mercy of her smiles!
Thus lovely, thus adorned, possessing all
Of bright or fair that can to woman fall,
The height of vanity might well be thought
Prerogative in her, and Nature's fault.
Yet gentle Amoret, in mind supreme
As well as charms, rejects the vainer theme;
And, half mistrustful of her beauty's store,
She barbs with wit those darts too keen before:—
Read in all knowledge that her sex should reach,
Though Greville,⁶ or the Muse, should deign to teach,
Fond to improve, nor tim'rous to discern
How far it is a woman's grace to learn;
In Millar's⁷ dialect she would not prove
Apollo's priestess, but Apollo's love,
Graced by those signs which truth delights to own,
The timid blush, and mild submitted tone:
Whate'er she says, though sense appear throughout,
Displays the tender hue of female doubt;
Decked with that charm, how lovely wit appears,
How graceful *science*, when that robe she wears!
Such too her talents, and her bent of mind,
As speak a sprightly heart by thought refined:
A taste for mirth, by contemplation schooled,
A turn for ridicule, by candor ruled,

A scorn of folly, which she tries to hide;
An awe of talent, which she owns with pride!
 Peace, idle Muse! no more thy strain prolong,
But yield a theme, thy warmest praises wrong;
Just to her merit, though thou canst not raise
Thy feeble verse, behold th' acknowledged praise
Has spread conviction through the envious train,
And cast a fatal gloom o'er Scandal's reign!
And lo! each pallid hag, with blistered tongue,
Mutters assent to all thy zeal has sung—
Owns all the colors just—the outline true:
Thee my inspirer, and my *model*—CREWE!

Prologue

Spoken by MR KING [8]

Written by D. GARRICK, ESQ. [9]

A School for Scandal! tell me, I beseech you,
Needs there a school—this modish art to teach you?
No need of lessons now;—the knowing think—
We might as well be taught to eat and drink;
Caus'd by a dearth of scandal, should the vapours [10]
Distress our fair ones—let 'em read the papers;
Their powerful mixtures such disorders hit;
Crave what you will—there's *quantum sufficit.* [11]
'Lord!' cries my Lady Wormwood (who loves tattle,
And puts much salt and pepper in her prattle),
Just ris'n at noon, all night at cards, when threshing
Strong tea and scandal—'Bless me, how refreshing!
Give me the papers, *Lisp*—how bold and free! [*Sips.*]
Last night Lord L. [*Sips.*] was caught with Lady D.
For aching heads what charming *sal volatile!* [12] [*Sips.*]
If Mrs B. will still continue flirting,
We hope she'll *draw,* or we'll *undraw* the curtain.
Fine satire, poz [13]—in public all abuse it,
But, by ourselves, [*sips*] our praise we can't refuse it.
Now, *Lisp,* read you—there, at that dash and star.' [14]
'Yes, ma'am—A certain Lord had best beware,
Who lives not twenty miles from Grosv'nor Square; [15]
For should he Lady W——find willing,—
Wormwood is bitter'—'Oh! that's me! the villain!
Throw it behind the fire, and never more
Let that vile paper *come within my door.*'
Thus at our friends we laugh, who feel the dart;
To reach *our* feelings, we ourselves must smart.
Is our young bard so young—to think that he
Can stop the full spring-tide of calumny?
Knows he the world so little, and its trade?

Alas! the devil's sooner *rais'd* than *laid*.
So strong, so swift, the monster there's no gagging:
Cut Scandal's head off, still the tongue is wagging.
Proud of your smiles once lavishly bestow'd,
Again our young Don Quixote[16] takes the road;
To show his gratitude he draws his pen,
And seeks this Hydra, Scandal, in his den.
From his fell gripe the frighted fair to save—
Tho' he should fall th' attempt must please the brave.
For your applause all perils he would through—
He'll fight—that's write—a cavalero true,
Till every drop of blood—that's ink—is spilt for you.

Act one.

SCENE I

[LADY SNEERWELL'S *house.*]

[LADY SNEERWELL *at the dressing-table.* MR SNAKE *drinking chocolate.*]

LADY SNEERWELL

The paragraphs, you say, Mr Snake, were all inserted?

SNAKE

They were, madam; and as I copied them myself in a feigned hand, there can be no suspicion whence they came.

LADY SNEERWELL

Did you circulate the report of Lady Brittle's intrigue with Captain Boastall?

SNAKE

That's in as fine a train as your ladyship could wish. In the common course of things, I think it must reach Mrs Clackit's ears within four-and-twenty hours; and then, you know, the business is as good as done.

LADY SNEERWELL

Why, truly, Mrs Clackit has a very pretty talent, and a great deal of industry.

SNAKE

True, madam, and has been tolerably successful in her day. To my knowledge she has been the cause of six matches being broken off, and three sons disinherited; of four forced elopements, and as many close confinements; nine separate maintenances, and two divorces. Nay, I have more than once traced her causing a *tête-à-tête* in the *Town and Country Magazine*,[17] when the parties, perhaps, had never seen each other's face before in the course of their lives.

LADY SNEERWELL

She certainly has talents, but her manner is gross.

SNAKE

'Tis very true.—She generally designs well, has a free tongue and a bold invention; but her colouring is too dark, and her outlines often extravagant. She wants that delicacy of tint, and mellowness of sneer, which distinguish your ladyship's scandal.

LADY SNEERWELL

You are partial, Snake.

SNAKE

Not in the least—everybody allows that Lady Sneerwell can do more with a word or look, than many can with the most laboured detail, even when they happen to have a little truth on their side to support it.

LADY SNEERWELL

Yes, my dear Snake; and I am no hypocrite to deny the satisfaction I reap from the success of my efforts. Wounded myself, in the early part of my life, by the envenomed tongue of slander, I confess I have since known no pleasure equal to the reducing others to the level of my own injured reputation.

SNAKE

Nothing can be more natural. But, Lady Sneerwell, there is one affair in which you have lately employed me, wherein, I confess, I am at a loss to guess your motives.

LADY SNEERWELL

I conceive you mean with respect to my neighbour, Sir Peter Teazle, and his family?

SNAKE

I do. Here are two young men, to whom Sir Peter has acted as a kind of guardian since their father's death; the eldest possessing the most amiable character, and universally well spoken of; the youngest, the most dissipated and extravagant young fellow in the kingdom, without friends or character: the former an avowed admirer of your ladyship's, and apparently your favourite; the latter attached to Maria, Sir Peter's ward, and confessedly beloved by her. Now on the face of these circumstances, it is utterly unaccountable to me, why you, the widow of a city knight,[18] with a good jointure,[19] should not close with[20] the passion

of a man of such character and expectations as Mr
Surface; and more so why you should be so uncommonly
earnest to destroy the mutual attachment subsisting between his brother Charles and Maria.

LADY SNEERWELL

Then at once to unravel this mystery, I must inform you,
that love has no share whatever in the intercourse between
Mr Surface and me.

SNAKE

No!

LADY SNEERWELL

His real attachment is to Maria, or her fortune; but finding in his brother a favoured rival, he has been obliged to
mask his pretensions, and profit by my assistance.

SNAKE

Yet still I am more puzzled why you should interest yourself in his success.

LADY SNEERWELL

How dull you are! Cannot you surmise the weakness which
I hitherto, through shame, have concealed even from you?
Must I confess that Charles, that libertine, that extravagant,
that bankrupt in fortune and reputation, that he it is for
whom I'm thus anxious and malicious, and to gain whom I
would sacrifice everything?

SNAKE

Now, indeed, your conduct appears consistent; but how
came you and Mr Surface so confidential?

LADY SNEERWELL

For our mutual interest. I have found him out a long time
since. I know him to be artful, selfish, and malicious—in
short, a sentimental knave; while with Sir Peter, and indeed
with all his acquaintance, he passes for a miracle of prudence, good sense, and benevolence.

SNAKE

Yes; yet Sir Peter vows he has not his equal in England,
and above all, he praises him as a man of sentiment.

LADY SNEERWELL

True—and with the assistance of his sentiment and hypocrisy he has brought Sir Peter entirely into his interest with
regard to Maria, while poor Charles has no friend in the
house, though, I fear, he has a powerful one in Maria's

heart, against whom we must direct our schemes.

[*Enter* SERVANT.]

SERVANT

Mr Surface.

LADY SNEERWELL

Show him up. [*Exit* SERVANT.] He generally calls about this time. I don't wonder at people giving him to me for a lover.

[*Enter* JOSEPH SURFACE.]

JOSEPH SURFACE

My dear Lady Sneerwell, how do you do today? Mr Snake, your most obedient.

LADY SNEERWELL

Snake has just been rallying me on our mutual attachment; but I have informed him of our real views. You know how useful he has been to us, and, believe me, the confidence is not ill-placed.

JOSEPH SURFACE

Madam, it is impossible for me to suspect a man of Mr Snake's sensibility and discernment.

LADY SNEERWELL

Well, well, no compliments now; but tell me when you saw your mistress, Maria—or, what is more material to me, your brother.

JOSEPH SURFACE

I have not seen either since I left you; but I can inform you that they never meet. Some of your stories have taken a good effect on Maria.

LADY SNEERWELL

Ah! my dear Snake! the merit of this belongs to you: but do your brother's distresses increase?

JOSEPH SURFACE

Every hour. I am told he has had another execution[21] in the house yesterday. In short, his dissipation and extravagance exceed anything I have ever heard of.

LADY SNEERWELL

Poor Charles!

JOSEPH SURFACE

True, madam; notwithstanding his vices, one can't help feeling for him. Aye poor Charles, indeed! I'm sure I wish it were in my power to be of any essential service to him;

for the man who does not share in the distresses of a brother, even though merited by his own misconduct, deserves—

LADY SNEERWELL

O Lud! you are going to be moral, and forget that you are among friends.

JOSEPH SURFACE

Egad, that's true!—I'll keep that sentiment till I see Sir Peter;—however, it is certainly a charity to rescue Maria from such a libertine, who, if he is to be reclaimed, can be so only by a person of your ladyship's superior accomplishments and understanding.

SNAKE

I believe, Lady Sneerwell, here's company coming: I'll go and copy the letter I mentioned to you.—Mr Surface, your most obedient. [*Exit* SNAKE.]

JOSEPH SURFACE

Sir, your very devoted.—Lady Sneerwell, I am very sorry you have put any further confidence in that fellow.

LADY SNEERWELL

Why so?

JOSEPH SURFACE

I have lately detected him in frequent conference with old Rowley, who was formerly my father's steward, and has never, you know, been a friend of mine.

LADY SNEERWELL

And do you think he would betray us?

JOSEPH SURFACE

Nothing more likely:—take my word for't, Lady Sneerwell, that fellow hasn't virtue enough to be faithful even to his own villainy.—Ah! Maria!

[*Enter* MARIA.]

LADY SNEERWELL

Maria, my dear, how do you do?—What's the matter?

MARIA

O there's that disagreeable lover[22] of mine, Sir Benjamin Backbite, has just called at my guardian's, with his odious uncle, Crabtree; so I slipped out, and ran hither to avoid them.

LADY SNEERWELL

Is that all?

JOSEPH SURFACE

If my brother Charles had been of the party, madam, perhaps you would not have been so much alarmed.

LADY SNEERWELL

Nay, now you are severe; for I dare swear the truth of the matter is, Maria heard *you* were here.—But, my dear, what has Sir Benjamin done, that you would avoid him?

MARIA

Oh, he has done nothing—but 'tis for what he has said: his conversation is a perpetual libel on all his acquaintance.

JOSEPH SURFACE

Ay, and the worst of it is, there is no advantage in not knowing him—for he'll abuse a stranger just as his best friend; and his uncle is as bad.

LADY SNEERWELL

Nay, but we should make allowance—Sir Benjamin is a wit and a poet.

MARIA

For my part, I confess, madam, wit loses its respect with me, when I see it in company with malice.—What do you think, Mr Surface?

JOSEPH SURFACE

Certainly, madam; to smile at the jest which plants a thorn in another's breast is to become a principal in the mischief.

LADY SNEERWELL

Pshaw!—there's no possibility of being witty without a little ill nature: the malice of a good thing is the barb that makes it stick.—What's your opinion, Mr Surface?

JOSEPH SURFACE

To be sure, madam; that conversation, where the spirit of raillery is suppressed, will ever appear tedious and insipid.

MARIA

Well, I'll not debate how far scandal may be allowable; but in a man, I am sure, it is always contemptible. We have pride, envy, rivalship, and a thousand motives to depreciate each other; but the male slanderer must have the cowardice of a woman before he can traduce one.

[*Enter* SERVANT.]

SERVANT

Madam, Mrs Candour is below, and, if your ladyship's at

leisure, will leave her carriage.

LADY SNEERWELL

Beg her to walk in.—[*Exit* SERVANT.] Now, Maria, here is a character to your taste; for, though Mrs Candour is a little talkative, everybody allows her to be the best-natured and best sort of woman.

MARIA

Yet with a very gross affectation of good nature and benevolence, she does more mischief than the direct malice of old Crabtree.

JOSEPH SURFACE

I'faith 'tis true, Lady Sneerwell: whenever I hear the current running against the characters of my friends, I never think them in such danger as when Candour undertakes their defence.

LADY SNEERWELL

Hush!—here she is!—

   [*Enter* MRS CANDOUR.]

MRS CANDOUR

My dear Lady Sneerwell, how have you been this century? —Mr Surface, what news do you hear?—though indeed it is no matter, for I think one hears nothing else but scandal.

JOSEPH SURFACE

Just so, indeed, ma'am.

MRS CANDOUR

Ah! Maria child,—what, is the whole affair off between you and Charles?—His extravagance, I presume—the town talks of nothing else.

MARIA

I am very sorry, ma'am, the town has so little to do.

MRS CANDOUR

True, true, child: but there's no stopping people's tongues. I own I was hurt to hear it, as I indeed was to learn, from the same quarter, that your guardian, Sir Peter, and Lady Teazle have not agreed lately as well as could be wished.

MARIA

'Tis strangely impertinent for people to busy themselves so.

MRS CANDOUR

Very true, child;—but what's to be done? People will talk —there's no preventing it. Why, it was but yesterday I

was told that Miss Gadabout had eloped with Sir Filagree
Flirt.—But, Lord! there is no minding what one hears;
though, to be sure, I had this from very good authority.

MARIA

Such reports are highly scandalous.

MRS CANDOUR

So they are, child—shameful! shameful! But the world is
so censorious, no character escapes.—Lord now! who
would have suspected your friend, Miss Prim, of an indiscretion? Yet such is the ill-nature of people, that they
say her uncle stopped her last week, just as she was step-
ping into the York diligence²² with her dancing-master.

MARIA

I'll answer for't there are no grounds for the report.

MRS CANDOUR

O no foundation in the world, I dare swear: no more,
probably, than for the story circulated last month, of
Mrs Festino's affair with Colonel Cassino;—though to be
sure, that matter was never rightly cleared up.

JOSEPH SURFACE

The licence of invention some people take is monstrous
indeed.

MARIA

'Tis so; but, in my opinion, those who report such things
are equally culpable.

MRS CANDOUR

To be sure they are; tale-bearers are as bad as the tale-
makers—'tis an old observation, and a very true one: but
what's to be done, as I said before? How will you prevent
people from talking? Today, Mrs Clackit assured me, Mr
and Mrs Honeymoon were at last become mere man and
wife, like the rest of their acquaintance. She likewise
hinted that a certain widow, in the next street, had got rid
of her dropsy and recovered her shape in a most surprising manner. And at the same time Miss Tattle, who was
by, affirmed, that Lord Buffalo had discovered his lady at
a house of no extraordinary fame; and that Sir Harry
Bouquet and Tom Saunter were to measure swords on a
similar provocation. But, Lord, do you think that I would
report these things! No, no! tale-bearers, as I said before,
are just as bad as the tale-makers.

JOSEPH SURFACE

Ah! Mrs Candour, if everybody had your forebearance and good nature!

MRS CANDOUR

I confess, Mr Surface, I cannot bear to hear people attacked behind their backs; and when ugly circumstances come out against our acquaintance I own I always love to think the best.—By-the-by, I hope 'tis not true that your brother is absolutely ruined?

JOSEPH SURFACE

I am afraid his circumstances are very bad indeed, madam.

MRS CANDOUR

Ah! I heard so—but you must tell him to keep up his spirits; everybody almost is in the same way—Lord Spindle, Sir Thomas Splint, Captain Quinze, and Mr Nickit—all up, I hear, within this week; so if Charles is undone, he'll find half his acquaintance ruined too, and that, you know, is a consolation.

JOSEPH SURFACE

Doubtless, ma'am—a very great one.

[*Enter* SERVANT.]

SERVANT

Mr Crabtree and Sir Benjamin Backbite.

[*Exit* SERVANT.]

LADY SNEERWELL

So, Maria, you see your lover pursues you; positively you shan't escape.

[*Enter* CRABTREE *and* SIR BENJAMIN BACKBITE.]

CRABTREE

Lady Sneerwell, I kiss your hand—Mrs Candour, I don't believe you are acquainted with my nephew, Sir Benjamin Backbite? Egad! ma'am, he has a pretty wit, and is a pretty poet too; isn't he, Lady Sneerwell?

SIR BENJAMIN

Oh, fie, uncle!

CRABTREE

Nay, egad it's true: I back him at a rebus or a charade against the best rhymer in the kingdom.—Has your ladyship heard the epigram he wrote last week on Lady Frizzle's feather catching fire?—Do Benjamin, repeat it, or the charade you made last night extempore at Mrs Drowzie's conversazione.[24] Come now;—your first is the name of a fish, your second a great naval commander, and—

SIR BENJAMIN

Uncle, now—prythee—

CRABTREE

I'faith, ma'am, 'twould surprise you to hear how ready he is at all these things.

LADY SNEERWELL

I wonder, Sir Benjamin, you never publish anything.

SIR BENJAMIN

To say truth, ma'am, 'tis very vulgar to print; and, as my little productions are mostly satires and lampoons on particular people, I find they circulate more by giving copies in confidence to the friends of the parties. However, I have some love elegies, which, when favoured with this lady's smiles, I mean to give the public.

CRABTREE

'Fore heaven, ma'am, they'll immortalize you!—you will be handed down to posterity, like Petrarch's Laura,[25] or Waler's Sacharissa.[26]

SIR BENJAMIN

Yes, madam, I think you will like them, when you shall see them on a beautiful quarto page, where a neat rivulet of text shall meander through a meadow of margin. 'Fore Gad, they will be the most elegant things of their kind!

CRABTREE

But, ladies, that's true—have you heard the news?

MRS CANDOUR

What, sir, do you mean the report of—

CRABTREE

No, ma'am, that's not it.—Miss Nicely is going to be married to her own footman.

MRS CANDOUR

Impossible!

CRABTREE

Ask Sir Benjamin.

SIR BENJAMIN

'Tis very true, ma'am: everything is fixed, and the wedding liveries bespoke.

CRABTREE

Yes—and they do say there were pressing reasons for it.

LADY SNEERWELL

Why, I have heard something of this before.

MRS CANDOUR

It can't be—and I wonder any one should believe such a story, of so prudent a lady as Miss Nicely.

SIR BENJAMIN

O Lud! ma'am, that's the very reason 'twas believed at once. She has always been so cautious and so reserved, that everybody was sure there was some reason for it at bottom.

MRS CANDOUR

Why, to be sure, a tale of scandal is as fatal to the credit of a prudent lady of her stamp as a fever is generally to those of the strongest constitutions. But there is a sort of puny sickly reputation, that is always ailing, yet will outlive the robuster characters of a hundred prudes.

SIR BENJAMIN

True, madam,—there are valetudinarians in reputation as well as constitution, who, being conscious of their weak part, avoid the least breath of air, and supply their want of stamina by care and circumspection.

MRS CANDOUR

Well, but this may be all a mistake. You know, Sir Benjamin, very trifling circumstances often give rise to the most injurious tales.

CRABTREE

That they do, I'll be sworn, ma'am.—Did you ever hear how Miss Piper came to lose her lover and her character last summer at Tunbridge?—Sir Benjamin, you remember it?

SIR BENJAMIN

Oh, to be sure!—the most whimsical circumstance.

LADY SNEERWELL

How was it, pray?

CRABTREE

Why, one evening, at Mrs Ponto's assembly, the conversation happened to turn on the difficulty of breeding Nova Scotia sheep in this country. Says a young lady in company, I have known instances of it; for Miss Letitia Piper,

a first cousin of mine, had a Nova Scotia sheep that produced her twins. What! cries the Lady Dowager Dundizzy
(who you know is as deaf as a post), has Miss Piper had
twins?—This mistake, as you may imagine, threw the
whole company into a fit of laughter. However, 'twas the
next day everywhere reported, and in a few days believed
by the whole town, that Miss Letitia Piper had actually
been brought to bed of a fine boy and girl.

LADY SNEERWELL

Strange, indeed!

CRABTREE

Matter of fact, I assure you.—O Lud! Mr Surface, pray
is it true that your uncle, Sir Oliver, is coming home?

JOSEPH SURFACE

Not that I know of, indeed, sir.

CRABTREE

He has been in the East Indies a long time. You can
scarcely remember him, I believe—Sad comfort, whenever
he returns, to hear how your brother has gone on!

JOSEPH SURFACE

Charles has been imprudent, sir, to be sure; but I hope no
busy people have already prejudiced Sir Oliver against
him—he may reform.

SIR BENJAMIN

To be sure he may: for my part, I never believed him to be
so utterly void of principle as people say; and though he
has lost all his friends, I am told nobody is better spoken
of by the Jews.

CRABTREE

That's true, egad, nephew. If the Old Jewry[27] was a ward,
I believe Charles would be an alderman:—no man more
popular there, 'fore Gad! I hear he pays as many annuities
as the Irish tontine;[28] and that, whenever he is sick, they
have prayers for the recovery of his health in all the
synagogues.

SIR BENJAMIN

Yet no man lives in greater splendour. They tell me, when
he entertains his friends he will sit down to dinner with a
dozen of his own securities; have a score of tradesmen
waiting in the antechamber, and an officer behind every
guest's chair.[29]

JOSEPH SURFACE

This may be entertainment to you, gentlemen, but you pay very little regard to the feelings of a brother.

MARIA

Their malice is intolerable!—Lady Sneerwell, I must wish you a good morning: I'm not very well. [*Exit* MARIA.]

MRS CANDOUR

O dear! she changes colour very much.

LADY SNEERWELL

Do, Mrs Candour, follow her; she may want assistance.

MRS CANDOUR

That I will, with all my soul, ma'am.—Poor dear creature, who knows what her situation may be! [*Exit.*]

LADY SNEERWELL

'Twas nothing but that she could not bear to hear Charles reflected on, notwithstanding their difference.

SIR BENJAMIN

The young lady's *penchant* is obvious.

CRABTREE

But, Benjamin, you must not give up the pursuit for that: —follow her, and put her into good humour. Repeat her some of your own verses. Come, I'll assist you.

SIR BENJAMIN

Mr Surface, I did not mean to hurt you; but depend on't your brother is utterly undone.

CRABTREE

O Lud, ay! undone as ever man was. Can't raise a guinea!

SIR BENJAMIN

Everything sold, I am told, that was movable.

CRABTREE

I have seen one that was at his house. Not a thing left but some empty bottles that were overlooked, and the family pictures, which I believe are framed in the wainscot.—

SIR BENJAMIN

And I'm very sorry also to hear some bad stories against him. [*Going.*]

CRABTREE

O! he has done many mean things, that's certain.

SIR BENJAMIN

But, however, as he's your brother—[*Going.*]

CRABTREE

We'll tell you all another opportunity. [*Exeunt.*]

LADY SNEERWELL

Ha! ha! 'tis very hard for them to leave a subject they have
not quite run down.

JOSEPH SURFACE

And I believe the abuse was no more acceptable to your
ladyship than to Maria.

LADY SNEERWELL

I doubt [30] her affections are further engaged than we
imagine. But the family are to be here this evening, so you
may as well dine where you are, and we shall have an
opportunity of observing further; in the meantime, I'll go
and plot mischief, and you shall study sentiment. [*Exeunt.*]

SCENE II

[SIR PETER TEAZLE'S *house.*]

[*Enter* SIR PETER.]

SIR PETER

When an old bachelor marries a young wife, what is he
to expect? 'Tis now six months since Lady Teazle made
me the happiest of men—and I have been the most
miserable dog ever since that ever committed wedlock!
We tiffed a little going to church, and came to a quarrel
before the bells had done ringing. I was more than once
nearly choked with gall during my honeymoon, and had
lost all comfort in life before my friends had done wishing
me joy. Yet I chose with caution—a girl bred wholly in
the country, who never knew luxury beyond one silk gown,
nor dissipation above the annual gala of a race ball. Yet
she now plays her part in all the extravagant fopperies of
the fashion and the town, with as ready a grace as if she
never had seen a bush or a grass-plot out of Grosvenor
Square! I am sneered at by all my acquaintance, and

paragraphed in the newspapers. She dissipates my fortune, and contradicts all my humours; yet the worst of it is, I doubt I love her, or I should never bear all this. However, I'll never be weak enough to own it.

[*Enter* ROWLEY.]

ROWLEY

O! Sir Peter, your servant; how is it with you, sir?

SIR PETER

Very bad, Master Rowley, very bad. I meet with nothing but crosses and vexations.

ROWLEY

What can have happened to trouble you since yesterday?

SIR PETER

A good question to a married man!

ROWLEY

Nay, I'm sure, Sir Peter, your lady can't be the cause of your uneasiness.

SIR PETER

Why, has anybody told you she was dead?

ROWLEY

Come, come, Sir Peter, you love her notwithstanding your tempers don't exactly agree.

SIR PETER

But the fault is entirely hers, Master Rowley. I am, myself, the sweetest-tempered man alive, and hate a teasing temper; and so I tell her a hundred times a day.

ROWLEY

Indeed!

SIR PETER

Ay; and what is very extraordinary, in all our disputes she is always in the wrong! But Lady Sneerwell, and the set she meets at her house, encourage the perverseness of her disposition.—Then, to complete my vexation, Maria, my ward, whom I ought to have the power of a father over, is determined to turn rebel too, and absolutely refuses the man whom I have long resolved on for her husband; meaning, I suppose, to bestow herself on his profligate brother.

ROWLEY

You know, Sir Peter, I have always taken the liberty to differ with you on the subject of these two young gentle-

men. I only wish you may not be deceived in your opinion
of the elder. For Charles, my life on't! he will retrieve
his errors yet. Their worthy father, once my honoured
master, was, at his years, nearly as wild a spark; yet, when
he died, he did not leave a more benevolent heart to
lament his loss.

SIR PETER

You are wrong, Master Rowley. On their father's death,
you know, I acted as a kind of guardian to them both,
till their uncle Sir Oliver's eastern liberality gave them an
early independence—of course, no person could have
more opportunities of judging of their hearts, and I was
never mistaken in my life. Joseph is indeed a model for the
young men of the age. He is a man of sentiment, and acts
up to the sentiments he professes; but, for the other, take
my word for't, if he had any grain of virtue by descent, he
has dissipated it with the rest of his inheritance. Ah! my
old friend, Sir Oliver, will be deeply mortified when he finds
how part of his bounty has been misapplied.

ROWLEY

I am sorry to find you so violent against the young man,
because this may be the most critical period of his fortune.
I came hither with news that will surprise you.

SIR PETER

What! let me hear.

ROWLEY

Sir Oliver is arrived, and at this moment in town.

SIR PETER

How! you astonish me! I thought you did not expect him
this month.

ROWLEY

I did not: but his passage has been remarkably quick.

SIR PETER

Egad, I shall rejoice to see my old friend. 'Tis sixteen years
since we met.—We have had many a day together:—but
does he still enjoin us not to inform his nephews of his
arrival?

ROWLEY

Most strictly. He means, before it is known, to make some
trial of their dispositions.

SIR PETER

Ah! There needs no art to discover their merits—he shall
have his way; but, pray, does he know I am married?

ROWLEY

Yes, and will soon wish you joy.

SIR BENJAMIN

What, as we drink health to a friend in a consumption!
Ah! Oliver will laugh at me. We used to rail at matrimony
together, but he has been steady to his text.—Well, he
must be soon at my house, though!—I'll instantly give
orders for his reception. But, Master Rowley, don't drop
a word that Lady Teazle and I ever disagree.

ROWLEY

By no means.

SIR PETER

For I should never be able to stand Noll's jokes; so I'll
have him think, Lord forgive me! that we are a very happy
couple.

ROWLEY

I understand you:—but then you must be very careful not
to differ while he is in the house with you.

SIR PETER

Egad, and so we must—and that's impossible. Ah! Master
Rowley, when an old bachelor marries a young wife, he
deserves—no—the crime carries its punishment along
with it. [*Exeunt.*]

End of the First Act.

Act two.

SCENE I

[SIR PETER TEAZLE'S *house*.]

[*Enter* SIR PETER *and* LADY TEAZLE.]

SIR PETER
Lady Teazle, Lady Teazle, I'll not bear it!

LADY TEAZLE
Sir Peter, Sir Peter, you may bear it or not, as you please;
but I ought to have my own way in everything, and what's
more, I will too. What! though I was educated in the
country, I know very well that women of fashion in London
are accountable to nobody after they are married.

SIR PETER
Very well, ma'am, very well;—so a husband is to have no
influence, no authority?

LADY TEAZLE
Authority! No, to be sure:—if you wanted authority over
me, you should have adopted me, and not married me: I
am sure you were old enough.

SIR PETER
Old enough!—aye, there it is! Well, well, Lady Teazle,
though my life may be made unhappy by your temper,
I'll not be ruined by your extravagance!

LADY TEAZLE
My extravagance! I'm sure I'm not more extravagant than
a woman of fashion ought to be.

SIR PETER
No, no, madam, you shall throw away no more sums on
such unmeaning luxury. 'Slife! to spend as much to furnish
your dressing-room with flowers in winter as would suffice

to turn the Pantheon[31] into a greenhouse, and give a *fête champêtre*[32] at Christmas.

LADY TEAZLE

Lord, Sir Peter, am I to blame, because flowers are dear in cold weather? You should find fault with the climate, and not with me. For my part, I'm sure, I wish it was spring all the year round, and that roses grew under one's feet!

SIR PETER

Oons! madam—if you had been born to this, I shouldn't wonder at your talking thus; but you forget what your situation was when I married you.

LADY TEAZLE

No, no, I don't; 'twas a very disagreeable one, or I should never have married you.

SIR PETER

Yes, yes, madam, you were then in somewhat an humbler style:—the daughter of a plain country squire. Recollect, Lady Teazle, when I saw you first, sitting at your tambour,[33] in a pretty figured linen gown, with a bunch of keys at your side, your hair combed smooth over a roll, and your apartment hung round with fruits in worsted, of your own working.

LADY TEAZLE

Oh, yes! I remember it very well, and a curious life I led! my daily occupation to inspect the dairy, superintend the poultry, make extracts from the family receipt-book, and comb my Aunt Deborah's lapdog.

SIR PETER

Yes, yes, madam, 'twas so indeed.

LADY TEAZLE

And then, you know, my evening amusements! To draw patterns for ruffles, which I had not the materials to make up; to play Pope Joan[34] with the curate; to read a sermon to my aunt; or to be stuck down to an old spinet to strum my father to sleep after a fox-chase.

SIR PETER

I am glad you have so good a memory. Yes, madam, these were the recreations I took you from; but now you must have your coach—*vis-à-vis*[35]—and three powdered footmen before your chair; and, in the summer, a pair of white cats[36] to draw you to Kensington Gardens.[37] No recollection, I suppose, when you were content to ride double, behind the butler, on a dock'd coach-horse?

LADY TEAZLE

No—I swear I never did that; I deny the butler and the coach-horse.

SIR PETER

This, madam, was your situation; and what have I done for you? I have made you a woman of fashion, of fortune, of rank;—in short, I have made you *my wife*.

LADY TEAZLE

Well, then,—and there is but one thing more you can make me to add to the obligation, that is—

SIR PETER

My widow, I suppose?

LADY TEAZLE

Hem! hem!

SIR PETER

I thank you, madam—but don't flatter yourself; for, though your ill conduct may disturb my peace of mind, it shall never break my heart, I promise you: however, I am equally obliged to you for the hint.

LADY TEAZLE

Then why will you endeavour to make yourself so disagreeable to me, and thwart me in every little elegant expense?

SIR PETER

'Slife, madam, I say, had you any of these little elegant expenses when you married me?

LADY TEAZLE

Lud, Sir Peter! would you have me be out of the fashion?

SIR PETER

The fashion, indeed! what had you to do with the fashion when you married me?

LADY TEAZLE

For my part, I should think you would like to have your wife thought a woman of taste.

SIR PETER

Aye—there again—taste—Zounds! madam, you had no taste when you married me!

LADY TEAZLE

That's very true, indeed, Sir Peter; and, after having married you, I am sure I should never pretend to taste

again. But now, Sir Peter, since we have finished our
daily jangle, I presume I may go to my engagement at
Lady Sneerwell's?

SIR PETER

Aye, there's another precious circumstance—a charming
set of acquaintance you have made there!

LADY TEAZLE

Nay, Sir Peter, they are all people of rank and fortune,
and remarkably tenacious of reputation.

SIR PETER

Yes, egad, they are tenacious of reputation with a vengeance; for they don't choose anybody should have a
character but themselves!—Such a crew! Ah! many a
wretch has rid on a hurdle[38] who has done less mischief
than these utterers of forged tales, coiners of scandal, and
clippers of reputation.

LADY TEAZLE

What, would you restrain the freedom of speech?

SIR PETER

Oh! they have made you just as bad as any one of the
society.

LADY TEAZLE

Why, I believe I do bear a part with a tolerable grace. But
I vow I bear no malice against the people I abuse. When I
say an ill-natured thing, 'tis out of pure good humour; and
I take it for granted, they deal exactly in the same manner
with me. But, Sir Peter, you know you promised to come
to Lady Sneerwell's too.

SIR PETER

Well, well, I'll call in just to look after my own character.

LADY TEAZLE

Then, indeed, you must make haste after me or you'll be
too late. So good-bye to you. [*Exit* LADY TEAZLE.]

SIR PETER

So—I have gained much by my intended expostulation:
yet with what a charming air she contradicts everything
I say, and how pleasantly she shows her contempt for my
authority! Well, though I can't make her love me, there
is great satisfaction in quarrelling with her; and I think
she never appears to such advantage as when she is doing
everything in her power to plague me. [*Exit.*]

SCENE II

[LADY SNEERWELL'S *house*.]

[LADY SNEERWELL, MRS CANDOUR, CRABTREE, SIR BENJAMIN BACKBITE, *and* JOSEPH SURFACE *discovered*, SERVANTS *attending with tea*.]

LADY SNEERWELL
Nay, positively, we will hear it.

JOSEPH SURFACE
Yes, yes, the epigram, by all means.

SIR BENJAMIN
Oh, plague on't, uncle! 'tis mere nonsense.

CRABTREE
No, no; 'fore Gad, very clever for an extempore!

SIR BENJAMIN
But, ladies, you should be acquainted with the circumstances. You must know, that one day last week, as Lady Betty Curricle was taking the dust in Hyde Park,[30] in a sort of a duodecimo phaeton,[40] she desired me to write some verses on her ponies; upon which I took out my pocketbook, and in one moment produced the following:

Sure never were seen two such beautiful ponies;
Other horses are clowns, but these macaronies:[41]
To give 'em this title I am sure isn't wrong.
Their legs are so slim, and their tails are so long.

CRABTREE
There, ladies, done in the smack of a whip, and on horseback too.

JOSEPH SURFACE
A very Phoebus,[42] mounted—indeed, Sir Benjamin!

SIR BENJAMIN
Oh dear sir,—trifles—trifles.

[*Enter* LADY TEAZLE *and* MARIA.]

MRS CANDOUR

I must have a copy.

LADY SNEERWELL

Lady Teazle, I hope we shall see Sir Peter?

LADY TEAZLE

I believe he'll wait on your ladyship presently.

LADY SNEERWELL

Maria, my love, you look grave. Come, you shall sit down to cards with Mr Surface.

MARIA

I take very little pleasure in cards—however, I'll do as your ladyship pleases.

LADY TEAZLE

[*Aside.*] I am surprised Mr Surface should sit down with her; I thought he would have embraced this opportunity of speaking to me, before Sir Peter came.

MRS CANDOUR

Now, I'll die, but you are so scandalous, I'll forswear your society.

LADY TEAZLE

What's the matter, Mrs Candour?

MRS CANDOUR

They'll not allow our friend Miss Vermillion to be handsome.

LADY SNEERWELL

Oh, surely she's a pretty woman.

CRABTREE

I am very glad you think so, madam.

MRS CANDOUR

She has a charming fresh colour.

LADY TEAZLE

Yes, when it is fresh put on.

MRS CANDOUR

Oh, fie! I'll swear her colour is natural: I have seen it come and go!

LADY TEAZLE

I dare swear you have, ma'am: it goes off at night, and comes again in the morning.

SIR BENJAMIN

True, ma'am, it not only comes and goes, but, what's more

—egad, her maid can fetch and carry it!

MRS CANDOUR

Ha! ha! ha! how I hate to hear you talk so! But surely, now, her sister *is,* or *was,* very handsome.

CRABTREE

Who? Mrs Evergreen? O Lord! she's six-and-fifty if she's an hour!

MRS CANDOUR

Now positively you wrong her; fifty-two or fifty-three is the utmost—and I don't think she looks more.

SIR BENJAMIN

Ah! there's no judging by her looks, unless one could see her face.

LADY SNEERWELL

Well, well, if Mrs Evergreen *does* take some pains to repair the ravages of time, you must allow she effects it with great ingenuity; and surely that's better than the careless manner in which the widow Ochre caulks her wrinkles.

SIR BENJAMIN

Nay, now, Lady Sneerwell, you are severe upon the widow. Come, come, 'tis not that she paints so ill—but, when she has finished her face, she joins it on so badly to her neck, that she looks like a mended statue, in which the connoisseur may see at once that the head's modern, though the trunk's antique!

CRABTREE

Ha! ha! ha! Well said, nephew!

MRS CANDOUR

Ha! ha! ha! Well, you make me laugh; but I vow I hate you for it.—What do you think of Miss Simper?

SIR BENJAMIN

Why, she has very pretty teeth.

LADY TEAZLE

Yes, and on that account, when she is neither speaking nor laughing (which very seldom happens), she never absolutely shuts her mouth, but leaves it always on a jar, as it were, thus—[*Shows her teeth.*]

MRS CANDOUR

How can you be so ill-natured?

LADY TEAZLE

Nay, I'll allow even that's better than the pains Mrs Prim takes to conceal her losses in front. She draws her mouth till it positively resembles the aperture of a poor's-box,⁴³ and all her words appear to slide out edgewise. As it were thus: *How do you do, madam? Yes, madam.*

LADY SNEERWELL

Very well, Lady Teazle; I see you can be a little severe.

LADY TEAZLE

In defence of a friend it is but justice.—But here comes Sir Peter to spoil our pleasantry.

[*Enter* SIR PETER TEAZLE.]

SIR PETER

Ladies, your most obedient. [*Aside.*] Mercy on me! here is the whole set! a character dead at every word, I suppose.

MRS CANDOUR

I am rejoiced you are come, Sir Peter. They have been so censorious—they will allow good qualities to nobody; not even good nature to our friend Mrs Pursy.

LADY TEAZLE

What, the fat dowager who was at Mrs Codrille's last night?

MRS CANDOUR

Nay, her bulk is her misfortune; and, when she takes so much pains to get rid of it, you ought not to reflect on her.

LADY SNEERWELL

That's very true, indeed.

LADY TEAZLE

Yes, I know she almost lives on acids and small whey; laces herself by pulleys; and often, in the hottest noon in summer, you may see her on a little squat pony, with her hair plaited up behind like a drummer's, and puffing round the Ring⁴⁴ on a full trot.

MRS CANDOUR

I thank you, Lady Teazle, for defending her.

SIR PETER

Yes, a good defence, truly.

MRS CANDOUR

But Sir Benjamin is as censorious as Miss Sallow.

CRABTREE

Yes, and she is a curious being to pretend to be censorious

—an awkward gawky, without any one good point under heaven.

MRS CANDOUR

Positively you shall not be so very severe. Miss Sallow is a relation of mine by marriage, and as for her person, great allowance is to be made; for, let me tell you, a woman labours under many disadvantages who tries to pass for a girl of six-and-thirty.

LADY SNEERWELL

Though, surely, she is handsome still—and for the weakness in her eyes, considering how much she reads by candle-light, it is not to be wondered at.

MRS CANDOUR

True, and then as to her manner; upon my word I think it is particularly graceful, considering she never had the least education; for you know her mother was a Welch milliner, and her father a sugar-baker⁴⁵ at Bristol.

SIR BENJAMIN

Ah! you are both of you too good-natured!

SIR PETER

[*Aside.*] Yes, damned good-natured! This their own relation! mercy on me!

MRS CANDOUR

For my part, I own I cannot bear to hear a friend ill spoken of.

SIR PETER

No, to be sure!

SIR BENJAMIN

And Mrs Candour is of so moral a turn, she can sit for an hour and hear Lady Stucco talk sentiment.

LADY TEAZLE

Nay, I vow Lady Stucco is very well with the dessert after dinner; for she's just like the French fruit⁴⁶ one cracks for mottoes—made up of paint and proverb.

MRS CANDOUR

Well, I never will join in ridiculing a friend; and so I constantly tell my cousin Ogle, and you all know what pretensions she has to be critical on beauty.

CRABTREE

Oh, to be sure! she has herself the oddest countenance that ever was seen; 'tis a collection of features from all the different countries of the globe.

SIR BENJAMIN

So she has, indeed——an Irish front——

CRABTREE

Caledonian locks——

SIR BENJAMIN

Dutch nose——

CRABTREE

Austrian lips——

SIR BENJAMIN

Complexion of a Spaniard——

CRABTREE

And teeth *à la Chinoise*——

SIR BENJAMIN

In short, her face resembles a *table d'hôte* at Spa[47]——
where no two guests are of a nation——

CRABTREE

Or a congress at the close of a general war——wherein all
the members, even to her eyes, appear to have a different
interest, and her nose and chin are the only parties likely to
join issue.

MRS CANDOUR

Ha! ha! ha!

SIR PETER

[*Aside.*] Mercy on my life!——a person they dine with twice
a week!

LADY SNEERWELL

Go, go; you are a couple of provoking toads.

MRS CANDOUR

Nay, but I vow you shall not carry the laugh off so——for
give me leave to say, that Mrs Ogle——

SIR PETER

Madam, madam, I beg your pardon——there's no stopping
these good gentlemen's tongues.——But when I tell you,
Mrs Candour, that the lady they are abusing is a particular
friend of mine, I hope you'll not take her part.

LADY SNEERWELL

Well said, Sir Peter! but you are a cruel creature——too
phlegmatic yourself for a jest, and too peevish to allow
wit in others.

SIR PETER

Ah! madam, true wit is more nearly allied to good-nature than your ladyship is aware of.

LADY TEAZLE

True, Sir Peter: I believe they are so near akin that they can never be united.

SIR BENJAMIN

Or rather, madam, suppose them to be man and wife, because one seldom sees them together.

LADY TEAZLE

But Sir Peter is such an enemy to scandal, I believe he would have it put down by Parliament.

SIR PETER

'Fore heaven, madam, if they were to consider the sporting with reputation of as much importance as poaching on manors, and pass an Act for the Preservation of Fame, I believe there are many who would thank them for the bill.

LADY SNEERWELL

O Lud! Sir Peter; would you deprive us of our privileges?

SIR PETER

Aye, madam; and then no person should be permitted to kill characters and run down reputations, but qualified old maids and disappointed widows.

LADY SNEERWELL

Go, you monster.

MRS CANDOUR

But, surely, you would not be quite so severe on those who only report what they hear?

SIR PETER

Yes, madam, I would have Law-Merchant [48] for them too; and in all cases of slander currency, whenever the drawer of the lie was not to be found, the injured parties should have a right to come on any of the indorsers.

CRABTREE

Well, for my part, I believe there never was a scandalous tale without some foundation.

LADY SNEERWELL

Come, ladies, shall we sit down to cards in the next room?

[*Enter* SERVANT, *who whispers* SIR PETER.]

SIR PETER

[*Apart.*] I'll be with them directly. I'll get away unperceived.

LADY SNEERWELL

Sir Peter, you are not going to leave us?

SIR PETER

Your ladyship must excuse me; I'm called away by
particular business. But I leave my character behind me.
[*Exit* SIR PETER.]

SIR BENJAMIN

Well—certainly, Lady Teazle, that lord of yours is a
strange being: I could tell you some stories of him would
make you laugh heartily—if he were not your husband.

LADY TEAZLE

Oh, pray don't mind that; come, do let's hear them. [LADY
T. *joins the rest of the company, going into the next room.*]

JOSEPH SURFACE

Maria, I see you have no satisfaction in this society.

MARIA

How is it possible I should? If to raise malicious smiles at
the infirmities or misfortunes of those who have never
injured us be the province of wit or humour, Heaven
grant me a double portion of dullness!

JOSEPH SURFACE

Yet they appear more ill-natured than they are—they have
no malice at heart.

MARIA

Then is their conduct still more contemptible; for, in my
opinion, nothing could excuse the intemperance of their
tongues, but a natural and uncontrollable bitterness of
mind.

JOSEPH SURFACE

But can you, Maria, feel thus for others, and be unkind to
me alone? Is hope to be denied the tenderest passion?

MARIA

Why will you distress me by renewing the subject?

JOSEPH SURFACE

Ah! Maria! you would not treat me thus, and oppose your
guardian, Sir Peter's will, but that I see that profligate
Charles is still a favoured rival.

MARIA

Ungenerously urged!—But whatever my sentiments are
for that unfortunate young man, be assured I shall not

feel more bound to give him up, because his distresses have lost him the regard even of a brother.

[*Enter* LADY TEAZLE *and comes forward.*]

JOSEPH SURFACE

Nay, but Maria, do not leave me with a frown: by all that's honest, I swear—[*Aside.*]—Gad's life, here's Lady Teazle.—You must not—no, you shall not—for, though I have the greatest regard for Lady Teazle—

MARIA

Lady Teazle!

JOSEPH SURFACE

Yet were Sir Peter once to suspect—

LADY TEAZLE

What is this, pray? Do you take her for me?—Child, you are wanted in the next room.—[*Exit* MARIA.]—What is all this, pray?

JOSEPH SURFACE

O, the most unlucky circumstance in nature! Maria has somehow suspected the tender concern I have for your happiness, and threatened to acquaint Sir Peter with her suspicions, and I was just endeavouring to reason with her when you came in.

LADY TEAZLE

Indeed! but you seemed to adopt a very tender mode of reasoning—do you usually argue on your knees?

JOSEPH SURFACE

Oh, she's a child, and I thought a little bombast.—But, Lady Teazle, when are you to give me your judgment on my library, as you promised?

LADY TEAZLE

No, no; I begin to think it would be imprudent, and you know I admit you as a lover no farther than fashion requires.

JOSEPH SURFACE

True—a mere platonic cicisbeo⁰—what every London wife is entitled to.

LADY TEAZLE

Certainly, one must not be out of the fashion. However, I have so many of my country prejudices left, that, though Sir Peter's ill-humour may vex me ever so, it never shall provoke me to—

JOSEPH SURFACE

The only revenge in your power. Well—I applaud your moderation.

LADY TEAZLE

Go—you are an insinuating wretch.—But we shall be missed—let us join the company.

JOSEPH SURFACE

But we had best not return together.

LADY TEAZLE

Well—don't stay; for Maria shan't come to hear any more of your reasoning, I promise you. [*Exit* LADY TEAZLE.]

JOSEPH SURFACE

A curious dilemma, truly, my politics have run me into! I wanted, at first, only to ingratiate myself with Lady Teazle, that she might not be my enemy with Maria; and I have, I don't know how, become her serious lover. Sincerely I begin to wish I had never made such a point of gaining so very good a character, for it has led me into so many cursed rogueries that I doubt I shall be exposed at last. [*Exit.*]

SCENE III

[SIR PETER TEAZLE'S *house.*]

[*Enter* ROWLEY *and* SIR OLIVER SURFACE.]

SIR OLIVER

Ha! ha! ha! so my old friend is married, hey?—a young wife out of the country.—Ha! ha! ha! that he should have stood bluff [30] to old bachelor so long, and sink into a husband at last!

ROWLEY

But you must not rally him on the subject, Sir Oliver: 'tis a tender point, I assure you, though he has been married only seven months.

SIR OLIVER

Then he has been just half a year on the stool of repentance! [61]—Poor Peter!—But you say he has entirely given up Charles,—never sees him, hey?

ROWLEY

His prejudice against him is astonishing, and I am sure greatly increased by a jealousy of him with Lady Teazle, which he had been industriously led into by a scandalous society in the neighbourhood, who have contributed not a little to Charles's ill name. Whereas the truth is, I believe, if the lady is partial to either of them, his brother is the favourite.

SIR OLIVER

Aye, I know there are a set of malicious, prating, prudent [62] gossips, both male and female, who murder characters to kill time; and will rob a young fellow of his good name, before he has years to know the value of it.—But I am not to be prejudiced against my nephew by such, I promise you.—No, no,—if Charles has done nothing false or mean, I shall compound for his extravagance. [63]

ROWLEY

Then, my life on't, you will reclaim him.—Ah, sir, it gives me new life to find that *your* heart is not turned against him, and that the son of my good old master has one friend, however, left.

SIR OLIVER

What, shall I forget, Master Rowley, when I was at his years myself? Egad, my brother and I were neither of us very prudent youths; and yet, I believe, you have not seen many better men than your old master was.

ROWLEY

Sir, 'tis this reflection gives me assurance that Charles may yet be a credit to his family.—But here comes Sir Peter.

SIR OLIVER

Egad, so he does!—Mercy on me!—he's greatly altered—and seems to have a settled married look! One may read *husband* in his face at this distance!

[*Enter* SIR PETER.]

SIR PETER

Ha! Sir Oliver—my old friend! Welcome to England a thousand times!

SIR OLIVER

Thank you—thank you, Sir Peter! and i'faith I am glad to find you well, believe me!

SIR PETER

Oh! 'tis a long time since we met—sixteen years, I doubt, Sir Oliver, and many a cross accident in the time.

SIR OLIVER

Aye. I have had my share. But what! I find you are married, hey, my old boy? Well, well—it can't be helped— and so—I wish you joy with all my heart!

SIR PETER

Thank you, thank you, Sir Oliver.—Yes, I have entered into—the happy state;—but we'll not talk of that now.

SIR OLIVER

True, true, Sir Peter; old friends should not begin on grievances at first meeting—no, no, no.

ROWLEY

[*To* SIR OLIVER.] Take care, pray, sir.

SIR OLIVER

Well—so one of my nephews is a wild young rogue, hey?

SIR PETER

Wild!—Ah! my old friend, I grieve for your disappointment there; he's a lost young man, indeed. However, his brother will make you amends; Joseph is, indeed, what a youth should be. Everybody in the world speaks well of him.

SIR OLIVER

I am sorry to hear it; he has too good a character to be an honest fellow. Everybody speaks well of him!—Pshaw! then he has bowed as low to knaves and fools as to the honest dignity of genius and virtue.

SIR PETER

What, Sir Oliver! do you blame him for not making enemies?

SIR OLIVER

Yes, if he has merit enough to deserve them.

SIR PETER

Well, well—you'll be convinced when you know him. 'Tis edification to hear him converse; he professes the noblest sentiments.

SIR OLIVER

Oh! plague of his sentiments! if he salutes me with a scrap of morality in his mouth, I shall be sick directly.— But, however, don't mistake me, Sir Peter; I don't mean to defend Charles's errors: but, before I form my judgement of either of them, I intend to make a trial of their hearts; and my friend Rowley and I have planned something for the purpose.

ROWLEY

And Sir Peter shall own he has been for once mistaken.

SIR PETER

Oh, my life on Joseph's honour.

SIR OLIVER

Well—come, give us a bottle of good wine, and we'll drink your lady's health, and tell you our scheme.

SIR PETER

Allons, then!

SIR OLIVER

And don't, Sir Peter, be so severe against your old friend's son. Odds my life! I am not sorry that he has run out of the course a little: for my part, I hate to see prudence clinging to the green suckers of youth; 'tis like ivy round a sapling, and spoils the growth of the tree. [*Exeunt.*]

End of the Second Act

Act three.

[SIR PETER TEAZLE'S *house*.]

[*Enter* SIR PETER TEAZLE, SIR OLIVER, *and* ROWLEY.]

SIR PETER
Well, then, we will see this fellow first, and have our wine afterwards:—but how is this, Master Rowley? I don't see the jet [54] of your scheme.

ROWLEY
Why, sir, this Mr Stanley, whom I was speaking of, is nearly related to them by their mother. He was once a merchant in Dublin, but has been ruined by a series of undeserved misfortunes. He has applied, by letter, since his confinement, both to Mr Surface and Charles: from the former he has received nothing but evasive promises of future service, while Charles has done all that his extravagance has left him power to do; and he is, at this time, endeavouring to raise a sum of money, part of which, in the midst of his own distresses, I know he intends for the service of poor Stanley.

SIR OLIVER
Ah!—he is my brother's son.

SIR PETER
Well, but how is Sir Oliver personally to—

ROWLEY
Why, sir, I will inform Charles and his brother that Stanley has obtained permission to apply personally to his friends, and, as they have neither of them ever seen him, let Sir Oliver assume his character, and he will have a fair opportunity, at least, of the benevolence of their dispositions:

and believe me, sir, you will find in the youngest brother
one who, in the midst of folly and dissipation, has still, as
our immortal bard expresses it,

> a heart to pity, and a hand
> Open as day, for melting charity.[65]

SIR PETER

Pshaw! What signifies his having an open hand or purse
either, when he has nothing left to give? Well, well—make
the trial, if you please. But where is the fellow whom you
brought for Sir Oliver to examine, relative to Charles's
affairs?

ROWLEY

Below, waiting his commands, and no one can give him
better intelligence. This, Sir Oliver, is a friendly Jew, who,
to do him justice, has done everything in his power to
bring your nephew to a proper sense of his extravagance.

SIR PETER

Pray let us have him in.

ROWLEY

[*Calls to* SERVANT.] Desire Mr Moses to walk upstairs.

SIR PETER

But, pray, why should you suppose he will speak the truth?

ROWLEY

Oh! I have convinced him that he has no chance of re-
covering certain sums advanced to Charles, but through the
bounty of Sir Oliver, who he knows is arrived; so that you
may depend on his fidelity to his own interests. I have
also another evidence in my power, one Snake, whom I
have detected in a matter little short of forgery, and shall
shortly produce him to remove some of your prejudices,
Sir Peter, relative to Charles and Lady Teazle.

SIR PETER

I have heard too much on that subject.

ROWLEY

Here comes the honest Israelite. [*Enter* MOSES.]—This is
Sir Oliver.

SIR OLIVER

Sir, I understand you have lately had great dealings with
my nephew, Charles.

MOSES

Yes, Sir Oliver, I have done all I could for him; but he was ruined before he came to me for assistance.

SIR OLIVER

That was unlucky, truly; for you have had no opportunity of showing your talents.

MOSES

None at all; I hadn't the pleasure of knowing his distresses till he was some thousands worse than nothing.

SIR OLIVER

Unfortunate, indeed!—But I suppose you have done all in your power for him, honest Moses?

MOSES

Yes, he owns that:—this very evening I was to have brought him a gentleman from the city, who does not know him, and will, I believe, advance him some money.

SIR PETER

What,—one Charles has never had money from before?

MOSES

Yes,—Mr Premium, of Crutched Friars,[56] formerly a broker.

SIR PETER

Egad, Sir Oliver, a thought strikes me!—Charles, you say, does not know Mr Premium?

MOSES

Not at all.

SIR PETER

Now then, Sir Oliver, you may have a better opportunity of satisfying yourself than by an old romancing tale of a poor relation: go with my friend Moses, and represent Premium, and then, I'll answer for it, you'll see your nephew in all his glory.

SIR OLIVER

Egad, I like this idea better than the other, and I may visit Joseph afterwards as Old Stanley.

SIR PETER

True—so you may.

ROWLEY

Well, this is taking Charles rather at a disadvantage, to be sure;—however, Moses, you understand Sir Peter, and will be faithful?

MOSES

You may depend upon me.—This is near the time I was to have gone.

SIR OLIVER

I'll accompany you as soon as you please, Moses.—But hold! I have forgot one thing—how the plague shall I be able to pass for a Jew?

MOSES

There's no need—the principal is Christian.

SIR OLIVER

Is he? I am very sorry to hear it. But, then again, an't I rather too smartly dressed to look like a money-lender?

SIR PETER

Not at all; 'twould not be out of character, if you went in your carriage—would it, Moses?

MOSES

Not in the least.

SIR OLIVER

Well—but how must I talk?—there's certainly some cant of usury and mode of treating that I ought to know.

SIR PETER

Oh! there's not much to learn. The great point, as I take it, is to be exorbitant enough in your demands—hey, Moses?

MOSES

Yes, that's a very great point.

SIR OLIVER

I'll answer for't I'll not be wanting in that. I'll ask him eight or ten per cent on the loan, at least.

MOSES

If you ask him no more than that, you'll be discovered immediately.

SIR OLIVER

Hey!—what, the plague!—how much then?

MOSES

That depends upon circumstances. If he appears not very anxious for the supply, you should require only forty or fifty per cent; but if you find him in great distress and want the moneys very bad, you must ask double.

SIR PETER

A good honest trade you're learning, Sir Oliver!

SIR OLIVER
Truly I think so—and not unprofitable.

MOSES
Then, you know, you haven't the moneys yourself, but are forced to borrow them for him of a friend.

SIR OLIVER
Oh! I borrow it of a friend, do I?

MOSES
And your friend is an unconscionable dog; but you can't help it!

SIR OLIVER
My friend an unconscionable dog, is he?

MOSES
Yes, and he himself has not the moneys by him, but is forced to sell stock at a great loss.

SIR OLIVER
He is forced to sell stock at a great loss, is he? Well, that's very kind of him.

SIR PETER
I'faith, Sir Oliver—Mr Premium, I mean, you'll soon be master of the trade. But, Moses! would not you have him run out [57] a little against the Annuity Bill? [58] That would be in character, I should think.

MOSES
Very much.

ROWLEY
And lament that a young man now must be at years of discretion before he is suffered to ruin himself?

MOSES
Aye, great pity!

SIR PETER
And abuse the public for allowing merit to an Act whose only object is to snatch misfortune and imprudence from the rapacious relief of usury, and give the minor the chance of inheriting his estate without being undone by coming into possession.

SIR OLIVER
So—so—Moses shall give me further instructions as we go together.

SIR PETER
You will not have much time, for your nephew lives hard

by.

SIR OLIVER

Oh! never fear: my tutor appears so able, that though
Charles lived in the next street, it must be my own fault
if I am not a complete rogue before I turn the corner.
[*Exeunt* SIR OLIVER *and* MOSES.]

SIR PETER

So, now, I think Sir Oliver will be convinced: you are
partial, Rowley, and would have prepared Charles for the
plot.

ROWLEY

No, upon my word, Sir Peter.

SIR PETER

Well, go bring me this Snake, and I'll hear what he has to
say presently.——I see Maria, and want to speak with her.
[*Exit* ROWLEY.] I should be glad to be convinced my suspicions of Lady Teazle and Charles were unjust. I have
never yet opened my mind on this subject to my friend
Joseph—I am determined I will do it—he will give me
his opinion sincerely. [*Enter* MARIA.] So, child, has Mr
Surface returned with you?

MARIA

No, sir; he was engaged.

SIR PETER

Well, Maria, do you not reflect, the more you converse
with that amiable young man, what return his partiality
for you deserves?

MARIA

Indeed, Sir Peter, your frequent importunity on this subject
distresses me extremely—you compel me to declare, that
I know no man who has ever paid me a particular attention whom I would not prefer to Mr Surface.

SIR PETER

So—here's perverseness! No, no, Maria, 'tis Charles only
whom you would prefer. 'Tis evident his vices and follies
have won your heart.

MARIA

This is unkind, sir. You know I have obeyed you in
neither seeing nor corresponding with him: I have heard
enough to convince me that he is unworthy my regard.
Yet I cannot think it culpable, if, while my understanding

severely condemns his vices, my heart suggests pity for his distresses.

SIR PETER
Well, well, pity him as much as you please; but give your heart and hand to a worthier object.

MARIA
Never to his brother!

SIR PETER
Go—perverse and obstinate! but take care, madam; you have never known what the authority of a guardian is: don't compel me to inform you of it.

MARIA
I can only say, you shall not have a just reason. 'Tis true, by my father's will, I am for a short period bound to regard you as his substitute; but must cease to think you so when you would compel me to be miserable. [*Exit* MARIA.]

SIR PETER
Was ever man so crossed as I am? everything conspiring to fret me! I had not been involved in matrimony a fortnight, before her father, a hale and hearty man, died, on purpose, I believe, for the pleasure of plaguing me with the care of his daughter. But here comes my helpmate—she appears in great good humour. How happy I should be if I could tease her into loving me, though but a little!

[*Enter* LADY TEAZLE.]

LADY TEAZLE
Lud! Sir Peter, I hope you haven't been quarrelling with Maria? It is not using me well to be ill-humoured when I am not by.

SIR PETER
Ah, Lady Teazle, you might have the power to make me good-humoured at all times.

LADY TEAZLE
I am sure I wish I had; for I want you to be in a charming sweet temper at this moment. Do be good-humoured now, and let me have two hundred pounds, will you?

SIR PETER
Two hundred pounds; what, an't I to be in a good humour without paying for it? But speak to me thus, and i'faith there's nothing I could refuse you. You shall have it; but

seal me a bond for the repayment.

LADY TEAZLE

[*Offering her hand.*] Oh, no—there—my note of hand will
do as well.

SIR PETER

And you shall no longer reproach me with not giving you
an independent settlement. I mean shortly to surprise
you;—but shall we always live thus, hey?

LADY TEAZLE

If you please. I'm sure I don't care how soon we leave
off quarrelling, provided you'll own you were tired first.

SIR PETER

Well—then let your future contest be, who shall be most
obliging.

LADY TEAZLE

I assure you, Sir Peter, good nature becomes you. You
look now as you did before we were married, when you
used to walk with me under the elms, and tell me stories
of what a gallant you were in your youth, and chuck me
under the chin, you would; and ask me if I thought I
could love an old fellow, who would deny me nothing—
didn't you?

SIR PETER

Yes, yes, and you were as kind and attentive—

LADY TEAZLE

Ay, so I was, and would always take your part, when my
acquaintance used to abuse you, and turn you into ridicule.

SIR PETER

Indeed!

LADY TEAZLE

Ay, and when my cousin Sophy has called you a stiff,
peevish old bachelor, and laughed at me for thinking of
marrying one who might be my father, I have always
defended you, and said, I didn't think you so ugly by any
means.

SIR PETER

Thank you.

LADY TEAZLE

And I dared say you'd make a very good sort of a husband.

SIR PETER

And you prophesied right; and we shall certainly now be

the happiest couple—

LADY TEAZLE

And never differ again?

SIR PETER

No, never—though at the same time, indeed, my dear
Lady Teazle, you must watch your temper very narrowly;
for in all our little quarrels, my dear, if you recollect, my
love, you always began first.

LADY TEAZLE

I beg your pardon, my dear Sir Peter: indeed, you always
gave the provocation.

SIR PETER

Now, see, my angel! take care—contradicting isn't the
way to keep friends.

LADY TEAZLE

Then, don't you begin it, my love!

SIR PETER

There, now! you—you are going on. You don't perceive,
my life, that you are just doing the very thing which you
know always makes me angry.

LADY TEAZLE

Nay, you know if you will be angry without any reason—
my dear—

SIR PETER

There! now you want to quarrel again.

LADY TEAZLE

No, I am sure I don't: but if you will be so peevish—

SIR PETER

There now, who begins first?

LADY TEAZLE

Why, you, to be sure. I said nothing—but there's no bearing your temper.

SIR PETER

No, no, madam; the fault's in your own temper.

LADY TEAZLE

Aye, you are just what my Cousin Sophy said you would
be.

SIR PETER

Your Cousin Sophy is a forward, impertinent gipsy.

LADY TEAZLE

You are a great bear, I am sure, to abuse my relations.

How dare you abuse my relations?

SIR PETER

Now may all the plagues of marriage be doubled on me, if ever I try to be friends with you any more!

LADY TEAZLE

So much the better.

SIR PETER

No, no, madam: 'tis evident you never cared a pin for me, and I was a madman to marry you—a pert, rural coquette, that had refused the honest 'squires in the neighbourhood!

LADY TEAZLE

And I am sure I was a fool to marry you—an old dangling bachelor, who was single at fifty, only because he never could meet with anyone who would have him.

SIR PETER

Aye, aye, madam; but you were pleased enough to listen to me: you never had such an offer before.

LADY TEAZLE

No! didn't I refuse Sir Tivy Terrier, who everybody said would have been a better match? for his estate is just as good as yours, and he has broke his neck since we have been married.

SIR PETER

I have done with you, madam! You are an unfeeling, ungrateful—but there's an end of everything. I believe you capable of everything that is bad. Yes, madam, I now believe the reports relative to you and Charles, madam.— Yes, madam, you and Charles are—not without grounds—

LADY TEAZLE

Take care, Sir Peter! you had better not insinuate any such thing! I'll not be suspected without cause, I promise you.

SIR PETER

Very well, madam, very well! a separate maintenance as soon as you please. Yes, madam, or a divorce! I'll make an example of myself for the benefit of all old bachelors.— Let us separate, madam.

LADY TEAZLE

[Enter TRIP.]

Agreed! agreed!—And now, my dear Sir Peter, we are of a mind once more, we may be the happiest couple—and never differ again, you know—ha! ha! ha! Well, you are

going to be in a passion, I see, and I shall only interrupt
you—so, bye! bye! [*Exit.*]

SIR PETER

Plagues and tortures! Can't I make her angry either! Oh,
I am the miserablest fellow! But I'll not bear her presuming
to keep her temper: no! she may break my heart, but she
shan't keep her temper. [*Exit.*]

SCENE II

[*At* CHARLES'S *house, a chamber.*]

[*Enter* TRIP, MOSES, *and* SIR OLIVER.]

TRIP

Here, Master Moses! if you'll stay a moment I'll try
whether Mr—what's the gentleman's name?

SIR OLIVER

Mr—[*Apart.*] Moses, what is my name?

MOSES

Mr Premium.

TRIP

Premium—very well. [*Exit, taking snuff.*]

SIR OLIVER

To judge by the servants, one would believe the master
was ruined. But what!—sure, this was my brother's house?

MOSES

Yes, sir; Mr Charles bought it of Mr Joseph, with the
furniture, pictures, etc., just as the old gentleman left it.
Sir Peter thought it a piece of extravagance in him.

SIR OLIVER

In my mind, the other's economy in selling it to him was
more reprehensible by half.

[*Enter* TRIP.]

TRIP

My master says you must wait, gentlemen: he has company, and can't speak with you yet.

SIR OLIVER

If he knew who it was wanted to see him, perhaps he would not have sent such a message?

TRIP

Yes, yes, sir; he knows you are here—I did not forget little Premium: no, no, no—

SIR OLIVER

Very well; and I pray, sir, what may be your name?

TRIP

Trip, sir; my name is Trip, at your service.

SIR OLIVER

Well, then, Mr Trip, you have a pleasant sort of place here, I guess?

TRIP

Why, yes—here are three or four of us pass our time agreeably enough; but then our wages are sometimes a little in arrear—and not very great either—but fifty pounds a year, and find our own bags and bouquets.[59]

SIR OLIVER

[*Aside.*] Bags and bouquets! halters and bastinadoes!

TRIP

And *à propos*, Moses, have you been able to get me that little bill discounted?

SIR OLIVER

[*Aside.*] Wants to raise money, too!—mercy on me! Has his distresses too, I warrant, like a lord, and affects creditors and duns.

MOSES

'Twas not to be done, indeed, Mr Trip.

TRIP

Good lack, you surprise me! My friend Brush has endorsed it, and I thought when he put his name at the back of a bill 'twas as good as cash.

MOSES

No! 'twouldn't do.

TRIP

A small sum—but twenty pounds. Hark'ee, Moses, do you think you couldn't get it me by way of annuity?

SIR OLIVER

[*Aside.*] An annuity! ha! ha! a footman raise money by way of annuity! Well done, luxury, egad!

MOSES

Well, but you must insure your place.

TRIP

Oh, with all my heart! I'll insure my place and, my life too, if you please.

SIR OLIVER

[*Aside.*] It's more than I would your neck.

TRIP

But then, Moses, it must be done before this d——d Register[60] takes place; one wouldn't like to have one's name made public, you know.

MOSES

No, certainly. But is there nothing you could deposit?

TRIP

Why, nothing capital of my master's wardrobe has dropped lately; but I could give you a mortgage on some of his winter clothes, with equity of redemption before November—or you shall have the reversion of the French velvet, or a post-obit[61] on the blue and silver:—these, I should think, Moses, with a few pair of point ruffles,[62] as a collateral security—hey, my little fellow?

MOSES

Well, well.

   [*Bell rings.*]

TRIP

Egad, I heard the bell! I believe, gentlemen, I can now introduce you. Don't forget the annuity, little Moses! This way, gentlemen: insure my place, you know.

SIR OLIVER

If the man be a shadow of the master, this is the temple of dissipation indeed! [*Exeunt.*]

SCENE III

   [CHARLES SURFACE, CARELESS, SIR TOBY BUMPER, *etc., discovered at a table, drinking wine.*]

CHARLES SURFACE

'Fore heaven, 'tis true!—there's the great degeneracy of the age. Many of our acquaintance have taste, spirit, and politeness; but, plague on't, they won't drink.

CARELESS

It is so, indeed, Charles! they give in to all the substantial luxuries of the table, and abstain from nothing but wine and wit.

CHARLES SURFACE

Oh, certainly society suffers by it intolerably; for now, instead of the social spirit of raillery that used to mantel over a glass of bright Burgundy, their conversation is become just like the Spa water they drink, which has all the pertness and flatulence of champagne without its spirit or flavour.

FIRST GENTLEMAN

But what are they to do who love play better than wine?

CARELESS

True! there's Harry diets himself for gaming, and is now under a hazard regimen.[63]

CHARLES SURFACE

Then he'll have the worst of it. What! you wouldn't train a horse for the course by keeping him from corn? For my part, egad, I'm never so successful as when I am a little merry; let me throw on a bottle of champagne, and I never lose—at least I never feel my losses, which is exactly the same thing.

SECOND GENTLEMAN

Ay, that I believe.

CHARLES SURFACE

And, then, what man can pretend to be a believer in love, who is an abjurer of wine? 'Tis the test by which the lover knows his own heart. Fill a dozen bumpers to a dozen beauties, and she that floats to the top is the maid that has bewitched you.

CARELESS

Now then, Charles, be honest, and give us your real favourite.

CHARLES SURFACE

Why, I have withheld her only in compassion to you. If I toast her, you must give a round of her peers, which is impossible—on earth.

CARELESS

Oh! then we'll find some canonized vestals or heathen goddesses that will do, I warrant!

CHARLES SURFACE

Here then, bumpers, you rogues! bumpers! Maria! Maria—

FIRST GENTLEMAN

Maria who?

CHARLES SURFACE

Oh, damn the surname!—'tis too formal to be registered in Love's calendar—but now, Sir Toby, beware, we must have beauty superlative.

CARELESS

Nay, never study, Sir Toby: we'll stand to the toast, though your mistress should want an eye, and you know you have a song will excuse you.

SIR TOBY

Egad, so I have! and I'll give him the song instead of the lady.

Song

> Here's to the maiden of bashful fifteen;
>   Here's to the widow of fifty;
> Here's to the flaunting extravagant quean,[66]
>   And here's to the housewife that's thrifty.

> *Chorus.*   Let the toast pass,—
>   Drink to the lass,
> I'll warrant she'll prove an excuse for a glass.

> Here's to the charmer whose dimples we prize;
>   Now to the maid who has none, sir;
> Here's to the girl with a pair of blue eyes,
>   And here's to the nymph with but *one,* sir.

> *Chorus.*   Let the toast pass,—
>   Drink to the lass,
> I'll warrant she'll prove an excuse for a glass.

> Here's to the maid with a bosom of snow;
>   Now to her that's as brown as a berry:

Here's to the wife with her face full of woe,
    And now to the damsel that's merry.

Chorus.   Let the toast pass,—
                Drink to the lass,
I'll warrant she'll prove an excuse for a glass.

For let 'em be clumsy, or let 'em be slim,
    Young or ancient, I care not a feather;
So fill a pint bumper quite up to the brim,
    And let us e'en toast them together.

Chorus.   Let the toast pass,—
                Drink to the lass,
I'll warrant she'll prove an excuse for a glass.

ALL
Bravo! Bravo!

[*Enter* TRIP *and whispers to* CHARLES.]

CHARLES SURFACE
Gentlemen, you must excuse me a little. Careless, take
the chair, will you?

CARELESS
Nay, prithee, Charles, what now? This is one of your
peerless beauties, I suppose, has dropt in by chance?

CHARLES SURFACE
No, faith! To tell you the truth, 'tis a Jew and a broker,
who are come by appointment.

CARELESS
Oh, damn it! let's have the Jew in.

FIRST GENTLEMAN
Ay, and the broker too, by all means.

SECOND GENTLEMAN
Yes, yes, the Jew and the broker.

CHARLES SURFACE
Egad, with all my heart!—Trip, bid the gentlemen walk
in.—[*Exit* TRIP.] Though there's one of them a stranger, I
can tell you.

CARELESS
Charles, let us give them some generous Burgundy, and
perhaps they'll grow conscientious.

CHARLES SURFACE

Oh, hang 'em, no! wine does but draw forth a man's natural qualities; and to make them drink would only be to whet their knavery.

[*Enter* TRIP, SIR OLIVER, *and* MOSES.]

CHARLES SURFACE

So, honest Moses, walk in: walk in, pray, Mr Premium—that's the gentleman's name, isn't it, Moses?

MOSES

Yes, sir.

CHARLES SURFACE

Set chairs, Trip—sit down, Mr Premium—glasses, Trip.—Sit down, Moses. Come, Mr Premium, I'll give you a sentiment; here's *Success to usury*—Moses, fill the gentleman a bumper.

MOSES

Success to usury!

CARELESS

Right, Moses—usury is prudence and industry, and deserves to succeed.

SIR OLIVER

Then—*here's all the success it deserves!*

CARELESS

No, no, that won't do, Mr Premium; you have demurred to the toast, and must drink it in a pint bumper.

FIRST GENTLEMAN

A pint bumper, at least.

MOSES

Oh, pray, sir, consider—Mr Premium's a gentleman.

CARELESS

And therefore loves good wine.

SECOND GENTLEMAN

Give Moses a quart glass—this is mutiny, and a high contempt for the chair.

CARELESS

Here, now for't! I'll see justice done, to the last drop of my bottle.

SIR OLIVER

Nay, pray, gentlemen—I did not expect this usage.

CHARLES SURFACE

No, hang it, you shan't! Mr Premium's a stranger.

SIR OLIVER

[*Aside.*] Odd! I wish I was well out of their company.

CARELESS

Plague on 'em then! if they won't drink, we'll not sit down with them. Come, Harry, the dice are in the next room—Charles, you'll join us when you have finished your business with these gentlemen?

CHARLES SURFACE

I will! I will!—[*Exeunt* GENTLEMEN.] Careless!

CARELESS

[*Returning.*] Well!

CHARLES SURFACE

Perhaps I may want you.

CARELESS

Oh, you know I am always ready: word, note, or bond, 'tis all the same to me. [*Exit.*]

MOSES

Sir, this is Mr Premium, a gentleman of the strictest honour and secrecy; and always performs what he undertakes. Mr Premium, this is—

CHARLES SURFACE

Pshaw! have done.—Sir, my friend Moses is a very honest fellow, but a little slow at expression: he'll be an hour giving us our titles. Mr Premium, the plain state of the matter is this: I am an extravagant young fellow who wants to borrow money—you I take to be a prudent old fellow, who has got money to lend. I am blockhead enough to give fifty per cent sooner than not have it; and you, I presume, are rogue enough to take an hundred if you can get it. Now, sir, you see we are acquainted at once, and may proceed to business without further ceremony.

SIR OLIVER

Exceeding frank, upon my word.—I see, sir, you are not a man of many compliments.

CHARLES SURFACE

Oh, no, sir! plain dealing in business I always think best.

SIR OLIVER

Sir, I like you the better for it—however, you are mistaken in one thing; I have no money to lend, but I believe I could procure some of a friend; but then he's an unconscionable dog. Isn't he, Moses? And must sell stock to accommodate you, mustn't he, Moses?

MOSES

Yes, indeed! You know I always speak the truth, and scorn to tell a lie!

CHARLES SURFACE

Right. People that speak truth generally do: but these are trifles, Mr Premium. What! I know money isn't to be bought without paying for't!

SIR OLIVER

Well—but what security could you give? You have no land, I suppose?

CHARLES SURFACE

Not a mole-hill, nor a twig, but what's in beau-pots* out of the window!

SIR OLIVER

Nor any stock, I presume?

CHARLES SURFACE

Nothing but live stock—and that's only a few pointers and ponies. But pray, Mr Premium, are you acquainted at all with any of my connexions?

SIR OLIVER

Why, to say the truth, I am.

CHARLES SURFACE

Then you must know that I have a dev'lish rich uncle in the East Indies, Sir Oliver Surface, from whom I have the greatest expectations?

SIR OLIVER

That you have a wealthy uncle, I have heard; but how your expectations will turn out is more, I believe, than you can tell.

CHARLES SURFACE

Oh, no!—there can be no doubt. They tell me I'm a prodigious favourite, and that he talks of leaving me everything.

SIR OLIVER

Indeed! this is the first I've heard of it.

CHARLES SURFACE

Yes, yes, 'tis just so. Moses knows 'tis true; don't you, Moses?

MOSES

Oh, yes! I'll swear to't.

SIR OLIVER

[*Aside.*] Egad, they'll persuade me presently I'm at Bengal.

CHARLES SURFACE

Now I propose, Mr Premium, if it's agreeable to you, a post-obit on Sir Oliver's life: though at the same time the old fellow has been so liberal to me, that I give you my word, I should be very sorry to hear that anything had happened to him.

SIR OLIVER

Not more than I should, I assure you. But the bond you mention happens to be just the worst security you could offer me—for I might live to a hundred and never recover the principal.

CHARLES SURFACE

Oh, yes, you would—the moment Sir Oliver dies, you know, you would come on me for the money.

SIR OLIVER

Then I believe I should be the most unwelcome dun you ever had in your life.

CHARLES SURFACE

What! I suppose you're afraid that Sir Oliver is too good a life?

SIR OLIVER

No, indeed I am not; though I have heard he is as hale and healthy as any man of his years in Christendom.

CHARLES SURFACE

There again, now, you are misinformed. No, no, the climate has hurt him considerably, poor uncle Oliver. Yes, yes, he breaks apace, I am told—and is so much altered lately that his nearest relations wouldn't know him.

SIR OLIVER

No! ha! ha! ha! so much altered lately that his nearest relations wouldn't know him! that's droll! egad—ha! ha! ha!

CHARLES SURFACE

Ha! ha!—you're glad to hear that, little Premium?

SIR OLIVER

No, no, I'm not.

CHARLES SURFACE

Yes, yes, you are—ha! ha! ha!—you know that mends your chance.

SIR OLIVER

But I'm told Sir Oliver is coming over; nay, some say he is actually arrived.

CHARLES SURFACE

Pshaw! Sure I must know better than you whether he's come or not. No, no, rely on't he's at this moment at Calcutta—isn't he, Moses?

MOSES

Yes, certainly.

SIR OLIVER

Very true, as you say, you must know better than I, though I have it from pretty good authority—haven't I, Moses?

MOSES

Yes, most undoubted!

SIR OLIVER

But, sir, as I understand you want a few hundred immediately—is there nothing you could dispose of?

CHARLES SURFACE

How do you mean?

SIR OLIVER

For instance, now, I have heard that your father left behind him a great quantity of massy old plate.

CHARLES SURFACE

O Lud!—that's gone long ago.—Moses can tell you how better than I can.

SIR OLIVER

[*Aside.*] Good lack! all the family race-cups and corporation bowls! [66]—Then it was also supposed that his library was one of the most valuable and complete—

CHARLES SURFACE

Yes, yes, so it was—vastly too much so for a private gentleman. For my part, I was always of a communicative disposition, so I thought it a shame to keep so much knowledge to myself.

SIR OLIVER

[*Aside.*] Mercy upon me! Learning that had run in the family like an heirloom!—Pray, what are become of the books?

CHARLES SURFACE

You must inquire of the auctioneer, master Premium, for I don't believe even Moses can direct you.

MOSES

I never meddle with books.

SIR OLIVER

So, so, nothing of the family property left, I suppose?

CHARLES SURFACE

Not much, indeed; unless you have a mind to the family
pictures. I have got a room full of ancestors above, and
if you have a taste for old paintings, egad, you shall have
them a bargain!

SIR OLIVER

Hey! what the devil! sure, you wouldn't sell your fore-
fathers, would you?

CHARLES SURFACE

Every man of 'em, to the best bidder.

SIR OLIVER

What! your great-uncles and aunts?

CHARLES SURFACE

Aye, and my grandfathers and grandmothers too.

SIR OLIVER

[*Aside.*] Now I give him up!—What the plague, have you
no bowels for your own kindred? Odd's life, do you take
me for Shylock in the play, that you would raise money
of me on your own flesh and blood?

CHARLES SURFACE

Nay, my little broker, don't be angry: what need you care,
if you have your money's worth?

SIR OLIVER

Well, I'll be the purchaser: I think I can dispose of the
family canvas.—[*Aside.*] Oh, I'll never forgive him this!
never!

[*Enter* CARELESS.]

CARELESS

Come, Charles, what keeps you?

CHARLES SURFACE

I can't come yet; i'faith, we are going to have a sale above
stairs; here's little Premium will buy all my ancestors!

CARELESS

Oh, burn your ancestors!

CHARLES SURFACE

No, he may do that afterwards, if he pleases. Stay, Careless,
we want you: egad, you shall be auctioneer; so come along

with us.

CARELESS

Oh, have with you, if that's the case. I can handle a hammer as well as a dice-box—a-going—a-going.

SIR OLIVER

[*Aside.*] Oh, the profligates!

CHARLES SURFACE

Come, Moses, you shall be appraiser, if we want one. Gad's life, little Premium, you don't seem to like the business?

SIR OLIVER

Oh, yes, I do, vastly! Ha! ha! ha! yes, yes, I think it a rare joke to sell one's family by auction—ha! ha!—[*Aside.*] Oh, the prodigal!

CHARLES SURFACE

To be sure! when a man wants money, where the plague should he get assistance, if he can't make free with his own relations? [*Exeunt.*]

End of the Third Act

Act four.

SCENE I

[*Picture room at* CHARLES'S *house.*]

[*Enter* CHARLES, SIR OLIVER, MOSES, *and* CARELESS.]

CHARLES SURFACE

Walk in, gentlemen, pray walk in;—here they are, the family of the Surfaces, up to the Conquest.

SIR OLIVER

And, in my opinion, a goodly collection.

CHARLES SURFACE

Ay, ay, these are done in the true spirit of portrait-painting; no *volunteer grace*[67] or expression. Not like the works of your modern Raphaels, who give you the strongest resemblance, yet contrive to make your portrait independent of you; so that you may sink the original and not hurt the picture. No, no; the merit of these is the inveterate likeness—all stiff and awkward as the originals, and like nothing in human nature besides.

SIR OLIVER

Ah! we shall never see such figures of men again.

CHARLES SURFACE

I hope not.—Well, you see, Master Premium, what a domestic character I am; here I sit of an evening surrounded by my family.—But come, get to your pulpit, Mr Auctioneer; here's an old gouty chair of my grandfather's will answer the purpose.

CARELESS

Ay, ay, this will do. But, Charles, I haven't a hammer; and what's an auctioneer without his hammer?

CHARLES SURFACE

Egad, that's true. What parchment have we here? *Richard*

heir to Thomas. Oh, our genealogy in full. Here, Careless —you shall have no common bit of mahogany, here's the family tree for you, you rogue,—this shall be your hammer, and now you may knock down my ancestors with their own pedigree.

SIR OLIVER

[*Aside.*] What an unnatural rogue!—an *ex post facto* parricide!

CARELESS

Yes, yes, here's a list of your generation indeed;—faith, Charles, this is the most convenient thing you could have found for the business, for 'twill not only serve as a hammer, but a catalogue into the bargain. But come, begin.—A-going, a-going, a-going!

CHARLES SURFACE

Bravo, Careless! Well, here's my great-uncle, Sir Richard Raveline, a marvellous good general in his day, I assure you. He served in all the Duke of Marlborough's[68] wars, and got that cut over his eye at the battle of Malplaquet.[69] What say you, Mr Premium?—look at him—there's a hero for you, not cut out of his feathers, as your modern clipt captains are, but enveloped in wig and regimentals, as a general should be.—What do you bid?

SIR OLIVER

[*Aside to Moses.*] Bid him speak.

MOSES

Mr Premium would have *you* speak.

CHARLES SURFACE

Why, then, he shall have him for ten pounds, and I'm sure that's not dear for a staff-officer.

SIR OLIVER

[*Aside.*] Heaven deliver me! his famous Uncle Richard for ten pounds!—Very well, sir, I take him at that.

CHARLES SURFACE

Careless, knock down my Uncle Richard.—Here, now, is a maiden sister of his, my great-aunt Deborah, done by Kneller,[70] in his best manner, and esteemed a very formidable likeness.—There she is, you see, a shepherdess feeding her flock.—You shall have her for five pounds ten—the sheep are worth the money.

SIR OLIVER

[*Aside.*] Ah! poor Deborah! a woman who set such value on herself!—Five pounds ten—she's mine.

CHARLES SURFACE

Knock down my Aunt Deborah!—Here, now, are two that were a sort of cousins of theirs—You see, Moses, these pictures were done some time ago, when beaux wore wigs, and the ladies their own hair.

SIR OLIVER

Yes, truly, head-dresses appear to have been a little lower in those days.

CHARLES SURFACE

Well, take this couple for the same.

MOSES

'Tis a good bargain.

CHARLES SURFACE

This, now, is a grandfather of my mother's, a learned judge, well known on the western circuit.—What do you rate him at, Moses?

MOSES

Four guineas.

CHARLES SURFACE

Four guineas!—Gad's life, you don't bid me the price of his wig.—Mr Premium, you have more respect for the woolsack; [n] do let us knock his lordship down at fifteen.

SIR OLIVER

By all means.

CARELESS

Gone!

CHARLES SURFACE

And there are two brothers of his, William and Walter Blunt, Esquires, both members of Parliament, and noted speakers, and what's very extraordinary, I believe, this is the first time they were ever bought or sold.

SIR OLIVER

That is very extraordinary, indeed! I'll take them at your own price, for the honour of Parliament.

CARELESS

Well said, little Premium!—I'll knock them down at forty.

CHARLES SURFACE

Here's a jolly fellow—I don't know what relation, but he

was mayor of Norwich: take him at eight pounds.

SIR OLIVER

No, no; six will do for the mayor.

CHARLES SURFACE

Come, make it guineas, and I'll throw you the two aldermen there into the bargain.

SIR OLIVER

They're mine.

CHARLES SURFACE

Careless, knock down the mayor and aldermen.—But, plague on't, we shall be all day retailing in this manner; do let us deal wholesale: what say you, little Premium? Give me three hundred pounds for the rest of the family in the lump.

CARELESS

Aye, aye, that will be the best way.

SIR OLIVER

Well, well, anything to accommodate you;—they are mine. But there is one portrait which you have always passed over.

CARELESS

What, that ill-looking little fellow over the settee?

SIR OLIVER

Yes, sir, I mean that; though I don't think him so ill-looking a little fellow, by any means.

CHARLES SURFACE

What, that?—Oh; that's my uncle Oliver; 'twas done before he went to India.

CARELESS

Your uncle Oliver! Gad, then you'll never be friends, Charles. That, now, to me, is as stern a looking rogue as ever I saw; an unforgiving eye, and a damned disinheriting countenance! an inveterate knave, depend on't. Don't you think so, little Premium?

SIR OLIVER

Upon my soul sir, I do not; I think it is as honest a looking face as any in the room, dead or alive;—but I suppose Uncle Oliver goes with the rest of the lumber[72]?

CHARLES SURFACE

No, hang it! I'll not part with poor Noll. The old fellow has been very good to me, and, egad, I'll keep his picture while I've a room to put it in.

SIR OLIVER

[*Aside.*] The rogue's my nephew after all!—But, sir, I have somehow taken a fancy to that picture.

CHARLES SURFACE

I'm sorry for't, for you certainly will not have it. Oons, haven't you got enough of them?

SIR OLIVER

[*Aside.*] I forgive him everything!—But sir, when I take a whim in my head, I don't value money, I'll give you as much for that as for all the rest.

CHARLES SURFACE

Don't tease me, master broker; I tell you I'll not part with it, and there's an end of it.

SIR OLIVER

[*Aside.*] How like his father the dog is.—Well, well, I have done.—I did not perceive it before, but I think I never saw such a striking resemblance.—Here is a draft for your sum.

CHARLES SURFACE

Why, 'tis for eight hundred pounds!

SIR OLIVER

You will not let Sir Oliver go?

CHARLES SURFACE

Zounds! no!—I tell you, once more.

SIR OLIVER

Then never mind the difference, we'll balance that another time—but give me your hand on the bargain; you are an honest fellow, Charles—I beg pardon, sir, for being so free.—Come, Moses.

CHARLES SURFACE

Egad, this is a whimsical old fellow! But hark'ee, Premium, you'll prepare lodgings for these gentlemen.

SIR OLIVER

Yes, yes, I'll send for them in a day or two.

CHARLES SURFACE

But hold; do now send a genteel conveyance for them, for I assure you, they were most of them used to ride in their own carriages.

SIR OLIVER

I will, I will—for all but Oliver.

CHARLES SURFACE
Aye, all but the little nabob.

SIR OLIVER
You're fixed on that?

CHARLES SURFACE
Peremptorily.

SIR OLIVER
[*Aside.*] A dear extravagant rogue!—Good-day!—Come,
Moses.—Let me hear now who dares call him profligate!
[*Exeunt* SIR OLIVER SURFACE *and* MOSES.]

CARELESS
Why, this is the oddest genius of the sort I ever met with!

CHARLES SURFACE
Egad, he's the prince of brokers, I think. I wonder how the
devil Moses got acquainted with so honest a fellow.—Ha!
here's Rowley; do, Careless, say I'll join the company in a
moment.

CARELESS
I will—but don't let that old blockhead persuade you to
squander any of that money on old musty debts, or any
such nonsense; for tradesmen, Charles, are the most
exorbitant fellows.

CHARLES SURFACE
Very true, and paying them is only encouraging them.

CARELESS
Nothing else.

CHARLES SURFACE
Aye, aye, never fear. [*Exit* CARELESS.] So! this was an odd
old fellow, indeed.—Let me see, two-thirds of this is mine
by right,—five hundred and thirty odd pounds. 'Fore
Heaven! I find one's ancestors are more valuable relations
than I took them for!—Ladies and gentlemen, your most
obedient and very grateful servant. [*Enter* ROWLEY.] Ha!
old Rowley! egad, you are just come in time to take leave
of your old acquaintance.

ROWLEY
Yes, I heard they were a-going. But I wonder you can
have such spirits under so many distresses.

CHARLES SURFACE
Why, there's the point! my distresses are so many, that I
can't afford to part with my spirits; but I shall be rich and

splenetic, all in good time. However, I suppose you are surprised that I am not more sorrowful at parting with so many near relations; to be sure, 'tis very affecting; but rot 'em, you see they never move a muscle, so why should I?

ROWLEY

There's no making you serious a moment.

CHARLES SURFACE

Yes, faith, I am so now. Here, my honest Rowley, here, get me this changed directly, and take a hundred pounds of it immediately, to old Stanley.

ROWLEY

A hundred pounds! Consider only—

CHARLES SURFACE

Gad's life, don't talk about it: poor Stanley's wants are pressing, and, if you don't make haste, we shall have someone call that has a better right to the money.

ROWLEY

Ah! there's the point I never will cease dunning you with the old proverb—

CHARLES SURFACE

'Be just before you're generous.'—Why, so I would if I could; but Justice is an old hobbling beldame, and I can't get her to keep pace with Generosity for the soul of me.

ROWLEY

Yet, Charles, believe me, one hour's reflection—

CHARLES SURFACE

Aye, aye, it's all very true; but, hark'ee, Rowley, while I have, by Heaven I'll give; so, damn your economy, and now for hazard. [*Exeunt.*]

SCENE II

[*The parlour.*]

[*Enter* SIR OLIVER *and* MOSES.]

MOSES

Well, sir, I think, as Sir Peter said, you have seen Mr

Charles in high glory; 'tis great pity he's so extravagant.

SIR OLIVER

True, but he would not sell my picture.

MOSES

And loves wine and women so much.

SIR OLIVER

But he would not sell my picture.

MOSES

And games[73] so deep.

SIR OLIVER

But he would not sell my picture.—Oh, here's Rowley.

[*Enter* ROWLEY.]

ROWLEY

So, Sir Oliver, I find you have made a purchase—

SIR OLIVER

Yes, yes, our young rake has parted with his ancestors like old tapestry.

ROWLEY

And here has he commissioned me to re-deliver you part of the purchase-money—I mean, though, in your necessitous character of old Stanley.

MOSES

Ah! there is the pity of all: he is so damned charitable.

ROWLEY

And I left a hosier and two tailors in the hall, who I'm sure, won't be paid, and this hundred would satisfy them.

SIR OLIVER

Well, well, I'll pay his debts, and his benevolence too.— But now I am no more a broker, and you shall introduce me to the elder brother as old Stanley.

ROWLEY

Not yet awhile; Sir Peter, I know, means to call there about this time.

[*Enter* TRIP.]

TRIP

Oh, gentlemen, I beg pardon for not showing you out; this way—Moses, a word. [*Exeunt* TRIP *and* MOSES.]

SIR OLIVER

There's a fellow for you—would you believe it, that puppy intercepted the Jew on our coming, and wanted to raise money before he got to his master!

ROWLEY
Indeed!
SIR OLIVER
Yes, they are now planning an annuity business.—Ah,
Master Rowley, in my days servants were content with the
follies of their masters, when they were worn a little
threadbare; but now, they have their vices, like their
birthday clothes,⁷⁴ with the gloss on. [*Exeunt.*]

SCENE III

[*A library.*]

[JOSEPH SURFACE *and a* SERVANT.]

JOSEPH SURFACE
No letter from Lady Teazle?
SERVANT
No, sir.
JOSEPH SURFACE
I am surprised she has not sent, if she is prevented from
coming. Sir Peter certainly does not suspect me. Yet I
wish I may not lose the heiress, through the scrape I have
drawn myself into with the wife; however, Charles's im-
prudence and bad character are great points in my
favour.
    [*Knock without.*]
SERVANT
Sir, I believe that must be Lady Teazle.
JOSEPH SURFACE
Hold!—See whether it is or not, before you go to the
door: I have a particular message for you if it should be
my brother.
SERVANT
'Tis her ladyship, sir; she always leaves the chair at the
milliner's in the next street.
JOSEPH SURFACE
Stay, stay: draw that screen before the window—that will
do;—my opposite neighbour is a maiden lady of so curious

a temper.—[SERVANT *draws the screen, and exit.*] I have
a difficult hand to play in this affair. Lady Teazle has
lately suspected my views on Maria; but she must by no
means be let into that secret,—at least, till I have her more
in my power.

[*Enter* LADY TEAZLE.]

LADY TEAZLE
What, sentiment in soliloquy? Have you been very im-
patient now?—O Lud! don't pretend to look grave—I vow
I couldn't come before.

JOSEPH SURFACE
Oh, Madam, punctuality is a species of constancy very
unfashionable in a lady of quality.

LADY TEAZLE
Upon my word, you ought to pity me. Do you know Sir
Peter is grown so ill-tempered to me of late, and so jealous
of Charles, too; that's the best of the story, isn't it?

JOSEPH SURFACE
[*Aside.*] I am glad my scandalous friends keep that up.

LADY TEAZLE
I am sure I wish he would let Maria marry him, and then
perhaps he would be convinced; don't you, Mr Surface?

JOSEPH SURFACE
[*Aside.*] Indeed I do not.—Oh, certainly I do! for then my
dear Lady Teazle would also be convinced how wrong her
suspicions were of my having any design on the silly girl.

LADY TEAZLE
Well, well, I'm inclined to believe you. But isn't it provoking, to have the most ill-natured things said of one?—And
there's my friend Lady Sneerwell has circulated I don't
know how many scandalous tales of me, and all without
any foundation, too—that's what vexes me.

JOSEPH SURFACE
Aye madam, to be sure, that is the provoking circumstance
—without foundation; yes, yes, there's the mortification,
indeed; for, when a scandalous story is believed against
one, there certainly is no comfort like the consciousness of
having deserved it.

LADY TEAZLE
No, to be sure, then I'd forgive their malice; but to attack
me, who am really so innocent, and who never say an ill-

natured thing of anybody—that is, of my friends; and then
Sir Peter, too, to have him so peevish, and so suspicious,
when I know the integrity of my own heart—indeed 'tis
monstrous!

JOSEPH SURFACE

But, my dear Lady Teazle, 'tis your own fault if you suffer
it. When a husband entertains a groundless suspicion of
his wife, and withdraws his confidence from her, the
original compact is broke, and she owes it to the honour of
her sex to endeavour to outwit him.

LADY TEAZLE

Indeed!—So that, if he suspects me without cause, it
follows, that the best way of curing his jealousy is to give
him reason for't?

JOSEPH SURFACE

Undoubtedly—for your husband should never be deceived
in you,—and in that case it becomes you to be frail in
compliment to his discernment.

LADY TEAZLE

To be sure, what you say is very reasonable, and when the
consciousness of my innocence—

JOSEPH SURFACE

Ah! my dear madam, there is the great mistake; 'tis this
very conscious innocence that is of the greatest prejudice
to you. What is it makes you negligent of forms, and careless of the world's opinion?—why, the consciousness of
your own innocence. What makes you thoughtless in your
conduct, and apt to run into a thousand little imprudences?
—why, the consciousness of your own innocence. What
makes you impatient of Sir Peter's temper, and outrageous
at his suspicions?—why, the consciousness of your innocence.

LADY TEAZLE

'Tis very true!

JOSEPH SURFACE

Now, my dear Lady Teazle, if you would but once make a
trifling *faux pas*, you can't conceive how cautious you
would grow, and how ready to humour and agree with your
husband.

LADY TEAZLE

Do you think so?

JOSEPH SURFACE

Oh, I'm sure on't; and then you would find all scandal would cease at once, for, in short, your character at present is like a person in a plethora, absolutely dying from too much health.

LADY TEAZLE

So, so; then I perceive your prescription is, that I must sin in my own defence, and part with my virtue to preserve my reputation?

JOSEPH SURFACE

Exactly so, upon my credit, ma'am.

LADY TEAZLE

Well, certainly this is the oddest doctrine, and the newest receipt for avoiding calumny!

JOSEPH SURFACE

An infallible one, believe me. Prudence, like experience, must be paid for.

LADY TEAZLE

Why, if my understanding were once convinced—

JOSEPH SURFACE

Oh, certainly, madam, your understanding should be convinced.—Yes, yes—Heaven forbid I should persuade you to do anything you thought wrong. No, no, I have too much honour to desire it.

LADY TEAZLE

Don't you think we may as well leave *honour* out of the argument?

JOSEPH SURFACE

Ah, the ill effects of your country education, I see, still remain with you.

LADY TEAZLE

I doubt they do indeed; and I will fairly own to you, that if I could be persuaded to do wrong, it would be by Sir Peter's ill usage sooner than your *honourable logic*, after all.

JOSEPH SURFACE

[*Taking her hand.*] Then, by his hand, which is unworthy of—[*Enter* SERVANT.] 'Sdeath, you blockhead—what do you want?

SERVANT

I beg pardon, sir, but I thought you would not choose Sir

Peter to come up without announcing him.

JOSEPH SURFACE

Sir Peter!—Oons and the devil!

LADY TEAZLE

Sir Peter! O Lud—I'm ruined—I'm ruined!

SERVANT

Sir, 'twasn't I let him in.

LADY TEAZLE

Oh! I'm quite undone! What will become of me now, Mr
Logic? Oh! he's on the stairs—I'll get behind here—and
if ever I'm so imprudent again—[*Goes behind the screen.*]

JOSEPH SURFACE

Give me that book. [*Sits down,* SERVANT *pretends to adjust
his chair. Enter* SIR PETER TEAZLE.]

SIR PETER

Aye, ever improving himself. Mr Surface, Mr Surface—

JOSEPH SURFACE

Oh, my dear Sir Peter, I beg your pardon. [*Gaping, throws
away the book.*] I have been dozing over a stupid book.—
Well, I am much obliged to you for this call. You haven't
been here, I believe, since I fitted up this room.—Books,
you know, are the only things I am a coxcomb in.

SIR PETER

'Tis very neat indeed.—Well, well, that's proper; and you
can make even your screen a source of knowledge—hung,
I perceive, with maps.

JOSEPH SURFACE

Oh, yes, I find great use in that screen.

SIR PETER

I dare say you must, certainly, when you want to find
anything in a hurry.

JOSEPH SURFACE

[*Aside.*] Aye, or to hide anything in a hurry either.

SIR PETER

Well, I have a little private business—

JOSEPH SURFACE

[*To* SERVANT.] You need not stay.

SERVANT

No, sir. [*Exit.*]

JOSEPH SURFACE

Here's a chair, Sir Peter—I beg—

SIR PETER

Well, now we are alone, there is a subject, my dear friend, on which I wish to unburthen my mind to you—a point of the greatest moment to my peace; in short, my good friend, Lady Teazle's conduct of late has made me very unhappy.

JOSEPH SURFACE

Indeed! I am very sorry to hear it.

SIR PETER

Aye, 'tis but too plain she has not the least regard for me; but, what's worse, I have pretty good authority to suspect she has formed an attachment to another.

JOSEPH SURFACE

You astonish me!

SIR PETER

Yes; and, between ourselves, I think I've discovered the person.

JOSEPH SURFACE

How! you alarm me exceedingly.

SIR PETER

Ah, my dear friend, I knew you would sympathize with me!

JOSEPH SURFACE

Yes—believe me, Sir Peter, such a discovery would hurt me just as much as it would you.

SIR PETER

I am convinced of it.—Ah! it is a happiness to have a friend whom we can trust even with one's family secrets. But have you no guess who I mean?

JOSEPH SURFACE

I haven't the most distant idea. It can't be Sir Benjamin Backbite!

SIR PETER

Oh no! What say you to Charles?

JOSEPH SURFACE

My brother! impossible! O no, Sir Peter, you must not credit the scandalous insinuations you may hear. No, no, Charles to be sure has been charged with many things of this kind, but I can never think he would meditate so gross an injury.

SIR PETER

Ah, my dear friend, the goodness of your own heart misleads you. You judge of others by yourself.

JOSEPH SURFACE

Certainly, Sir Peter, the heart that is conscious of its own integrity is ever slow to credit another's treachery.

SIR PETER

True; but your brother has no sentiment—you never hear him talk so.

JOSEPH SURFACE

Yet I can't but think Lady Teazle herself has too much principle.

SIR PETER

Aye, but what is principle against the flattery of a handsome, lively young fellow?

JOSEPH SURFACE

That's very true.

SIR PETER

And then, you know, the difference of our ages makes it very improbable that she should have any great affection for me; and if she were to be frail, and I were to make it public, why the town would only laugh at me—the foolish old bachelor, who had married a girl.

JOSEPH SURFACE

That's true, to be sure—they *would* laugh.

SIR PETER

Laugh—aye, and make ballads, and paragraphs, and the devil knows what of me.

JOSEPH SURFACE

No—you must never make it public.

SIR PETER

But then again—that the nephew of my old friend, Sir Oliver, should be the person to attempt such a wrong, hurts me more nearly.

JOSEPH SURFACE

Aye, there's the point.—When ingratitude barbs the dart of injury, the wound has double danger in it.

SIR PETER

Aye—I, that was, in a manner, left his guardian: in whose house he had been so often entertained! who never in my life denied him—my advice!

JOSEPH SURFACE

Oh, 'tis not to be credited! There may be a man capable of

such baseness, to be sure; but, for my part, till you can give me positive proofs, I cannot but doubt it. However, if it should be proved on him, he is no longer a brother of mine—I disclaim kindred with him: for the man who can break the laws of hospitality, and attempt the wife of his friend, deserves to be branded as the pest of society.

SIR PETER

What a difference there is between you! What noble sentiments!

JOSEPH SURFACE

Yet, I cannot suspect Lady Teazle's honour.

SIR PETER

I am sure I wish to think well of her, and to remove all ground of quarrel between us. She has lately reproached me more than once with having made no settlement on her; and, in our last quarrel, she almost hinted that she should not break her heart if I was dead. Now, as we seem to differ in our ideas of expense, I have resolved she shall have her own way, and be her own mistress in that respect for the future; and, if I were to die, she will find I have not been inattentive to her interest while living. Here, my friend, are the drafts of two deeds, which I wish to have your opinion on.—By one, she will enjoy eight hundred a year independent while I live; and, by the other, the bulk of my fortune at my death.

JOSEPH SURFACE

This conduct, Sir Peter, is indeed truly generous.—[*Aside.*] I wish it may not corrupt my pupil.

SIR PETER

Yes, I am determined she shall have no cause to complain, though I would not have her acquainted with the latter instance of my affection yet awhile.

JOSEPH SURFACE

[*Aside.*] Nor I, if I could help it.

SIR PETER

And now, my dear friend, if you please, we will talk over the situation of your hopes with Maria.

JOSEPH SURFACE

Oh, no, Sir Peter; another time, if you please.

SIR PETER

I am sensibly chagrined at the little progress you seem to

make in her affections.

JOSEPH SURFACE

[*Softly.*] I beg you will not mention it. What are my disappointments when your happiness is in debate!—[*Aside.*]
'Sdeath, I shall be ruined every way!

SIR PETER

And though you are averse to my acquainting Lady Teazle
with *your* passion, I'm sure she's not your enemy in the
affair.

JOSEPH SURFACE

Pray, Sir Peter, now, oblige me. I am really too much
affected by the subject we have been speaking of, to bestow
a thought on my own concerns. The man who is entrusted
with his friend's distresses can never—[*Enter* SERVANT.]
Well, sir?

SERVANT

Your brother, sir, is speaking to a gentleman in the street,
and says he knows you are within.

JOSEPH SURFACE

'Sdeath, blockhead, I'm not within—I'm out for the day.

SIR PETER

Stay—hold—a thought has struck me:—you shall be at
home.

JOSEPH SURFACE

Well, well, let him up.—[*Exit* SERVANT. *Aside.*] He'll
interrupt Sir Peter, however.

SIR PETER

Now, my good friend, oblige me, I entreat you. Before
Charles comes, let me conceal myself somewhere—then
do you tax him on the point we have been talking on, and
his answer may satisfy me at once.

JOSEPH SURFACE

Oh, fie, Sir Peter! would you have me join in so mean a
trick?—to trepan[75] my brother too?

SIR PETER

Nay, you tell me you are *sure* he is innocent; if so, you
do him the greatest service by giving him an opportunity
to clear himself, and you will set my heart at rest. Come,
you shall not refuse me: here, behind the screen will be—
hey! what the devil! there seems to be one listener here
already—I'll swear I saw a petticoat!

JOSEPH SURFACE

Ha! ha! ha! Well, this is ridiculous enough. I'll tell you, Sir Peter, though I hold a man of intrigue to be a most despicable character, yet you know, it does not follow that one is to be an absolute Joseph either! Hark'ee, 'tis a little French milliner,—a silly rogue that plagues me,—and having some character to lose, on your coming, sir, she ran behind the screen.

SIR PETER

Ah! you rogue! But, egad, she has overheard all I have been saying of my wife.

JOSEPH SURFACE

Oh, 'twill never go any farther, you may depend upon it!

SIR PETER

No! then, faith, let her hear it out.—Here's a closet will do as well.

JOSEPH SURFACE

Well, go in there.

SIR PETER

Sly rogue! sly rogue. [*Goes into the closet.*]

JOSEPH SURFACE

A narrow escape, indeed! and a curious situation I'm in, to part man and wife in this manner.

LADY TEAZLE

[*Peeping.*] Couldn't I steal off?

JOSEPH SURFACE

Keep close, my angel!

SIR PETER

[*Peeping.*] Joseph, tax him home.

JOSEPH SURFACE

Back, my dear friend!

LADY TEAZLE

Couldn't you lock Sir Peter in?

JOSEPH SURFACE

Be still, my life!

SIR PETER

[*Peeping.*] You're sure the little milliner won't blab?

JOSEPH SURFACE

In, in, my dear Sir Peter!—'Fore Gad, I wish I had a key to the door.

   [*Enter* CHARLES SURFACE.]

CHARLES SURFACE

Holla! brother, what has been the matter? Your fellow would not let me up at first. What! have you had a Jew or a wench with you?

JOSEPH SURFACE

Neither, brother, I assure you.

CHARLES SURFACE

But what has made Sir Peter steal off? I thought he had been with you.

JOSEPH SURFACE

He *was,* brother; but, hearing you were coming, he did not choose to stay.

CHARLES SURFACE

What! was the old gentleman afraid I wanted to borrow money of him!

JOSEPH SURFACE

No, sir; but I am sorry to find, Charles, you have lately given that worthy man grounds for great uneasiness.

CHARLES SURFACE

Yes, yes, yes, they tell me I do that to a great many worthy men—But how so, pray?

JOSEPH SURFACE

To be plain with you, brother—he thinks you are endeavouring to gain Lady Teazle's affections from him.

CHARLES SURFACE

Who, I? O Lud! not I, upon my word. Ha! ha! ha! ha! so the old fellow has found out that he has got a young wife, has he?—or, what is worse, has her ladyship discovered she has an old husband?

JOSEPH SURFACE

This is no subject to jest upon, brother. He who can laugh—

CHARLES SURFACE

True, true, as you were going to say—then, seriously, I never had the least idea of what you charge me with, upon my honour.

JOSEPH SURFACE

[*Aloud.*] Well, it will give Sir Peter great satisfaction to hear this.

CHARLES SURFACE

To be sure, I once thought the lady seemed to have taken

a fancy to me; but, upon my soul, I never gave her the least encouragement:—besides, you know my attachment to Maria.

JOSEPH SURFACE

But sure, brother, even if Lady Teazle had betrayed the fondest partiality for you—

CHARLES SURFACE

Why, look'ee, Joseph, I hope I shall never deliberately do a dishonourable action; but if a pretty woman was purposely to throw herself in my way—and that pretty woman married to a man old enough to be her father—

JOSEPH SURFACE

Well—

CHARLES SURFACE

Why, I believe I should be obliged to borrow a little of your morality, that's all.—But, brother, do you know now that you surprise me exceedingly, by naming me with Lady Teazle; for i'faith, I always understood *you* were her favourite.

JOSEPH SURFACE

Oh, for shame, Charles! This retort is foolish.

CHARLES SURFACE

Nay, I swear I have seen you exchange such significant glances—

JOSEPH SURFACE

Nay, nay, sir, this is no jest.

CHARLES SURFACE

Egad, I'm serious. Don't you remember one day, when I called here—

JOSEPH SURFACE

Nay, prithee, Charles—

CHARLES SURFACE

And found you together—

JOSEPH SURFACE

Zounds, sir, I insist—

CHARLES SURFACE

And another time, when your servant—

JOSEPH SURFACE

Brother, brother, a word with you!—[*Aside.*] Gad, I must stop him.

CHARLES SURFACE
Informed, I say, that—

JOSEPH SURFACE
Hush! I beg your pardon, but Sir Peter has overheard all
we have been saying. I knew you would clear yourself, or
I should not have consented.

CHARLES SURFACE
How, Sir Peter! Where is he?

JOSEPH SURFACE
Softly; there! [*Points to the closet.*]

CHARLES SURFACE
Oh, 'fore Heaven, I'll have him out. Sir Peter, come forth!

JOSEPH SURFACE
No, no—

CHARLES SURFACE
I say, Sir Peter, come into court.—[*Pulls in* SIR PETER.]
What! my old guardian!—What! turn inquisitor, and take
evidence, incog?

SIR PETER
Give me your hand, Charles—I believe I have suspected
you wrongfully; but you mustn't be angry with Joseph—
'twas my plan!

CHARLES SURFACE
Indeed!

SIR PETER
But I acquit you. I promise you I don't think near so ill
of you as I did: what I have heard has given me great
satisfaction.

CHARLES SURFACE
Egad, then, 'twas lucky you didn't hear any more. Wasn't
it, Joseph?

SIR PETER
Ah! you would have retorted on him.

CHARLES SURFACE
Aye, aye, that was a joke.

SIR PETER
Yes, yes, I know his honour too well.

CHARLES SURFACE
But you might as well have suspected *him* as *me* in this
matter, for all that. Mightn't he, Joseph?

SIR PETER
Well, well, I believe you.

JOSEPH SURFACE
Would they were both out of the room!

[*Enter* SERVANT, *and whispers* JOSEPH SURFACE.]

SIR PETER
And in future, perhaps, we may not be such strangers.

SERVANT
Lady Sneerwell is below, and says she will come up.

JOSEPH SURFACE
[*To the* SERVANT.] Lady Sneerwell! Gad's life, she mustn't
come here. Gentlemen, I beg pardon—I must wait on you
downstairs; here's a person come on particular business.

CHARLES SURFACE
Well, you can see him in another room. Sir Peter and I
have not met a long time, and I have something to say to
him.

JOSEPH SURFACE
[*Aside.*] They must not be left together.—[*To Charles.*]
I'll send this man away, and return directly.—Sir Peter,
not a word of the French milliner.

SIR PETER
Oh, not for the world!—[*Exit* JOSEPH.] Ah, Charles, if you
associated more with your brother, one might indeed hope
for your reformation. He is a man of sentiment.—Well,
there is nothing in the world so noble as a man of sentiment.

CHARLES SURFACE
Pshaw! he is too moral by half;—and so apprehensive of
his good name, as he calls it, that I suppose he would as
soon let a priest into his house as a girl.

SIR PETER
No, no,—come, come,—you wrong him. No, no, Joseph
is no rake, but he is no such saint in that respect either.—
[*Aside.*] I have a great mind to tell him—we should have
a laugh.

CHARLES SURFACE
Oh, hang him! he's a very anchorite, a young hermit!

SIR PETER
Hark'ee—you must not abuse him: he may chance to
hear of it again, I promise you.

CHARLES SURFACE
Why, you won't tell him?

SIR PETER
No—but—this way.—[*Aside.*] Egad, I'll tell him. Hark'ee,
have you a mind to have a good laugh at Joseph?

CHARLES SURFACE
I should like it of all things.

SIR PETER
Then, i'faith, we will!—[*Whispers.*] I'll be quit with him for
discovering me. He had a girl with him when I called.

CHARLES SURFACE
What! Joseph? you jest.

SIR PETER
Hush!—a little French milliner—and the best of the jest
is—she's in the room now.

CHARLES SURFACE
[*Looking at the closet.*] The devil she is!

SIR PETER
[*Points to the screen.*] Hush! I tell you.

CHARLES SURFACE
Behind the screen! Odds life, let's unveil her!

SIR PETER
No, no—he's coming—you shan't, indeed!

CHARLES SURFACE
Oh, egad, we'll have a peep at the little milliner!

SIR PETER
Not for the world!—Joseph will never forgive me.

CHARLES SURFACE
I'll stand by you—

SIR PETER
Odds, here he is!
  [JOSEPH SURFACE *enters just as* CHARLES SURFACE
  throws down the screen.]

CHARLES SURFACE
Lady Teazle, by all that's wonderful!

SIR PETER
Lady Teazle, by all that's damnable!

CHARLES SURFACE
Sir Peter, this is one of the smartest French milliners I
ever saw. Egad, you seem all to have been diverting yourselves here at hide and seek, and I don't see who is out

of the secret. Shall I beg your ladyship to inform me? Not
a word!—Brother, will you be pleased to explain this
matter? What! is Morality dumb too?—Sir Peter, though
I found you in the dark, perhaps you are not so now! All
mute! Well—though I can make nothing of the affair, I
suppose you perfectly understand one another—so I'll
leave you to yourselves.—[*Going.*] Brother, I'm sorry to
find you have given that worthy man grounds for so much
uneasiness.—Sir Peter! there's nothing in the world so
noble as a man of sentiment! [*Exit* CHARLES. *They stand
for some time looking at each other.*]

JOSEPH SURFACE

Sir Peter—notwithstanding—I confess—that appearances
are against me—if you will afford me your patience—I
make no doubt—but I shall explain everything to your
satisfaction.

SIR PETER

If you please, sir.

JOSEPH SURFACE

The fact is, sir—that Lady Teazle, knowing my pretensions
to your ward, Maria—I say, sir, Lady Teazle, being apprehensive of the jealousy of your temper—and knowing
my friendship to the family—she, sir, I say—called here—
in order that—I might explain these pretensions—but on
your coming—being apprehensive—as I said—of your
jealousy—she withdrew—and this, you may depend on it,
is the whole truth of the matter.

SIR PETER

A very clear account, upon my word; and I dare swear
the lady will vouch for every article of it.

LADY TEAZLE

For not one word of it, Sir Peter!

SIR PETER

How! don't you think it worth while to agree in the lie.

LADY TEAZLE

There is not one syllable of truth in what that gentleman
has told you.

SIR PETER

I believe you, upon my soul, ma'am!

JOSEPH SURFACE

[*Aside.*] 'Sdeath, madam, will you betray me?

LADY TEAZLE

Good Mr Hypocrite, by your leave, I'll speak for myself.

SIR PETER

Aye, let her alone, sir; you'll find she'll make out a better story than you, without prompting.

LADY TEAZLE

Hear me, Sir Peter!—I came here on no matter relating to your ward, and even ignorant of this gentleman's pretensions to her. But I came, seduced by his insidious arguments, at least to listen to his pretended passion, if not to sacrifice your honour to his baseness.

SIR PETER

Now, I believe, the truth is coming out indeed!

JOSEPH SURFACE

The woman's mad!

LADY TEAZLE

No, sir—she has recovered her senses, and your own arts have furnished her with the means.—Sir Peter, I do not expect you to credit me—but the tenderness you expressed for me, when I am sure you could not think I was a witness to it, has penetrated so to my heart, that had I left the place without the shame of this discovery, my future life should have spoken the sincerity of my gratitude. As for that smooth-tongued hypocrite, who would have seduced the wife of his too credulous friend, while he affected honourable addresses to his ward—I behold him now in a light so truly despicable, that I shall never again respect myself for having listened to him. [*Exit.*]

JOSEPH SURFACE

Notwithstanding all this, Sir Peter, Heaven knows—

SIR PETER

That you are a villain! and so I leave you to your conscience.

JOSEPH SURFACE

You are too rash, Sir Peter; you *shall* hear me. The man who shuts out conviction by refusing to—

SIR PETER

O damn your sentiments. [*Exeunt,* SURFACE *following and speaking.*]

End of Fourth Act

Act five.

SCENE I

[*The library*.]

[*Enter* JOSEPH SURFACE *and* SERVANT.]

JOSEPH SURFACE
Mr Stanley!—and why should you think I would see him?
you must know he comes to ask something.
SERVANT
Sir, I should not have let him in, but that Mr Rowley came
to the door with him.
JOSEPH SURFACE
Pshaw! blockhead! to suppose that I should now be in a
temper to receive visits from poor relatives!—Well, why
don't you show the fellow up?
SERVANT
I will, sir.—Why, sir, it was not my fault that Sir Peter
discovered my lady—
JOSEPH SURFACE
Go, fool!—[*Exit* SERVANT.] Sure Fortune never played a
man of my policy[76] such a trick before! My character with
Sir Peter, my hopes with Maria, destroyed in a moment!
I'm in a rare humour to listen to other people's distresses!
I shan't be able to bestow even a benevolent sentiment on
Stanley.—So! here he comes, and Rowley with him. I must
try to recover myself, and put a little charity into my face,
however. [*Exit. Enter* SIR OLIVER *and* ROWLEY.]
SIR OLIVER
What! does he avoid us?—That was he, was it not?
ROWLEY
It was, sir. But I doubt you are come a little too abruptly.

His nerves are so weak, that the sight of a poor relation may be too much for him. I should have gone first to break it to him.

SIR OLIVER

Oh, plague of his nerves! Yet this is he whom Sir Peter extols as a man of the most benevolent way of thinking!

ROWLEY

As to his way of thinking, I cannot pretend to decide, for, to do him justice, he appears to have as much speculative benevolence as any private gentleman in the kingdom, though he is seldom so sensual as to indulge himself in the exercise of it.

SIR OLIVER

Yet he has a string of charitable sentiments, I suppose, at his fingers' ends.

ROWLEY

Or, rather, at his tongue's end, Sir Oliver; for I believe there is no sentiment he has more faith in than that 'Charity begins at home.'

SIR OLIVER

And his, I presume, is of that domestic sort; it never stirs abroad at all.

ROWLEY

I doubt you'll find it so;—but he's coming. I mustn't seem to interrupt you; and you know, immediately as you leave him, I come in to announce your arrival in your real character.

SIR OLIVER

True; and afterwards you'll meet me at Sir Peter's.

ROWLEY

Without losing a moment. [*Exit.*]

SIR OLIVER

I don't like the complaisance of his features.

[*Enter* JOSEPH SURFACE.]

JOSEPH SURFACE

Sir, I beg you ten thousand pardons for keeping you a moment waiting.—Mr Stanley, I presume.

SIR OLIVER

At your service.

JOSEPH SURFACE

Sir, I beg you will do me the honour to sit down—I entreat

you, sir.

SIR OLIVER

Dear sir—there's no occasion.—[*Aside.*] Too civil by half.

JOSEPH SURFACE

I have not the pleasure of knowing you, Mr Stanley; but
I am extremely happy to see you look so well. You were
nearly related to my mother, I think, Mr Stanley?

SIR OLIVER

I was sir;—so nearly that my present poverty, I fear, may
do discredit to her wealthy children, else I should not have
presumed to trouble you.

JOSEPH SURFACE

Dear sir, there needs no apology:—He that is in distress,
though a stranger, has a right to claim kindred with the
wealthy. I am sure I wish I was one of that class, and had
it in my power to offer you even a small relief.

SIR OLIVER

If your uncle, Sir Oliver, were here, I should have a friend.

JOSEPH SURFACE

I wish he was, sir, with all my heart: you should not want
an advocate with him, believe me, sir.

SIR OLIVER

I should not need one—my distresses would recommend
me. But I imagined his bounty had enabled you to become
the agent of his charity.

JOSEPH SURFACE

My dear sir, you were strangely misinformed. Sir Oliver
is a worthy man, a very worthy sort of man; but avarice,
Mr Stanley, is the vice of age. I will tell you, my good
sir, in confidence, what he has done for me has been a
mere nothing; though people, I know, have thought otherwise, and, for my part, I never chose to contradict the
report.

SIR OLIVER

What! has he never transmitted you bullion—rupees—
pagodas[77]?

JOSEPH SURFACE

Oh, dear sir, nothing of the kind!—No, no—a few presents
now and then—china, shawls, congou tea, avadavats, and
Indian crackers[78]—little more, believe me.

SIR OLIVER

[*Aside.*] Here's gratitude for twelve thousand pounds!—
Avadavats and Indian crackers!

JOSEPH SURFACE

Then, my dear sir, you have heard, I doubt not, of the
extravagance of my brother; there are very few would
credit what I have done for that unfortunate young man.

SIR OLIVER

[*Aside.*] Not I, for one!

JOSEPH SURFACE

The sums I have lent him!—Indeed I have been exceedingly to blame; it was an amiable weakness—however—I
don't pretend to defend it—and now I feel it doubly
culpable, since it has deprived me of the pleasure of
serving *you*, Mr Stanley, as my heart dictates.

SIR OLIVER

[*Aside.*] Dissembler!—Then, sir, you can't assist me?

JOSEPH SURFACE

At present, it grieves me to say, I cannot; but, whenever I
have the ability, you may depend upon hearing from me.

SIR OLIVER

I am extremely sorry—

JOSEPH SURFACE

Not more than I, believe me;—to pity, without the power
to relieve, is still more painful than to ask and be denied.

SIR OLIVER

Kind sir, your most obedient humble servant.

JOSEPH SURFACE

You leave me deeply affected, Mr Stanley.—William, be
ready to open the door.

SIR OLIVER

O, dear sir, no ceremony.

JOSEPH SURFACE

Your very obedient.

SIR OLIVER

Your most obsequious.

JOSEPH SURFACE

You may depend upon hearing from me, whenever I can
be of service.

SIR OLIVER

Sweet sir, you are too good.

JOSEPH SURFACE

In the meantime I wish you health and spirits.

SIR OLIVER

Your ever grateful and perpetual humble servant.

JOSEPH SURFACE

Sir, yours as sincerely.

SIR OLIVER

[*Aside.*] Charles!—you are my heir. [*Exit.*]

JOSEPH SURFACE

This is one bad effect of a good character; it invites application from the unfortunate, and there needs no small degree of address to gain the reputation of benevolence without incurring the expense. The silver ore of pure charity is an expensive article in the catalogue of a man's good qualities; whereas the sentimental French plate I use instead of it makes just as good a show, and pays no tax.

[*Enter* ROWLEY.]

ROWLEY

Mr Surface, your servant: I was apprehensive of interrupting you, though my business demands immediate attention, as this note will inform you.

JOSEPH SURFACE

Always happy to see Mr Rowley.—How!—[*Reads the letter.*] Oliver Surface!—My uncle arrived!

ROWLEY

He is, indeed: we have just parted—quite well, after a speedy voyage, and impatient to embrace his worthy nephew.

JOSEPH SURFACE

I am astonished!—William! stop Mr Stanley, if he's not gone.

ROWLEY

Oh! he's out of reach, I believe.

JOSEPH SURFACE

Why did you not let me know this when you came in together?

ROWLEY

I thought you had particular business;—but I must be gone to inform your brother, and appoint him here to meet his uncle. He will be with you in a quarter of an hour.

JOSEPH SURFACE

So he says. Well, I am strangely overjoyed at his coming.
—[*Aside.*] Never, to be sure, was anything so damned unlucky!

ROWLEY

You will be delighted to see how well he looks.

JOSEPH SURFACE

Oh! I'm rejoiced to hear it.—[*Aside.*] Just at this time!

ROWLEY

I'll tell him how impatiently you expect him.

JOSEPH SURFACE

Do, do; pray give my best duty and affection. Indeed, I
cannot express the sensations I feel at the thought of
seeing him.—[*Exit* ROWLEY.] Certainly his coming just at
this time is the cruellest piece of ill fortune. [*Exit.*]

SCENE II

[SIR PETER TEAZLE'S.]

[*Enter* MRS CANDOUR *and* MAID.]

MAID

Indeed, ma'am, my lady will see nobody at present.

MRS CANDOUR

Did you tell her it was her friend Mrs Candour?

MAID

Yes, ma'am; but she begs you will excuse her.

MRS CANDOUR

Do go again.—I shall be glad to see her, if it be only for a
moment, for I am sure she must be in great distress.—[*Exit*
MAID.] Dear heart, how provoking! I'm not mistress of
half the circumstances! We shall have the whole affair in
the newspapers, with the names of the parties at full
length, before I have dropped the story at a dozen houses.
[*Enter* SIR BENJAMIN BACKBITE.] Oh, Sir Benjamin! you
have heard, I suppose—

SIR BENJAMIN
Of Lady Teazle and Mr Surface—

MRS CANDOUR
And Sir Peter's discovery—

SIR BENJAMIN
Oh, the strangest piece of business, to be sure!

MRS CANDOUR
Well, I never was so surprised in my life. I am so sorry for
all parties, indeed.

SIR BENJAMIN
Now, I don't pity Sir Peter at all: he was so extravagantly
partial to Mr Surface.

MRS CANDOUR
Mr Surface! Why, 'twas with Charles Lady Teazle was
detected.

SIR BENJAMIN
No such thing!—Mr Surface is the gallant.

MRS CANDOUR
No, no! Charles is the man. 'Twas Mr Surface brought
Sir Peter on purpose to discover them.

SIR BENJAMIN
I tell you I had it from one—

MRS CANDOUR
And I have it from one—

SIR BENJAMIN
Who had it from one, who had it—

MRS CANDOUR
From one immediately—but here comes Lady Sneerwell;
perhaps she knows the whole affair.

[*Enter* LADY SNEERWELL.]

LADY SNEERWELL
So, my dear Mrs Candour, here's a sad affair of our friend
Teazle!

MRS CANDOUR
Aye, my dear friend, who could have thought it?

LADY SNEERWELL
Well, there is no trusting to appearances; though indeed,
she was always too lively for me.

MRS CANDOUR
To be sure, her manners were a little too free; but then
she was very young!

LADY SNEERWELL
And had, indeed, some good qualities.

MRS CANDOUR
So she had, indeed. But have you heard the particulars?

LADY SNEERWELL
No; but everybody says that Mr Surface—

SIR BENJAMIN
Aye, there; I told you Mr Surface was the man.

MRS CANDOUR
No, no, indeed, the assignation was with Charles.

LADY SNEERWELL
With Charles! You alarm me, Mrs Candour!

MRS CANDOUR
Yes, yes, he was the lover. Mr Surface, to do him justice,
was only the informer.

SIR BENJAMIN
Well, I'll not dispute with you, Mrs Candour; but, be it
which it may, I hope that Sir Peter's wound will not—

MRS CANDOUR
Sir Peter's wound! Oh, mercy! I didn't hear a word of their
fighting.

LADY SNEERWELL
Nor I, a syllable.

SIR BENJAMIN
No! what, no mention of the duel?

MRS CANDOUR
Not a word.

SIR BENJAMIN
Oh Lord, yes, yes: they fought before they left the room.

LADY SNEERWELL
Pray let us hear.

MRS CANDOUR
Aye, do oblige us with the duel.

SIR BENJAMIN
'Sir,' says Sir Peter, immediately after the discovery, 'you
are a most ungrateful fellow.'

MRS CANDOUR
Aye, to Charles—

SIR BENJAMIN
No, no—to Mr Surface—'a most ungrateful fellow; and
old as I am, sir,' says he, 'I insist on immediate satisfaction.'

MRS CANDOUR

Aye, that must have been to Charles; for 'tis very un-
likely Mr Surface should go fight in his own house.

SIR BENJAMIN

'Gad's life, ma'am, not at all—'giving me immediate
satisfaction,'—On this, ma'am, Lady Teazle, seeing Sir
Peter in such danger, ran out of the room in strong
hysterics, and Charles after her, calling out for hartshorn
and water; then, madam, they began to fight with swords—

[*Enter* CRABTREE.]

CRABTREE

With pistols, nephew—pistols: I have it from undoubted
authority.

MRS CANDOUR

Oh, Mr Crabtree, then it is all true!

CRABTREE

Too true, indeed, madam, and Sir Peter dangerously
wounded—

SIR BENJAMIN

By a thrust in *seconde*[70] quite through his left side—

CRABTREE

By a bullet lodged in the thorax.

MRS CANDOUR

Mercy on me! Poor Sir Peter!

CRABTREE

Yes, madam; though Charles would have avoided the
matter, if he could.

MRS CANDOUR

I knew Charles was the person.

SIR BENJAMIN

My uncle, I see, knows nothing of the matter.

CRABTREE

But Sir Peter taxed him with the basest ingratitude—

MRS CANDOUR

What I told you, you know—

CRABTREE

Do, nephew, let me speak! and insisted on immediate—

SIR BENJAMIN

Just as I said—

CRABTREE

Odds life, nephew, allow others to know something too!

A pair of pistols lay on the bureau (for Mr Surface, it seems, had come home the night before late from Salthill, where he had been to see the Montem[80] with a friend, who has a son at Eton), so, unluckily, the pistols were left charged.

SIR BENJAMIN

I heard nothing of this.

CRABTREE

Sir Peter forced Charles to take one, and they fired, it seems, pretty nearly together. Charles's shot took effect, as I tell you, and Sir Peter's missed; but, what is very extraordinary, the ball struck against a little bronze Shakespeare that stood over the fireplace, grazed out of the window at a right angle, and wounded the postman, who was just coming to the door with a double letter[81] from Northamptonshire.

SIR BENJAMIN

My uncle's account is more circumstantial, I confess; but I believe mine is the true one for all that.

LADY SNEERWELL

[*Aside.*] I am more interested in this affair than they imagine, and must have better information. [*Exit.*]

SIR BENJAMIN

[*After a pause, looking at each other.*] Ah! Lady Sneerwell's alarm is very easily accounted for.

CRABTREE

Yes, yes, they certainly *do* say—but that's neither here nor there.

MRS CANDOUR

But, pray, where is Sir Peter at present?

CRABTREE

Oh! they brought him home, and he is now in the house, though the servants are ordered to deny him.

MRS CANDOUR

I believe so, and Lady Teazle, I suppose, attending him.

CRABTREE

Yes, yes; and I saw one of the faculty[82] enter just before me.

SIR BENJAMIN

Hey! who comes here?

CRABTREE
Oh, this is he: the physician, depend on't.

MRS CANDOUR
Oh, certainly! it must be the physician; and now we shall know.

[*Enter* SIR OLIVER.]

CRABTREE
Well, doctor, what hopes?

MRS CANDOUR
Aye, doctor, how's your patient?

SIR BENJAMIN
Now, doctor, isn't it a wound with a small-sword?

CRABTREE
A bullet lodged in the thorax, for a hundred.

SIR OLIVER
Doctor! a wound with a small-sword! and a bullet in the thorax? What! are you mad, good people?

SIR BENJAMIN
Perhaps, sir, you are not a doctor?

SIR OLIVER
Truly, I am to thank you for my degree, if I am.

CRABTREE
Only a friend of Sir Peter's, then, I presume. But, sir, you must have heard of his accident?

SIR OLIVER
Not a word!

CRABTREE
Not of his being dangerously wounded?

SIR OLIVER
The devil he is!

SIR BENJAMIN
Run through the body—

CRABTREE
Shot in the breast—

SIR BENJAMIN
By one Mr Surface—

CRABTREE
Aye, the younger.

SIR OLIVER
Hey! what the plague! you seem to differ strangely in your accounts: however, you agree that Sir Peter is dangerously

wounded.

SIR BENJAMIN

Oh, yes, we agree there.

CRABTREE

Yes, yes, I believe there can be no doubt in that.

SIR OLIVER

Then, upon my word, for a person in that situation, he is
the most imprudent man alive; for here he comes, walking
as if nothing at all was the matter. [*Enter* SIR PETER.] Odds
heart, Sir Peter, you are come in good time, I promise you;
for we had just given you over!

SIR BENJAMIN

Egad, uncle, this is the most sudden recovery!

SIR OLIVER

Why, man, what do you do out of bed with a small-sword
through your body, and a bullet lodged in your thorax?

SIR PETER

A small-sword and a bullet!

SIR OLIVER

Aye, these gentlemen would have killed you without law
or physic, and wanted to dub me a doctor, to make me an
accomplice.

SIR PETER

Why, what is all this?

SIR BENJAMIN

We rejoice, Sir Peter, that the story of the duel is not true,
and are sincerely sorry for your other misfortune.

SIR PETER

[*Aside.*] So, so; all over the town already.

CRABTREE

Though, Sir Peter, you were certainly vastly to blame to
marry at all at your years.

SIR PETER

Sir, what business is that of yours?

MRS CANDOUR

Though, indeed, as Sir Peter made so good a husband, he's
very much to be pitied.

SIR PETER

Plague on your pity, ma'am! I desire none of it.

SIR BENJAMIN

However, Sir Peter, you must not mind the laughing and

jests you will meet with on the occasion.

SIR PETER

Sir, sir, I desire to be master in my own house.

CRABTREE

'Tis no uncommon case, that's one comfort.

SIR PETER

I insist on being left to myself: without ceremony—I insist on your leaving my house directly!

MRS CANDOUR

Well, well, we are going; and depend on't, we'll make the best report of you we can. [*Exit.*]

SIR PETER

Leave my house!

CRABTREE

And tell how hardly you've been treated. [*Exit.*]

SIR PETER

Leave my house!

SIR BENJAMIN

And how patiently you bear it. [*Exit.*]

SIR PETER

Fiends! vipers! furies! Oh! that their own venom would choke them!

SIR OLIVER

They are very provoking indeed, Sir Peter.

[*Enter* ROWLEY.]

ROWLEY

I heard high words: what has ruffled you, sir?

SIR PETER

Pshaw! what signifies asking? Do I ever pass a day without my vexations?

SIR OLIVER

Well, I'm not inquisitive. I come only to tell you, that I have seen both my nephews in the manner we proposed.

SIR PETER

A precious couple they are!

ROWLEY

Yes, and Sir Oliver is convinced that your judgement was right, Sir Peter.

SIR OLIVER

Yes, I find Joseph is indeed the man, after all.

ROWLEY
Aye, as Sir Peter says, he is a man of sentiment.

SIR OLIVER
And acts up to the sentiments he professes.

ROWLEY
It certainly is edification to hear him talk.

SIR OLIVER
Oh, he's a model for the young men of the age!—But how's this, Sir Peter? you don't join us in your friend Joseph's praise, as I expected.

SIR PETER
Sir Oliver, we live in a damned wicked world, and the fewer we praise the better.

ROWLEY
What! do you say so, Sir Peter, who were never mistaken in your life?

SIR PETER
Pshaw! plague on you both! I see by your sneering you have heard the whole affair. I shall go mad among you!

ROWLEY
Then, to fret you no longer, Sir Peter, we are indeed acquainted with it all. I met Lady Teazle coming from Mr Surface's so humbled, that she deigned to request me to be her advocate with you.

SIR PETER
And does Sir Oliver know all too?

SIR OLIVER
Every circumstance.

SIR PETER
What, of the closet—and the screen, hey?

SIR OLIVER
Yes, yes, and the little French milliner. Oh, I have been vastly diverted with the story! Ha! ha! ha!

SIR PETER
'Twas very pleasant.

SIR OLIVER
I never laughed more in my life, I assure you: ha! ha! ha!

SIR PETER
Oh, vastly diverting! ha! ha! ha!

ROWLEY
To be sure, Joseph with his sentiments! ha! ha! ha!

SIR PETER

Yes, his sentiments! Ha! ha! ha! Hypocritical villain!

SIR OLIVER

Aye, and that rogue Charles to pull Sir Peter out of the
closet: ha! ha! ha!

SIR PETER

Ha! ha! 'twas devilish entertaining, to be sure!

SIR OLIVER

Ha! ha! ha! Egad, Sir Peter, I should like to have seen
your face when the screen was thrown down: ha! ha!

SIR PETER

Yes, my face when the screen was thrown down: ha! ha!
ha! Oh, I must never show my head again!

SIR OLIVER

But come, come, it isn't fair to laugh at you neither, my
old friend; though, upon my soul, I can't help it.

SIR PETER

Oh, pray don't restrain your mirth on my account: it does
not hurt me at all! I laugh at the whole affair myself. Yes,
yes, I think being a standing jest for all one's acquaintance
a very happy situation. Oh, yes, and then of a morning to
read the paragraphs about Mr S——, Lady T——, and
Sir P——, will be so diverting! I shall certainly leave town
tomorrow and never look mankind in the face again.

ROWLEY

Without affectation, Sir Peter, you may despise the ridicule
of fools: but I see Lady Teazle going towards the next
room; I am sure you must desire a reconciliation as
earnestly as she does.

SIR OLIVER

Perhaps my being here prevents her coming to you. Well,
I'll leave honest Rowley to mediate between you; but he
must bring you all presently to Mr Surface's, where I am
now returning, if not to reclaim a libertine, at least to
expose hypocrisy.

SIR PETER

Ah, I'll be present at your discovering yourself there with
all my heart; though 'tis a vile unlucky place for discoveries.

ROWLEY

We'll follow.

[*Exit* SIR OLIVER.]

SIR PETER
She is not coming here, you see, Rowley.

ROWLEY
No, but she has left the door of that room open, you perceive. See, she is in tears.

SIR PETER
Certainly a little mortification appears very becoming in a wife. Don't you think it will do her good to let her pine a little?

ROWLEY
Oh, this is ungenerous in you!

SIR PETER
Well, I know not what to think. You remember the letter I found of hers evidently intended for Charles!

ROWLEY
A mere forgery, Sir Peter, laid in your way on purpose. This is one of the points which I intend Snake shall give you conviction of.

SIR PETER
I wish I were once satisfied of that. She looks this way. What a remarkably elegant turn of the head she has! Rowley, I'll go to her.

ROWLEY
Certainly.

SIR PETER
Though, when it is known that we are reconciled people will laugh at me ten times more.

ROWLEY
Let them laugh, and retort their malice only by showing them you are happy in spite of it.

SIR PETER
I'faith, so I will! and, if I'm not mistaken, we may yet be the happiest couple in the country.

ROWLEY
Nay, Sir Peter, he who once lays aside suspicion—

SIR PETER
Hold, Master Rowley! if you have any regard for me, never let me hear you utter anything like a sentiment: I have had enough of them to serve me the rest of my life. [*Exeunt.*]

SCENE III

[*The library*.]

[*Enter* JOSEPH SURFACE *and* LADY SNEERWELL.]

LADY SNEERWELL
Impossible! Will not Sir Peter immediately be reconciled
to Charles, and of consequence no longer oppose his union
with Maria? The thought is distraction to me.

JOSEPH SURFACE
Can passion furnish a remedy?

LADY SNEERWELL
No, nor cunning either. Oh! I was a fool, an idiot, to
league with such a blunderer!

JOSEPH SURFACE
Surely, Lady Sneerwell, I am the greatest sufferer; yet
you see I bear the accident with calmness.

LADY SNEERWELL
Because the disappointment doesn't reach your heart;
your interest only attached you to Maria. Had you felt for
her what I have for that ungrateful libertine, neither your
temper nor hypocrisy could prevent your showing the
sharpness of your vexation.

JOSEPH SURFACE
But why should your reproaches fall on me for this disappointment?

LADY SNEERWELL
Are you not the cause of it? What had you to bate in your
pursuit of Maria to pervert Lady Teazle by the way? Had
you not a sufficient field for your roguery in blinding Sir
Peter, and supplanting your brother, but you must endeavour to seduce his wife? I hate such an avarice of
crimes; 'tis an unfair monopoly, and never prospers.

JOSEPH SURFACE
Well, I admit I have been to blame. I confess I deviated

from the direct road of wrong, but I don't think we're so totally defeated neither.

LADY SNEERWELL

No!

JOSEPH SURFACE

You tell me you have made a trial of Snake since we met, and that you still believe him faithful to us?

LADY SNEERWELL

I do believe so.

JOSEPH SURFACE

And that he has undertaken, should it be necessary, to swear and prove, that Charles is at this time contracted by vows and honour to your ladyship, which some of his former letters to you will serve to support?

LADY SNEERWELL

This, indeed, might have assisted.

JOSEPH SURFACE

Come, come; it is not too late yet. [*Knocking at the door.*] But hark! this is probably my uncle, Sir Oliver: retire to that room; we'll consult further when he's gone.

LADY SNEERWELL

Well, but if *he* should find you out too?

JOSEPH SURFACE

Oh, I have no fear of that. Sir Peter will hold his tongue for his own credit's sake—and you may depend on it I shall soon discover Sir Oliver's weak side!

LADY SNEERWELL

I have no diffidence[88] of your abilities: only be constant to one roguery at a time. [*Exit* LADY SNEERWELL.]

JOSEPH SURFACE

I will, I will!—So! 'tis confounded hard, after such bad fortune, to be baited by one's confederate in evil. Well, at all events, my character is so much better than Charles's, that I certainly—hey!—what—this is not Sir Oliver, but old Stanley again. Plague on't that he should return to tease me just now—I shall have Sir Oliver come and find him here—and—[*Enter* SIR OLIVER.] Gad's life, Mr Stanley, why have you come back to plague me at this time? You must not stay now, upon my word.

SIR OLIVER

Sir, I hear your uncle Oliver is expected here, and though

he has been so penurious to you, I'll try what he'll do for me.

JOSEPH SURFACE

Sir, 'tis impossible for you to stay now, so I must beg.— Come any other time, and I promise you, you shall be assisted.

SIR OLIVER

No: Sir Oliver and I must be acquainted.

JOSEPH SURFACE

Zounds, sir! then I insist on your quitting the room directly.

SIR OLIVER

Nay, sir—

JOSEPH SURFACE

Sir, I insist on't:—here, William! show this gentleman out. Since you compel me, sir, not one moment—this is such insolence.

[*Enter* CHARLES.]

CHARLES SURFACE

Heyday! what's the matter now? What the devil, have you got hold of my little broker here? Zounds, brother, don't hurt little Premium. What's the matter, my little fellow?

JOSEPH SURFACE

So! he has been with you, too, has he?

CHARLES SURFACE

To be sure he has. Why, he's as honest a little—But sure, Joseph, you have not been borrowing money too, have you?

JOSEPH SURFACE

Borrowing! no! But, brother, you know we expect Sir Oliver here every—

CHARLES SURFACE

O Gad, that's true! Noll mustn't find the little broker here, to be sure.

JOSEPH SURFACE

Yet, Mr Stanley insists—

CHARLES SURFACE

Stanley! why his name's Premium.

JOSEPH SURFACE

No, no, Stanley.

CHARLES SURFACE

No, no, Premium.

JOSEPH SURFACE

Well, no matter which—but—

CHARLES SURFACE

Aye, aye, Stanley or Premium, 'tis the same thing, as you say; for I suppose he goes by half a hundred names, besides A. B. at the coffee-house.[84]

[*Knocking.*]

JOSEPH SURFACE

'Sdeath! here's Sir Oliver at the door. Now I beg, Mr Stanley—

CHARLES SURFACE

Aye, aye, and I beg, Mr Premium—

SIR OLIVER

Gentlemen—

JOSEPH SURFACE

Sir, by heaven you shall go!

CHARLES SURFACE

Aye, out with him, certainly.

SIR OLIVER

This violence—

JOSEPH SURFACE

'Tis your own fault.

CHARLES SURFACE

Out with him, to be sure. [*Both forcing* SIR OLIVER *out. Enter* SIR PETER *and* LADY TEAZLE, MARIA, *and* ROWLEY.]

SIR PETER

My old friend, Sir Oliver—hey! What in the name of wonder!—here are dutiful nephews—assault their uncle at his first visit!

LADY TEAZLE

Indeed, Sir Oliver, 'twas well we came in to release you.

ROWLEY

Truly, it was; for I perceive, Sir Oliver, the character of old Stanley was not a protection to you.

SIR OLIVER

Nor of Premium either: the necessities of the former could not extort a shilling from that benevolent gentleman; and with the other I stood a chance of faring worse than my ancestors, and being knocked down without being bid for.

JOSEPH SURFACE
Charles!

CHARLES SURFACE
Joseph!

JOSEPH SURFACE
'Tis now complete!

CHARLES SURFACE
Very.

SIR OLIVER
Sir Peter, my friend, and Rowley too, look on that elder nephew of mine. You know what he has already received from my bounty; and you also know how gladly I would have regarded half my fortune as held in trust for him: judge, then, my disappointment in discovering him to be destitute of truth, charity and gratitude!

SIR PETER
Sir Oliver, I should be more surprised at this declaration, if I had not myself found him to be selfish, treacherous, and hypocritical.

LADY TEAZLE
And if the gentleman pleads not guilty to these, pray let him call *me* to his character.

SIR PETER
Then, I believe, we need add no more: if he knows himself, he will consider it as the most perfect punishment that he is known to the world.

CHARLES SURFACE
[*Aside.*] If they talk this way to Honesty, what will they say to me, by-and-by?

SIR OLIVER
As for that prodigal, his brother, there—

CHARLES SURFACE
[*Aside.*] Aye, now comes my turn: the damned family pictures will ruin me.

JOSEPH SURFACE
Sir Oliver—uncle, will you honour me with a hearing?

CHARLES SURFACE
[*Aside.*] Now, if Joseph would make one of his long speeches, I might recollect myself a little.

SIR OLIVER
[*To* JOSEPH.] I suppose you would undertake to justify

yourself?

JOSEPH SURFACE

I trust I could.

SIR OLIVER

Pshaw!—nay, if you desert your roguery in this distress and try to be justified, you have even less principle than I thought you had. [*Turns from him in contempt.*] Well, sir! [*to* CHARLES]—and you would justify yourself too, I suppose?

CHARLES SURFACE

Not that I know of, Sir Oliver.

SIR OLIVER

What!—Little Premium has been let too much into the secret, I suppose?

CHARLES SURFACE

True, sir; but they were *family* secrets, and should not be mentioned again, you know.

ROWLEY

Come, Sir Oliver, I know you cannot speak of Charles's follies with anger.

SIR OLIVER

Odd's heart, no more I can; nor with gravity either.— Sir Peter, do you know the rogue bargained with me for all his ancestors; sold me judges and generals by the foot, and maiden aunts as cheap as broken china.

CHARLES SURFACE

To be sure, Sir Oliver, I did make a little free with the family canvas, that's the truth on't. My ancestors may rise in judgement against me, there's no denying it; but believe me sincere when I tell you—and upon my soul I would not say so if I was not—that if I do not appear mortified at the exposure of my follies, it is because I feel at this moment the warmest satisfaction at seeing you, my liberal benefactor.

SIR OLIVER

Charles, I believe you. Give me your hand again: the ill-looking little fellow over the settee has made your peace.

CHARLES SURFACE

Then, sir, my gratitude to the original is still increased.

LADY TEAZLE

Yet, I believe, Sir Oliver, here is one whom Charles is still more anxious to be reconciled to.

SIR OLIVER

Oh, I have heard of his attachment there; and with the young lady's pardon, if I construe right—that blush—

SIR PETER

Well, child, speak your sentiments.

MARIA

Sir, I have little to say, but that I shall rejoice to hear that he is happy; for me—whatever claim I had to his attention, I willingly resign to one who has a better title.

CHARLES SURFACE

How, Maria!

SIR PETER

Heyday! what's the mystery now?—While he appeared an incorrigible rake, you would give your hand to no one else; and now that he is likely to reform I'll warrant you won't have him.

MARIA

His own heart and Lady Sneerwell know the cause.

CHARLES SURFACE

Lady Sneerwell!

JOSEPH SURFACE

Brother, it is with great concern I am obliged to speak on this point, but my regard to justice compels me, and Lady Sneerwell's injuries can no longer be concealed. [*Goes to door. Enter* LADY SNEERWELL.]

ALL

Lady Sneerwell!

SIR PETER

So! another French milliner! Egad, he has one in every room in the house, I suppose!

LADY SNEERWELL

Ungrateful Charles! Well may you be surprised, and feel for the indelicate situation your perfidy has forced me into.

CHARLES SURFACE

Pray, uncle, is this another plot of yours? For, as I have life, I don't understand it.

JOSEPH SURFACE

I believe, sir, there is but the evidence of one person more necessary to make it extremely clear.

SIR PETER

And that person, I imagine, is Mr Snake.—Rowley, you
were perfectly right to bring him with you, and pray let
him appear.

ROWLEY

Walk in, Mr Snake. [*Enter* SNAKE.] I thought his testimony
might be wanted; however, it happens unluckily, that he
comes to confront Lady Sneerwell, not to support her.

LADY SNEERWELL

A villain! Treacherous to me at last!—Speak, fellow, have
you too conspired against me?

SNAKE

I beg your ladyship ten thousand pardons: you paid me
extremely liberally for the lie in question; but I un-
fortunately have been offered double to speak the truth.

LADY SNEERWELL

The torments of shame and disappointment on you all!

LADY TEAZLE

Hold, Lady Sneerwell—before you go, let me thank you
for the trouble you and that gentleman have taken, in
writing letters from me to Charles, and answering them
yourself; and let me also request you to make my respects
to the Scandalous College, of which you are president, and
inform them, that Lady Teazle, licentiate,²⁵ begs leave to
return the diploma they granted her, as she leaves off practice, and kills characters no longer.

LADY SNEERWELL

You too, madam—provoking—insolent—May your husband live these fifty years! [*Exit.*]

SIR PETER

Oons! what a fury!

LADY TEAZLE

A malicious creature it is.

SIR PETER

Hey! not for her last wish?

LADY TEAZLE

Oh, no!

SIR OLIVER

Well, sir, and what have you to say now?

JOSEPH SURFACE

Sir, I am so confounded, to find that Lady Sneerwell could

be guilty of suborning Mr Snake in this manner, to impose
on us all, that I know not what to say: however, lest her
revengeful spirit should prompt her to injure my brother,
I had certainly better follow her directly. [*Exit.*]

SIR PETER

Moral to the last drop!

SIR OLIVER

Ay, and marry her, Joseph, if you can. Oil and vinegar,
egad! you'll do very well together.

ROWLEY

I believe we have no more occasion for Mr Snake at
present?

SNAKE

Before I go, I beg pardon once for all, for whatever uneasiness I have been the humble instrument of causing to
the parties present.

SIR PETER

Well, well, you have made atonement by a good deed at
last.

SNAKE

But I must request of the company that it shall never be
known.

SIR PETER

Hey!—what the plague!—Are you ashamed of having done
a right thing once in your life?

SNAKE

Ah, sir, consider,—I live by the badness of my character;
and, if it were once known that I had been betrayed into
an honest action, I should lose every friend I have in the
world.

SIR PETER

Here's a precious rogue!

SIR OLIVER

Well, well—we'll not traduce you by saying anything in
your praise, never fear.

   [*Exit* SNAKE.]

LADY TEAZLE

See, Sir Oliver, there needs no persuasion now to reconcile
your nephew and Maria.

SIR OLIVER

Aye, aye, that's as it should be, and, egad, we'll have the

wedding to-morrow morning.

CHARLES SURFACE

Thank you, my dear uncle.

SIR PETER

What, you rogue! don't you ask the girl's consent first?

CHARLES SURFACE

Oh, I have done that a long time—a minute ago—and she has looked *yes*.

MARIA

For shame, Charles!—I protest, Sir Peter, there has not been a word.

SIR OLIVER

Well, then, the fewer the better:—may your love for each other never know abatement.

SIR PETER

And may you live as happily together as Lady Teazle and I—intend to do.

CHARLES SURFACE

Rowley, my old friend, I am sure you congratulate me; and I suspect that I owe you much.

SIR OLIVER

You do, indeed, Charles.

ROWLEY

If my efforts to serve you had not succeeded you would have been in my debt for the attempt; but deserve to be happy, and you overpay me.

SIR PETER

Aye, honest Rowley always said you would reform.

CHARLES SURFACE

Why, as to reforming, Sir Peter, I'll make no promises, and that I take to be a proof that I intend to set about it. But here shall be my monitor—my gentle guide.—Ah! can I leave the virtuous path those eyes illumine?

Though thou, dear maid, shouldst waive thy beauty's
     sway,
Thou still must rule, because I will obey:
An humble fugitive from Folly view,
No sanctuary near but Love [*to the audience*] and you:
You can, indeed, each anxious fear remove,
For even Scandal dies if you approve.

                      End of the Fifth Act

Epilogue

[*By Mr Colman.*] [86]

[*Spoken by* MRS ABINGTON *in the character of* LADY
TEAZLE.]

I, who was late so volatile and gay,
Like a trade wind must now blow all one way,
Bend all my cares, my studies, and my vows,
To one dull rusty weathercock—my spouse!
So wills our virtuous bard—the pye-ball'd Bayes[87]
Of crying epilogues and laughing plays!
Old bachelors, who marry smart young wives,
Learn from our play to regulate your lives:
Each bring his dear to town, all faults upon her—
London will prove the very source of honour.
Plung'd fairly in, like a cold bath it serves,
When principles relax,—to brace the nerves:
Such is my case—and yet I must deplore
That the gay dream of dissipation's o'er:
And say, ye fair, was ever lively wife,
Born with a genius for the highest life,
Like me untimely blasted in her bloom,
Like me condemn'd to such a dismal doom?
Save money—when I just knew how to *waste* it!
Leave London—just as I began to taste it!

Must I then watch the early crowing cock,
The melancholy ticking of a clock;
In a lone rustic hall for ever pounded,[88]
With dogs, cats, rats, and squalling brats surrounded?
With humble curate can I now retire
(While good Sir Peter boozes with the squire),
And at backgammon mortify my soul,
That pants for loo,[89] or flutters at a vole.[90]
Seven's the main![91] Dear sound! that must expire,
Lost at hot cockles[92] round a Christmas fire;

The transient hour of fashion too soon spent,
Farewell the tranquil mind, farewell content! [93]
Farewell the *plumèd* head, the cushion'd *tête,*
That takes the cushion from its proper seat!
That spirit-stirring drum! [94]—card-drums I mean,
Spadille[95]—odd trick—pam[96]—basto[97]—king and queen!
And you, ye knockers, that, with brazen throat,
The welcome visitors' approach denote;
Farewell!—all quality of high renown,
Pride, pomp, and circumstance of glorious Town!
Farewell! your revels I partake no more,
And Lady Teazle's occupation's o'er!
And this I told our bard; he smiled, and said 'twas clear,
I ought to play deep tragedy next year.
Meanwhile he drew wise morals from his play,
And in these solemn periods stalk'd away:—
'Blest were the fair like you; her faults who stopt,
And closed her follies when the curtain dropt!
No more in vice or error to engage,
Or play the fool at large on life's great stage.'

Notes

SHE STOOPS TO CONQUER

1. *By David Garrick, Esq.:* Garrick, at Dr. Johnson's instigation, wrote the prologue to make up for the fact that he turned down the play (see introduction).

2. *Mr. Woodward:* a London comedian. He was supposed to play Tony Lumpkin, but turned the part down as being too vulgar.

3. *''Tis not alone . . . are no plasters':* a paraphrase of Hamlet's speech in Act I, Sc. ii, ll. 77–85.

4. *Shuter:* Edward (Ned) Shuter played the role of Hardcastle in the original production of *She Stoops to Conquer.*

5. *Doctor:* Goldsmith claimed this title (see introduction).

6. *Draughts:* acts.

7. *within:* at box office.

8. *basket:* a container on the outside rear of the stagecoach, used for carrying baggage and, occasionally, passengers.

9. *Prince Eugene and the Duke of Marlborough:* They led British and Austrian armies against the French in the War of Spanish Succession (1701–13).

10. *Darby . . . Joan:* a happy old couple from popular ballads.

11. *quotha!:* says she! A term of contempt like "indeed!"

12. *horse-pond:* for a ducking.

13. *snub:* check, rein.

14. *The Three Pigeons:* a neighboring alehouse.

15. *exciseman:* taxcollector.

16. *whimsical:* odd.

17. *improvements:* the landscaped grounds of the estate.

18. *Allons:* "Arise" or "Come on."

19. *knock himself down:* offer himself as at an auction.

20. *Lethes . . . Styxes . . . Stygians:* rivers of Hades in Roman mythology. ("Stygian" is form of "Styx.")

21. *Quis . . . Quaes . . . Quods:* masculine, feminine and neuter nominative singular of common Latin pronouns "who," "which," "what."

22. *Methodist:* Tony, as the son of an upper-class family, would have probably belonged to the Anglican Church and would have had little use for the austere reforms of Methodism.

23. *pigeon:* "fool" or "gull."

24. *jorum:* drinking bowl.

25. *Water Parted:* song from the opera *Artaxerxes* by Thomas Arne.

26. *Ariadne:* an opera by Handel.

27. *postchaise:* closed carriage drawn by relays of horses.

28. *woundily:* excessively.

29. *Father-in-law:* stepfather.

30. *wanted no ghost:* reference to Act I, Sc. V of Hamlet.

31. *duchesses of Drury Lane:* prostitutes.

32. *Denain:* a battle in 1712. Marlborough was not present.

33. *ventre d'or:* gold-fronted.

34. *'for us that sell ale':* ordinary people.

35. *Heyder Ally . . . Ally Cawn . . . Ally Croaker:* The first two were Indian sultans; the last one was the hero of an Irish street song.

36. *Westminster Hall:* center of London law courts.

37. *battle of Belgrade:* battle in which Prince Eugene defeated the Turks in 1717.

38. *All upon the high rope:* Playing the big shot.

39. *Joiners Company:* carpenter's guild; *Corporation:* organization of merchants.

40. *Florentine . . . shaking pudding . . . taffety cream:* a Florentine is a spiced meat pie; a shaking pudding is a jelly and cream concoction (*blanc mange*); taffety cream is a velvety cream dessert.

41. *made dished:* recipes containing combinations of foods, more popular with the French than with the English.

42. *India Director:* an officer of the East India Company.

43. *Ranelagh, St. James's, or Tower Wharf:* Hastings is insulting Mrs. Hardcastle; Ranelagh and St. James's are fashionable sections of greater London, while Tower Wharf is a sort of Coney Island.

44. *tête-à-tête:* column of scandalous revelations published in *Town and Country* (see *School for Scandal,* note 17).

45. *head:* coiffure.

46. *dégagée:* graceful.

47. *friseur:* hairdresser.

48. *inoculation:* The first type of smallpox inoculation was introduced in 1718.

49. *tête:* wig.

50. *Mrs. Niece:* "Mistress, my niece."

51. *the complete housewife:* a popular guide on household

economy, home remedies and the like.

52. *Quincy:* Dr. John Quince, author of *Complete English Dispensatory.*

53. *Anon:* How's that?

54. *mauvaise honte:* false modesty.

55. *Bully Dawson:* a notorious ruffian of the early part of the eighteenth century.

56. *bobs:* pendants.

57. *cracker:* firecracker.

58. *Morrice:* Do a morrice dance.

59. *marcasites:* ornaments of fool's gold (pyrites).

60. *rose and table-cut things:* ways of cutting gems of smaller size. Larger gems are brilliant cut.

61. *catherine wheel:* a pinwheel firecracker.

62. *Cherry in the Beaux 'Stratagem:* the innkeeper's daughter in Farquhar's comedy (1707).

63. *Lion . . . Angel . . . Lamb:* names frequently given to private rooms at an inn.

64. *salute:* kiss.

65. *I never nicked . . . ames-ace:* At Hazard, a dice game which was a forerunner of craps, seven was the highest throw and two aces (snake eyes) was the lowest.

66. *To the side scene:* addressing someone in the wings (see introduction).

67. *liberty and Fleet Street forever:* a popular political slogan of the day.

68. *Rake's Progress:* a famous series of paintings by Hogarth.

69. *Dullissimo Maccaroni:* the most stupid fop of all.

70. *Whistlejacket:* a racehorse.

71. *haspicholls:* harpsichords.

72. *izzard:* the letter Z.

73. *baskets:* basket-hilted swords.

74. *circumbendibus:* roundabout way.

75. *kept:* resorted.

76. *We have our exits and our entrances:* adapted from Shakespeare's *As You Like It* (Act II, Sc. vii, l. 141).

77. *cits:* city-dwellers.

78. *caro:* dearest.

79. *Nancy Dawson:* a popular song of the time.

80. *Che Faro:* an aria from Gluck's opera *Orfeo*.

81. *Heinel:* a popular continental dancer; *Cheapside:* a popular marketplace.

82. *spadille:* the one of spades in the card game Ombre.

83. *Bayes:* a character in the play *The Rehearsal* by George Villiers, Duke of Buckingham. Bayes was an aspiring author.

84. *J. Craddock, Esq.:* a friend of Goldsmith.

85. *roratorio:* oratorio.

THE RIVALS

1. *sergeant-at-law:* equivalent to a doctor of civil law, at that time the highest ranked barrister in English courts.

2. *sons of Phoebus:* Phoebus is Apollo, the patron god of the arts. Sons of Phoebus were therefore poets.

3. *Fleet:* the debtors' prison in Fleet Street.

4. *bays:* laurel branches. They were worn in the form

of a wreath and in ancient times were a symbol of victory. Afterward they were the mark of a poet.

5. *Full-bottomed heroes:* lawyers with full wigs.

6. *dread court:* the theatre audience.

7. *No writ . . . to Drury Lane:* no appeal can be made to Drury Lane, the rival theatre of Covent Garden (see introduction).

8. *transportation:* exile in the colonies.

9. *this form:* She points to Thalia, the Muse of comedy, whose figure adorned one side of the theatre proscenium.

10. *her sister's hand:* Melpomene, the Muse of tragedy, adorns one side of the theatre proscenium.

11. *Harry Woodward . . . Dunstal . . . Quick . . . Ned Shuter . . . Barsanti . . . Mrs. Green:* actors in the original cast of the play (see Dramatis Personæ).

12. *Odd's:* a corruption of the word "God's," frequently used at the time in combination with various expressions, often with no clear meaning.

13. *Zounds:* a corruption of "God's wounds," originally a strong oath.

14. *thread-papers:* papers folded to hold skeins of thread.

15. *a mort:* a lot.

16. *pump-room:* a hall where people gathered to drink the water of the hot springs.

17. *wig:* Wigs at this time were going out of style in London.

18. *ton:* tone, the fashion or vogue.

19. *thoff:* though.

20. *carrots:* his own red hair.

21. *bob:* short wig.

22. *Gyde's porch:* the entrance to the lower assembly rooms at Bath.

23. *The Reward of Constancy . . . The Fatal Connection . . . The Mistakes of the Heart . . . The Delicate Distress, or the Memoirs of Lady Woodford:* All these novels were mildly sensational love stories of gushing sentimentality.

24. *The Gordian Knot . . . Peregrine Pickle . . . The Tears of Sensibility . . . Humphrey Clinker . . . The Memoirs of a Lady of Quality, written by Herself . . . The Sentimental Journey:* The novels Lucy brought were generally of a higher literary quality than of those Lydia requested; though they were still not what a protected young lady should have been reading. *Peregrine Pickle* and *Humphrey Clinker* by Tobias Smolett and *The Sentimental Journey* by Lawrence Sterne are today considered classics in our language.

25. *The Whole Duty of Man:* a popular work of moral platitudes.

26. *few blonds:* pieces of lace made from raw silk.

27. *sal volatile:* an aromatic solution of ammonium carbonate; smelling salts.

28. *intercourse:* exchange of letters.

29. *rout:* a large reception or party.

30. *coz:* cousin, a term applied to relatives and to close friends.

31. *Mrs. Chapone . . . Fordyce's Sermons:* These books were considered highly moral and exactly what a young lady should be reading.

32. *torn away:* to make curl papers for setting the hair.

33. *Lord Chesterfield's Letters:* considered appropriate literature for any young person.

34. *illiterate:* Mrs. Malaprop means, of course, "obliterate." The reader will find dozens of such word confusions

in Mrs. Malaprop's speeches. In fact any such mistake in speech is today called a "malapropism."

35. *black art:* black magic.

36. *simplicity:* lack of sophistication.

37. *black paduasoy:* a strong silk material.

38. *disbanded chairmen:* Chairmen pushed invalids around Bath in wheel chairs. "Disbanded" means "unemployed."

39. *minority waiters:* Meaning not clear. It could mean "unemployed waiters," or "tide waiting" men who were dockworkers.

40. *reversion of a good fortune:* "Reversion" is an English legal term. The expression means that Absolute will eventually inherit a fortune from his father.

41. *farrago:* mixture.

42. *eccentric planet:* a planet that apparently follows no fixed orbit.

43. *Squallante:* tinkling; *rumblante:* "Rollante" is a rolling effect in music. "Rumblante" is Acres' word for a rumbling, rolling effect; *quiverante:* Acres' word for a quivering musical effect; *minums and crotchets:* half notes and quarter notes.

44. *When absent from my soul's delight; Go gentle gales; My heart's my own, my will is free:* All these were popular songs of the period.

45. *race ball:* a dance held after a day of races.

46. *watchfulness:* sleeplessness.

47. *looby:* a clumsy fellow.

48. *frogs and tambours:* "Frogs" are ornamental loops or buttonholes sewn into clothes; "tambour" is embroidery.

49. *cashier:* discard.

50. *Cox's Museum:* an exhibit of mechanical and orna-

mental objects. The mechanical bull was one of the exhibits.

51. *I'll lodge . . . trustees:* I'll leave you an estate of a dollar.

52. *habeas corpus:* a legal process which releases a person from unjust detention.

53. *address:* manners.

54. *anchorite:* hermit.

55. *Promethean torch:* in mythology, Prometheus was the Titan who first brought fire to mankind.

56. *person:* vain concern with appearance.

57. *virago:* a shrew.

58. *antipodes:* the other side of the earth.

59. *monkeyrony:* macaroni. In the eighteenth century the word meant a fop or a dandy.

60. *balancing, and chasing, and boring:* dance terms; the last two are corruptions of "chassé" and "bourée."

61. *cotillons:* French dances.

62. *allemandes:* German dances.

63. *pas:* dance step.

64. *anti-gallican:* anti-French.

65. *We wear no swords here:* Swords were forbidden by custom at Bath.

66. *play:* Shakespeare's *King Lear* loosely quoted (Act II, Sc. IV, l. 283).

67. *cormorants:* literally a sea bird, but figuratively a greedy person.

68. *sharps and snaps:* swords and pistols.

69. *Hamlet says in the play:* To fully appreciate the extent

of Mrs. Malaprop's butchering of Shakespeare, see *Hamlet*, Act III, Sc. IV, ll. 56–59.

70. *quinsy:* a sore throat.

71. *side-front:* profile.

72. *Bedlam:* Bethlehem Hospital for the insane.

73. *Youth's the season made for joy:* from the *Beggar's Opera.*

74. *Cerberus:* mythological three-headed dog which guarded the gates of Hades.

75. *"not unsought be won":* From *Paradise Lost* (Book VIII, l. 503).

76. *Smithfield bargain:* a hard bargain; in other words, a marriage bargain.

77. *Scotch parson:* Couples frequently eloped to Scotland, particularly to Gretna Green, where marriages were performed without delay.

78. *fire-office:* insurance company.

79. *Derbyshire petrifactions:* The wells of Matlock in Derbyshire yielded petrified objects.

80. *quietus:* death.

81. *cit:* city-dweller.

THE SCHOOL FOR SCANDAL

1. *Mrs. Crewe:* Mrs. John Crewe, a famous beauty of the period, and a friend of the Sheridans (see introduction).

2. *Amoret:* a character from Spenser's *Faerie Queene.* She personified beauty.

3. *Reynolds:* Sir Joshua Reynolds, the famous portrait painter of the time. He had painted Mrs. Crewe.

4. *Granby's cheek:* Lady Mary Isabella, wife of the Marquis of Granby.

5. *Devon's eyes:* the Duchess of Devonshire.

6. *Greville:* Mrs. Fulke Greville, mother of Mrs. Crewe. Sheridan had dedicated his play *The Critic* to her.

7. *Millar's:* Lady Millar was widely known for her literary gatherings at Bath.

8. *Mr. King:* original Sir Peter Teazle, (see Dramatis Personæ).

9. *D. Garrick, Esq.:* David Garrick, famous actor of the time (see introduction).

10. *vapours:* blues.

11. *quantum sufficit:* plenty.

12. *sal volatile:* aromatic spirits of ammonia (smelling salts).

13. *poz:* positively.

14. *dash and star:* method of making veiled reference to those involved in scandals.

15. *Grosv'nor Square:* a fashionable section of London.

16. *Don Quixote:* Cervantes' famous novel, *Don Quixote*, had ridiculed the romantic novel; Sheridan's earlier play, *The Rivals,* had ridiculed sentimental comedy (see introduction).

17. *tête-à-tête in the Town and Country Magazine:* magazine sketches, appearing monthly, of fashionable intrigue and scandals.

18. *city knight:* a merchant who had been knighted.

19. *good jointure:* good estate from her husband.

20. *close with:* come together with.

21. *another execution:* a sheriff's sale of household goods to meet the terms of a judgment for debt.

22. *lover:* suitor.

23. *York diligence:* York stagecoach.

24. *conversazione:* a semiformal gathering to discuss art or literature.

25. *Petrarch's Laura:* Laura was the lady to whom Petrarch, the Italian poet, dedicated his sonnets.

26. *Waller's Sacharissa:* Edmund Waller, the seventeenth-century English poet, wrote lyrics in honor of Lady Dorothy Sydney, whom he called Sacharissa.

27. *old Jewry:* a London street which was frequented by moneylenders.

28. *Irish tontine:* a system of insurance used by the Irish Parliament to raise revenues.

29. *an officer behind every guest's chair:* a bailiff ready to confiscate the chair for debt.

30. *doubt:* doubt not or suspect.

31. *Pantheon:* a London concert hall.

32. *fête champêtre:* garden party.

33. *tambour:* embroidery frame.

34. *Pope Joan:* a game of cards.

35. *vis-à-vis:* face to face.

36. *white cats:* white horses.

37. *Kensington Gardens:* a public park in London.

38. *rid on a hurdle:* carried to the gallows in an open cart.

39. *Hyde Park:* London park frequented by people of fashion.

40. *duodecimo phaeton:* small carriage.

41. *macaronies:* dandies or fops.

42. *Phoebus:* the god Apollo.

43. *aperture of a poor's-box:* the slit in the top of the box placed in church to receive contributions for the poor.

44. *Ring:* fashionable drive in Hyde Park.

45. *sugar-baker:* confectioner.

46. *French fruit:* artificial fruits with slips of paper containing brief sayings; much like Chinese "fortune cookies."

47. *Spa:* a watering place in Belgium which has given its name to all such places today.

48. *Law-Merchant:* mercantile law. Sir Peter would make them as legally responsible as people who make contracts.

49. *cicisbeo:* an escort or gigolo to a married woman. He would escort her to public functions but was not necessarily a true lover.

50. *bluff:* firm.

51. *stool of repentance:* Scottish churches often had a stool placed in front of pulpit on which a penitent sinner sat.

52. *prudent:* worldly wise, therefore cynical.

53. *compound for his extravagance:* make up for his excess extravagance.

54. *jet:* design.

55. *a heart to pity . . . charity:* from Shakespeare's Henry IV, Part II, Act IV, Sc. iv, ll. 31–32. It actually reads "a tear for pity," etc.

56. *Crutched Friars:* street near the Tower of London.

57. *run out:* "pop off," speak his mind.

58. *Annuity Bill:* The bill was passed shortly after this play was first presented. The bill was designed to protect survivors from unscrupulous annuity sharks.

59. *bags and bouquets:* footman's livery. In other words

the servants had to buy their own uniforms out of their wages.

60. *Register:* the Annuities Bill (see note 58). After the bill was passed, editions of this play dropped this reference.

61. *post-obit:* "after the obituary," in other words the blue and silver were payable after death.

62. *point ruffles:* ruffles made of very fine lace.

63. *hazard regimen:* keeping fit for playing dice, with a pun on "hazardous."

64. *quean:* a prostitute.

65. *beau-pots:* window boxes.

66. *race-cups and corporation-bowls:* trophies, loving cups, and the like.

67. *volunteer grace:* natural grace.

68. *Duke of Marlborough's:* famous British general and statesman (1650–1722).

69. *Malplaquet:* Marlborough defeated the French here in 1709, although the English took heavier losses than the French.

70. *Kneller:* Sir Godfrey Kneller, a popular portrait painter.

71. *woolsack:* symbol of the law. The Lord Chancellor's seat in House of Lords is the Woolsack.

72. *lumber:* the other pictures, frames, and the like.

73. *games:* gambles.

74. *birthday clothes:* elegant dress worn at the king's birthday party.

75. *trepan:* entrap.

76. *policy:* cunning.

77. *rupees, pagodas:* silver and gold coins of India.

78. *congou tea, avadavats, Indian crackers:* a black Chinese tea, Indian songbirds, gayly colored firecrackers.

79. *seconde:* a parrying position in fencing.

80. *Salthill where he had been to see the Montem:* the Montem was a fair or carnival held yearly (at Salthill) by students of Eton.

81. *double letter:* oversized letter.

82. *one of the faculty:* a medical professor.

83. *diffidence:* doubt.

84. *A. B. at the coffee-house:* The letters were used instead of a name to make discreet appointments at coffee-houses.

85. *licentiate:* a holder of a university diploma which acts as a licence to practice the profession.

86. *Mr. Colman:* George Colman, a playwright and theatre manager.

87. *Bayes:* see *She Stoops to Conquer,* note 83.

88. *pounded:* closed up.

89. *loo:* lanterloo, a card game.

90. *vole:* winning all the tricks.

91. *Seven's the main:* a number called by the caster in a dice game (hazard).

92. *hot cockles:* a game in which a kneeling, blindfolded man must guess who hit him.

93. *Farewell . . . content:* This and the next eight lines parody a speech from Shakespeare's *Othello* (Act III, Sc. iii. ll. 347–57).

94. *drum:* card party.

95. *Spadille:* the ace of spades.

96. *pam:* the Jack of clubs.

97. *basto:* the ace of clubs.